# COLLECTIVIST ECONOMIC PLANNING

# COLLECTIVIST
# ECONOMIC PLANNING

## CRITICAL STUDIES ON
## THE POSSIBILITIES OF SOCIALISM

*By* N. G. PIERSON, LUDWIG v. MISES,
GEORG HALM & ENRICO BARONE

*EDITED WITH AN INTRODUCTION*
*AND A CONCLUDING ESSAY*
*BY*
FRIEDRICH A. HAYEK

[ 1933 ]

AUGUSTUS M. KELLEY · PUBLISHERS
*CLIFTON 1975*

First Edition 1935

( *London*: George Routledge & Sons, Ltd., 1935 )


Reprinted 1975 *by*

# Augustus M. Kelley Publishers

*Clifton New Jersey 07012*

By *Arrangement with* ROUTLEDGE AND KEGAN PAUL, LTD.

H B
97.5
.H36
1975

**Library of Congress Cataloging in Publication Data**

Hayek, Friedrich August von, 1899-     ed.
   Collectivist economic planning; critical studies on
the possibilities of socialism.

   (Reprints of economic classics)
   Reprint of the 1935 ed. published by G. Routledge,
London.
   Bibliography:  p.
   1.  Marxian economics.  2.  Economic policy.
3.  Socialism.  I.  Pierson, Nikolaas Gerard, 1839-1909.
II.  Title.
[HB97.5.H36  1974]          335          74-7272
ISBN 0-678-00782-9

PRINTED IN THE UNITED STATES OF AMERICA
*by* SENTRY PRESS, NEW YORK, N. Y. 10013
*Bound by* A. HOROWITZ & SON, CLIFTON, N. J.

# CONTENTS

# I

# THE NATURE AND HISTORY OF THE PROBLEM

## By F. A. HAYEK

## 1. THE UNSEEN PROBLEM

THERE is reason to believe that we are at last entering an era of reasoned discussion of what has long uncritically been assumed to be a reconstruction of society on rational lines. For more than half a century, the belief that deliberate regulation of all social affairs must necessarily be more successful than the apparent haphazard interplay of independent individuals has continuously gained ground until to-day there is hardly a political group anywhere in the world which does not want central direction of most human activities in the service of one aim or another. It seemed so easy to improve upon the institutions of a free society which had come more and more to be considered as the result of mere accident, the product of a peculiar historical growth which might as well have taken a different direction. To bring order to such a chaos, to apply reason to the organization of society, and to shape it deliberately in every detail according to human wishes and the common ideas of justice seemed the only course of action worthy of a reasonable being.

But at the present day it is clear—it would probably be admitted by all sides—that during the greater part of the growth of this belief, some of the most serious problems of such a reconstruction have not even been recognized, much less successfully answered. For many years discussion of socialism—and for the greater part of the period it was only from socialism proper that the movement sprang—turned almost exclusively on ethical and psychological issues. On the one hand there was the general question whether justice required a re-organization of society on socialist lines and what principles of the distribution of income were to be regarded as just. On the other hand there was the question whether men in general could be trusted to have the moral and psychological qualities which were dimly seen to be essential if a socialist system was to work. But although this latter question does raise some of the real difficulties, it does not really touch the heart of the problem. What was questioned was only whether the authorities in the new state would be in a position to make people carry out their plans properly. Only the practical possibility of the execution of the plans was called in question, not whether planning, even in the ideal case where these difficulties were absent, would

2

achieve the desired end. The problem seemed therefore to be " only " one of psychology or education, the
" only " meaning that after initial difficulties these
obstacles would certainly be overcome.

If this were true, then the economist would have
nothing to say on the feasibility of such proposals, and
indeed it is improbable that any scientific discussion of
their merits would be possible. It would be a problem
of ethics, or rather of individual judgments of value, on
which different people might agree or disagree, but on
which no reasoned arguments would be possible. Some
of the questions might be left to the psychologist to
decide, if he has really any means of saying what men
would be like under entirely different circumstances.
Apart from this no scientist, and least of all the economist,
would have anything to say about the problems of
Socialism. And many people believing that the knowledge of the economist is only applicable to the problems
of a capitalist society (i.e. to problems arising out of
peculiar human institutions which would be absent in
a world organized on different lines), still think this to
be the case.


## 2. ECONOMIC AND TECHNOLOGICAL PROBLEMS

Whether this widespread belief is based on a clear
conviction that there would be no economic problems
in a socialist world, or whether it simply proves that
the people who hold it do not know what economic
problems are, is not always evident. Probably usually
the latter. This is not at all surprising. The big
economic problems which the economist sees and which
he contends will also have to be solved in a collectivist

3

society, are not problems which at present are solved deliberately by anybody in the sense in which the economic problems of a household reach solution. In a purely competitive society nobody bothers about any but his own economic problems. There is therefore no reason why the existence of economic problems, in the sense in which the economist uses the term, should be known to others. But the distribution of available resources between different uses which is the economic problem is no less a problem for society than for the individual, and although the decision is not consciously made by anybody, the competitive mechanism does bring about some sort of solution.

No doubt if it were put in this general way everybody would be ready to admit that such a problem exists. But few realize that it is fundamentally different not only in difficulty but also in character from the problems of engineering. The increasing preoccupation of the modern world with problems of an engineering character tends to blind people to the totally different character of the economic problem, and is probably the main cause why the nature of the latter was less and less understood. At the same time everyday terminology used in discussing either sort of problem has greatly enhanced the confusion. The familiar phrase of " trying to get the greatest results from the given means " covers both problems. The metallurgist who seeks for a method which will enable him to extract a maximum amount of metal from a given quantity of ore, the military engineer who tries to build a bridge with a given number of men in the shortest possible time, or the optician who endeavours to construct a telescope which will enable the astronomer to penetrate to still

4

more distant stars, all are concerned solely with technological problems. The common character of these
problems is determined by the singleness of their purpose in every case, the absolutely determined nature of
the ends to which the available means are to be devoted.
Nor does it alter the fundamental character of the
problem if the means available for a definite purpose
is a fixed amount of money to be spent on factors of
production with given prices. From this point of view
the industrial engineer who decides on the best method
of production of a given commodity on the basis of
given prices is concerned only with technological problems although he may speak of his trying to find the
most economical method. But the only element which
makes his decision *in its effects* an economic one is not
any part of his calculations but only the fact that he
uses, as a basis for these calculations, prices as he finds
them on the market.

The problems which the director of all economic
activities of a community would have to face would
only be similar to those solved by an engineer if the
order of importance of the different needs of the community were fixed in such a definite and absolute way
that provision for one could always be made irrespective
of cost. If it were possible for him first to decide on
the best way to produce the necessary supply of, say,
food as the most important need, as if it were the only
need, and would think about the supply, say of clothing,
only if and when some means were left over after the
demand for food had been fully satisfied, then there
would be no economic problem. For in such a case
nothing would be left over except what could not possibly
be used for the first purpose, either because it could

5

not be turned into food or because there was no further demand for food. The criterion would simply be whether the possible maximum of foodstuffs had been produced or whether the application of different methods might not lead to a greater output. But the task would cease to be merely technological in character and would assume an entirely different nature if it were further postulated that as many resources as possible should be left over for other purposes. Then the question arises what *is* a greater quantity of resources. If one engineer proposed a method which would leave a great deal of land but only little labour for other purposes, while another would leave much labour and little land, how in the absence of any standard of value could it be decided which was the greater quantity? If there were only one factor of production this could be decided unequivocally on merely technical grounds, for then the main problem in every line of production would again be reduced to one of getting the maximum quantity of product out of any given amount of the same resources. The remaining economic problem of how much to produce in every line of production would in this case be of a very simple and almost negligible nature. As soon as there are two or more factors, however, this possibility is not present.

The economic problem arises therefore as soon as different purposes compete for the available resources. And the criterion of its presence is that costs have to be taken into account. Cost here, as anywhere, means nothing but the advantages to be derived from the use of given resources in other directions. Whether this is simply the use of part of the possible working day for recreation, or the use of material resources in an alter-

6

native line of production, makes little difference. It is clear that decisions of this sort will have to be made in any conceivable kind of economic system, wherever one has to choose between alternative employments of given resources. But the decisions between two possible alternative uses cannot be made in the absolute way which was possible in our earlier example. Even if the director of the economic system were quite clear in his mind that the food of one person is always more important than the clothing of another, that would by no means necessarily imply that it is also more important than the clothing of two or ten others. How critical the question is becomes clearer if we look at the less elementary wants. It may well be that although the need for one additional doctor is greater than the need for one additional school teacher, yet under conditions where it costs three times as much to train an additional doctor as it costs to train an additional school teacher, three additional school teachers may appear preferable to one doctor.

As has been said before, the fact that in the present order of things such economic problems are not solved by the conscious decision of anybody has the effect that most people are not conscious of their existence. Decisions whether and how much to produce a thing are economic decisions in this sense. But the making of such a decision by a single individual is only part of the solution of the economic problem involved. The person making such a decision makes it on the basis of given prices. The fact that by this decision he influences these prices to a certain, probably very small, extent will not influence his choice. The other part of the problem is solved by the functioning of the price system. But it is solved in a way which only a systematic study of the working of this system reveals. It has been already suggested that it is not necessary for the working of this system, that anybody should understand it. But people are not likely to let it work if they do not understand it.

The real situation in this respect is very well reflected in the popular estimate of the relative merits of the economists and the engineer. It is probably no exaggeration to say that to most people the engineer is the person who actually does things and the economist the odious individual who sits back in his armchair and explains why the well-meaning efforts of the former are frustrated. In a sense this is not untrue. But the implication that the forces which the economist studies and the engineer is likely to disregard are unimportant and ought to be disregarded is absurd. It needs the special training of the economist to see that the spontaneous forces which limit the ambitions of the engineer themselves provide a way of solving a problem which otherwise would have to be solved deliberately.

## 3. The Decay of Economic Insight

There are, however, other reasons besides the increasing conspicuousness of the elaborate modern technique of production which are responsible for our contemporary failure to see the existence of economic problems. It was not always so. For a comparatively short period in the middle of last century, the degree to which the economic problems were seen and understood by the general public was undoubtedly much higher than it is at present. But the classical system of political economy whose extraordinary influence facilitated this understanding had been based on insecure and in parts definitely faulty foundations, and its popularity had been achieved at the price of a degree of over-simplification which proved to be its undoing. It was only much later, after its teaching had lost influence, that the gradual reconstruction of economic theory showed that what defects there were in its basic concepts had invalidated its explanation of the working of the economic system to a much smaller degree than had at first seemed probable. But in the interval irreparable harm had been done. The downfall of the classical system tended to discredit the very idea of theoretical analysis, and it was attempted to substitute for an understanding of the why of economic phenomena a mere description of their occurrence. In consequence, the comprehension of the nature of the economic problem, the achievement of generations of teaching, was lost. The economists who were still interested in general analysis were far too much concerned with the reconstructing of the purely abstract foundations of economic science to exert a noticeable influence on opinion regarding policy.

It was largely owing to this temporary eclipse of analytical economics that the real problems connected with the suggestions of a planned economy have received so surprisingly little careful examination. But this eclipse itself was by no means only due to the inherent weaknesses and the consequent need for reconstruction of the old economics. Nor would it have had the same effect if it had not coincided with the rise of another movement definitely hostile to rational methods in economics. The common cause which at the same time undermined the position of economic theory and furthered the growth of a school of socialism, which positively discouraged any speculation of the actual working of the society of the future, was the rise of the so-called historical school in economics.[1] For it was the essence of the standpoint of this school. that the laws of economics could only be established by the application to the material of history of the methods of the natural sciences. And the nature of this material is such that any such attempt is bound to degenerate into mere record and description and a total scepticism concerning the existence of any laws at all.

It is not difficult to see why this should happen. In all sciences except those which deal with social phenomena all that experience shows us is the result of processes which we cannot directly observe and which it is our task to reconstruct. All our conclusions concerning the nature of these processes are of necessity hypothetical, and the only test of the validity of these hypotheses is that they prove equally applicable to the explanation of other phenomena. And what enables us to arrive by this process of induction at the formulation of general laws or hypotheses regarding the process of causation is the fact that the possibility of experimenting, of observing the repetition of the same phenomena under identical conditions, shows the existence of definite regularities in the observed phenomena.

In the social sciences, however, the situation is the exact reverse. On the one hand, experiment is impossible, and we have therefore no knowledge of definite regularities in the complex phenomena in the same

[1] Some of the points on which I can only touch here I have developed at somewhat greater length in my inaugural address on the Trend of Economic Thinking, *Economica*, May, 1933.

sense as we have in the natural sciences. But on the other hand the position of man, midway between natural and social phenomena—of the one of which he is an effect and of the other a cause—brings it about that the essential basic facts which we need for the explanation of social phenomena are part of common experience, part of the stuff of our thinking. In the social sciences it is the elements of the complex phenomena which are known beyond the possibility of dispute. In the natural sciences they can only be at best surmised. The existence of these elements is so much more certain than any regularities in the complex phenomena to which they give rise, that it is they which constitute the truly empirical factor in the social sciences. There can be little doubt that it is this different position of the empirical factor in the process of reasoning in the two groups of disciplines which is at the root of much of the confusion with regard to their logical character. There can be no doubt, the social as well as natural sciences have to employ deductive reasoning. The essential difference is that in the natural sciences the process of deduction has to start from some hypothesis which is the result of inductive generalizations, while in the social sciences it starts directly from known empirical elements and uses them to find the regularities in the complex phenomena which direct observations cannot establish. They are, so to speak, empirically deductive sciences, proceeding from the known elements to the regularities in the complex phenomena which cannot be directly established. But this is not the place to discuss questions of methodology for their own sake. Our concern is only to show how it came that in the era of the great triumphs of empiricism in the natural sciences the attempt to force the same empirical methods on the social sciences was bound to lead to disaster. To start here at the wrong end, to seek for regularities of complex phenomena which could never be observed twice under identical conditions, could not but lead to the conclusion that there were no general laws, no inherent necessities determined by the permanent nature of the constituting elements, and that the only task of economic science in particular was a description of historical change. It was only with this abandonment of the appropriate methods of procedure, well established in the classical period, that it began to be thought that there were no other laws of social life than those made by men, that all observed phenomena were all only the product of social or legal institutions, merely " historical categories " and not in any way arising out of the basic economic problems which humanity has to face.

## 4. The Attitude of Marxism

In many respects the most powerful school of socialism the world has so far seen is essentially a product of this kind of " Historismus ".  Although in some points Karl Marx adopted the tools of the classical economists, he made little use of their main permanent contribution, their analysis of competition.  But he did wholeheartedly accept the central contention of the historical school that most of the phenomena of economic life were not the result of permanent causes but only the product of a special historical development.  It is no accident that the country where the historical school had had the greatest vogue, Germany, was also the country where Marxism was most readily accepted.

The fact that this most influential school of socialism was so closely related to the general antitheoretical tendencies in the social sciences of the time had a most profound effect on all further discussion of the real problems of socialism.  Not only did the whole outlook create a peculiar inability to see any of the permanent economic problems which are independent of the historical framework, but Marx and the Marxians also proceeded, quite consistently, positively to discourage any inquiry into the actual organization and working of the socialist society of the future.  If the change was to be brought about by the inexorable logic of history, if it was the inevitable result of evolution, there was little need for knowing in detail what exactly the new society would be like.  And if nearly all the factors which determined economic activity in the present society would be absent, if there would be no problems in the new society except those determined by the new institutions which the process of historical change would have created, then there was indeed little possibility of solving any of its problems beforehand.  Marx himself had only scorn and ridicule for any such attempt deliberately to construct a working plan of such an " utopia ".  Only occasionally, and then in this negative form, do we find in his works statements about what the new society would *not* be like.  One may search his writings in vain for any definite statement of the general principles on which the economic activity in the socialist community would be directed.[1]

---

[1] A useful collection of the different allusions to this problem in Marx's works, particularly in the *Randglossen zum Gothaer Programm* (1875), will be found in K. Tisch, *Wirtschaftsrechnung und Verteilung im zentralistisch organisierten sozialistischen Gemeinwesen*, 1932, pp. 110-15.

Marx's attitude on this point had a lasting effect on the socialist of his school. To speculate about the actual organization of the socialist society immediately stigmatized the unfortunate writer as being "unscientific", the most dreaded condemnation to which a member of the "scientific" school of socialism could expose himself. But even outside the Marxian camp the common descent of all modern branches of socialism from some essentially historical or "institutional" view of economic phenomena had the effect of successfully smothering all attempts to study the problems any constructive socialist policy would have to solve. As we shall see later, it was only in reply to criticism from the outside that this task was ultimately undertaken.

### 5. SOCIALISM AND PLANNING

We have now reached a point where it becomes necessary clearly to separate several different aspects of the programmes which we have so far lumped together as socialistic. For the earlier part of the period in which the belief in central planning grew it is historically justified to identify, without much qualification, the idea of socialism and that of planning. And in so far as the main economic problems are concerned, this is still the case to-day. Yet it must be admitted that in many other respects modern socialists and other modern planners are fully entitled to disclaim any responsibility for each other's programmes. What we must distinguish here are the ends aimed at and the means which have been proposed or are in fact necessary for the purpose. The ambiguities which exist in this connection arise out of the fact that the means necessary to achieve the ends of socialism in the narrower sense may be used for other ends, and that the problems with which we are concerned arise out of the means and not the ends.

The common end of all socialism in the narrower sense, of " proletarian " socialism, is the improvement of the position of the propertyless classes of society by a redistribution of income derived from property. This implies collective ownership of the material means of production and collectivist direction and control of their use. The same collectivist methods may, however, be applied in the service of quite different ends. An aristocratic dictatorship, for example, may use the same methods to further the interest of some racial or other *élite* or in the service of some other decidedly anti-equalitarian purpose. The situation is further complicated by the fact that the method of collectivist ownership and control which is essential for any of these attempts to dissociate the distribution of income from the private ownership of the means of production, admits of application in different degrees. For the present it will be convenient to use the term socialism to describe the traditional socialist ends and to use the term planning to describe the method, although later we shall use socialism in the wider sense. In the narrower sense of the term it can be said, then, that it is possible to have much planning with little socialism or little planning and much socialism. The method of planning in any case can certainly be used for purposes which have nothing to do with the ethical aims of socialism. Whether it is equally possible to dissociate socialism completely from planning—and the criticism directed against the

15

method have led to attempts in this direction—is a question which we shall have to investigate later.

That it is possible, not only in theory but also in practice, to separate the problem of the method from that of the end is very fortunate for the purposes of scientific discussion. On the validity of the ultimate ends science has nothing to say. They may be accepted or rejected, but they cannot be proved or disproved. All that we can rationally argue about is whether and to what extent given measures will lead to the desired results. If, however, the method in question were only proposed as a means for one particular end it might prove difficult, in practice, to keep the argument about the technical question and the judgments of value quite apart. But since the same problem of means arises in connection with altogether different ethical ideals, one may hope that it will be possible to keep value judgments altogether out of the discussion.

The common condition necessary for the achievement of a distribution of income which is independent of individual ownership of resources—the common proximate end of socialism and other anti-capitalistic movements—is that the authority which decides on the principles of this distribution should also have control over the resources. Now whatever the substance of these principles of distribution, these ideas about the just or otherwise desirable division of income, they must be similar in one purely formal but highly important respect : they must be stated in the form of a scale of importance of a number of competing individual ends. It is this formal aspect, this fact that one central authority has to solve the economic problem of distributing a limited amount of resources between a practically infinite number of competing purposes, that constitutes the problem of socialism as a method. And the fundamental question is whether it is possible under the complex conditions of a large modern society for such a central authority to carry out the implications of any such scale of values with a reasonable degree of accuracy, with a degree of success equalling or approaching the results of competitive capitalism, not whether any particular set of values of this sort is in any way superior to another. It is the methods common to socialism in the narrower sense and all the other modern movements for a planned society, not the particular ends of socialism with which we are here concerned.

## 6. THE TYPES OF SOCIALISM

Since in all that follows we shall be concerned only with the methods to be employed and not with the ends aimed at, from now onwards it will be convenient to use the term socialism in this wider sense. In this sense it covers therefore any case of collectivist control of productive resources, no matter in whose interest this control is used. But while we need for our purpose no further definition of the concrete ends followed, there is still need for a further definition of the exact methods we want to consider. There are, of course, many kinds of socialism, but the traditional names of these different types, like communism, syndicalism, guild socialism, have never quite corresponded to the classification of methods which we want, and most of them have in recent times become so closely connected with political parties rather than with definite programmes, that they are hardly useful for our purpose.

What is relevant for us is essentially the degree to which the central control and direction of the resources is carried in each of the different types. To see to what extent variation on this point is possible it is perhaps best to begin with the most familiar type of socialism and then examine to what extent its arrangements can be altered in different directions.

The programme which is at once the most widely advocated and has the greatest *prima facie* plausibility provides not only for collective ownership but also for unified central direction of the use of all material resources of production. At the same time it envisages continued freedom of choice in consumption and continued freedom of the choice of occupation. At least it is essentially in this form that Marxism has been interpreted by the social-democratic parties on the Continent, and it is the form in which socialism is imagined by the greatest number of people. It is in this form too that socialism has been most widely discussed ; most of the more recent criticism is focused on this variety. Indeed, so widely has it been treated as the only important socialist programme that in most discussions on the economic problems of socialism the authors concerned have neglected to specify which kind of socialism they had in mind. This has had somewhat unfortunate effects. For it never became quite clear whether particular objections or criticisms applied only to this particular form or to all the forms of socialism.

For this reason right from the outset it is necessary to keep the alternative possibilities in mind, and to consider at every stage of the discussion carefully whether any particular problem arises out of the assumptions which must underlie any socialist programme or whether they are only due to assumptions made in some particular case. Freedom of the choice of the consumer or freedom of occupation, for example, are by no means necessary attributes of any socialist programme, and although earlier socialists have generally repudiated the suggestion that socialism would abolish these freedoms, more recently criticisms of the socialist position have been met by the answer that the supposed difficulties would arise only if they were retained : and that it was by no means too high a price for the other advantages of socialism if their abolition should prove necessary. It is therefore necessary to consider this extreme form of socialism equally with the others. It corresponds in most respects to what in the past used to be called communism, i.e. a system where not only the means of production but all goods were collectively owned and where, in addition to this, the central authority would also be in a position to order any person to do any task.

This kind of society where everything is centrally directed may be regarded as the limiting case of a long series of other systems of a lesser degree of centralization. The more familiar type discussed already stands somewhat further in the direction of decentralization. But it still involves planning on a most extensive scale—minute direction of practically all productive activity by one central authority. The earlier systems of more decentralized socialism like guild-socialism or syndicalism need not concern us here since it seems now to be fairly generally admitted that they provide no mechanism whatever for a rational direction of economic activity. More recently, however, there has arisen, again mainly in response to criticism, a tendency among socialist thinkers to reintroduce a certain degree of competition into their schemes in order to overcome the difficulty which they admit would arise in the case of completely centralized planning. There is no need at this stage to consider in detail the forms in which competition between individual producers may be combined with socialism. This will be done later on. But it is necessary from the outset to be aware of them. This for two reasons : in the first place in order to remain conscious throughout the further discussion that the completely centralized direction of all economic activity which is generally regarded as typical of all socialism, may conceivably be varied to some extent; secondly—and even more important—in order that we may see clearly what degree of central control must be retained in order that we may reasonably speak of socialism, or what are the minimum assumptions which will still entitle us to regard a system as coming within our field. Even if collective ownership of productive resources should be found to be compatible with competitive determination of the purposes for which individual units of resources are to be used and the method of their employment, we must still assume that the question, who is to exercise command over a given quantity of resources for the community, or with what amount of resources the different "entrepreneurs" are to be entrusted, will have to be decided by one central authority. This seems to be the minimum assumption consistent with the idea of collective ownership, the smallest degree of central control which would still enable the community to retain command over the income derived from the material means of production.

## 7. PLANNING AND CAPITALISM

Without some such central control of the means of production, planning in the sense in which we have used the term ceases to be a problem. It becomes unthinkable. This would probably be agreed by the majority of economists of all camps, although most other people who believe in planning still think of it as something which could be rationally attempted inside the framework of a society based on private property. In fact, however, if by planning is meant the actual direction of productive activity by authoritative prescription, either of the quantities to be produced, the methods of production to be used, or the prices to be fixed, it can be easily shown, not that such a thing is impossible, but that any isolated measure of this sort will cause reactions which will defeat its own end, and that any attempt to act consistently will necessitate further and further measures of control until all economic activity is brought under one central authority.

It is impossible within the scope of this discussion of socialism to enter further into this separate problem of state intervention in a capitalistic society. It is mentioned here only to say explicitly that it is excluded from our considerations. In our opinion well-accepted analysis shows that it does not provide an alternative which can be rationally chosen or which can be expected to provide a stable or satisfactory solution of any of the problems to which it is applied.[1]

But here again it is necessary to guard against misunderstanding. To say that partial planning of the kind we are alluding to is irrational is, however, not

[1] *Cf.* L. v. Mises, *Interventionismus*, Jena, 1929.

equivalent to saying that the only form of capitalism which can be rationally advocated is that of complete *laissez faire* in the old sense. There is no reason to assume that the historically given legal institutions are necessarily the most " natural " in any sense. The recognition of the principle of private property does not by any means necessarily imply that the particular delimitation of the contents of this right as determined by the existing laws are the most appropriate. The question as to which is the most appropriate permanent framework which will secure the smoothest and most efficient working of competition is of the greatest importance and one which it must be admitted has been sadly neglected by economists.

But on the other hand, to admit the possibility of changes in the legal framework is not to admit the possibility of a further type of planning in the sense in which we have used the word so far. There is an essential distinction here which must not be overlooked ; the distinction between a permanent legal framework so devised as to provide all the necessary incentives to private initiative to bring about the adaptations required by any change, and a system where such adaptations are brought about by central direction. And it is this, and not the question of the maintenance of the existing order *versus* the introduction of new institutions, which is the real issue. In a sense both systems can be described as being the product of rational planning. But in the one case this planning is concerned only with the permanent framework of institutions and may be dispensed with if one is willing to accept the institutions which have grown in a slow historical process, while in the other it has to deal with day-to-day changes of every sort.

There can be no doubt that planning of this sort involves changes of a type and magnitude hitherto unknown in human history. It is sometimes urged that the changes now in progress are merely a return to the social forms of the pre-industrial era. But this is a

he mediæval guild system ... estrictions to commerce ... e not used as a means ... ivity. They were prob- ... rmanent framework for ... have been devised, but ... nanent framework inside ... vidual initiative had free ... se the old apparatus of ... it of almost day-to-day ... e probably already gone ... of central planning of ... been attempted before. ... which we have started, ... and to combat the self- ... isolated act of planning, we shall certainly embark upon an experiment which has no parallel in history. But even at this stage we have gone very far. If we are to judge the potentialities aright it is necessary to realize that the system under which we live choked up with attempts at partial planning and restrictionism is almost as far from any system of capitalism which could be rationally advocated as it is different from any consistent system of planning. It is important to realize in any investigation of the possibilities of planning that it is a fallacy to suppose capitalism as it exists to-day is the alternative. We are certainly as far from capitalism in its pure form as we are from any system of central planning. The world of to-day is just interventionist chaos.

## 8. The Basis of Modern Criticism

Classical political economy broke down mainly because it failed to base its explanation of the fundamental phenomenon of value on the same analysis of the springs of economic activity which it had so successfully applied to the analysis of the more complex phenomena of competition. The labour theory of value was the product of a search after some illusory substance of value rather than an analysis of the behaviour of the economic subject. The decisive step in the progress of economics was taken when economists began to ask what exactly were the circumstances which made individuals behave towards goods in a particular way. And to ask the question in this form led immediately to the recognition that to attach a definite significance or value to the units of different goods was a necessary step in the solution of the general problem which arises everywhere when a multiplicity of ends compete for a limited quantity of means.

The omnipresence of this problem of value wherever there is rational action was the basic fact from which a systematic exploration of the forms, under which it would make its appearance under different organizations of economic life, could proceed. And up to a certain point from the very beginning the problems of a centrally directed economy found a prominent place in the expositions of modern economics. It was obviously so much simpler to discuss the fundamental problems on the assumption of the existence of a *single*

24

scale of values consistently followed than on the assumption of a multiplicity of individuals following their personal scales, that in the early chapters of the new systems the assumption of a communist state was frequently used—and used with considerable advantage —as an expository device.[1] But it was used only to demonstrate that any solution would necessarily give rise to essentially the same value phenomena—rent, wages, and interest, etc.—which we actually observe in a competitive society, and the authors then generally proceeded to show how the interaction of independent activities of the individuals produced these phenomena spontaneously without inquiring further whether they could be produced in a complex modern society by any other means. The mere absence of an agreed common scale of values seemed to deprive that problem of any practical importance. It is true that some of the earlier writers of the new school not only thought that they had actually solved the problem of socialism but also believed that their utility calculus provided a means which made it possible to combine individual utility scale into a scale of ends objectively valid for society as a whole. But it is now generally recognized that this latter belief was just an illusion and that there is no scientific criterion which would enable us to compare or assess the relative importance of needs of different persons, although conclusions implying such illegitimate interpersonal comparisons of utilities can probably still be found in discussions of special problems.

But it is evident that as the progress of the analysis of the competitive system revealed the complexity of the problems which it solved spontaneously, economists

[1] *Cf.* particularly F. v. Wieser, *Natural Value*, London, 1893, *passim*.

became more and more sceptical about the possibility of solving the same problems by deliberate decision. It is perhaps worth noting that as early as 1854 the most famous among the predecessors of the modern " marginal utility " school, the German, H. H. Gossen, had come to the conclusion that the central economic authority projected by the communists would soon find that it had set itself a task which far exceeded the powers of individual men.[1] Among the later economists of the modern school the point in which already Gossen based his objection, the difficulty of rational calculation when there is no private property, was frequently hinted at. It was particularly clearly put by Professor Cannan, who stressed the fact that the aims of socialists and communists could only be achieved by " abolishing both the institution of private property and the practice of exchange, without which value, in any reasonable sense of the word, cannot exist ".[2] But beyond general statements of this sort, critical examination of the possibilities of a socialist economic policy made little head-

[1] H. H. Gossen, *Entwicklung der Gesetze des Menschlichen Verkehrs und der daraus fliessenden Regeln für menschliches Handeln*, Braunschweig, 1854, p. 231 : " Dazu folgt aber ausserdem aus den im vorstehenden gefundenen Sätzen über das Geniessen, und infolgedessen über das Steigen und Sinken des Werthes jeder Sache mit Verminderung und Vermehrung der Masse und der Art, *dass nur durch Feststellung des Privateigenthums der Massstab gefunden wird zur Bestimmung der Quantität, welche den Verhältnissen angemessen am Zweckmässigsten von jedem Gegenstand zu produzieren ist.* Darum würde denn die von Communisten projectierte Zentralbehörde zur Verteilung der verschiedenen Arbeiten sehr bald die Erfahrung machen, dass sie sich eine Aufgabe gestellt habe, deren Lösung die Kräfte einzelner Menschen weit übersteigt " (italics in the original).

[2] E. Cannan, *A History of the Theories of Production and Distribution*, 1893, 3rd edition, 1917, p. 395. Professor Cannan has later also made an important contribution to the problem of the international

26

way, for the simple reason that no concrete socialist proposal of how these problems would be overcome existed to be examined.[1]

It was only early in the present century that at last a general statement of the kind we have just examined concerning the impracticability of socialism by the eminent Dutch economist, N. G. Pierson, provoked K. Kautsky, then the leading theoretician of Marxian socialism, to break the traditional silence about the actual working of the future socialist state, and to give in a lecture, still somewhat hesitantly and with many apologies, a description of what would happen on the Morrow of the Revolution.[2] But Kautsky only showed that he was not even really aware of the problem which the economists had seen. He thus gave Pierson the opportunity to demonstrate in detail, in an article which first appeared in the Dutch *Economist*, that a socialist state would have its problems of value just as any other economic system and that the task socialists had to solve was to show how in the absence of a pricing system the value of different goods was to be determined. This article is the first important contribution to the modern discussion of the economic aspects of socialism, and although it remained practically unknown outside of

relation between socialist states. *Cf.* his essay on " The Incompatibility of Socialism and Nationalism " in *The Economic Outlook*, London, 1912.

[1] A completely neglected attempt to solve the problem from the socialist side, which shows at least some realization of the real difficulty, was made by G. Sulzer, *Die Zukunft des Sozialismus*, Dresden, 1899.

[2] An English translation of this lecture, originally given in Delft on April 24, 1902, and soon afterwards published in German, together with that of another lecture given two days earlier at the same place, was published in London, 1907, under the title, *The Social Revolution and On the Morrow of the Social Revolution*.

Holland and was only made accessible in a German version after the discussion had been started independently by others, it remains of special interest as the only important discussion of these problems published before the War. It is particularly valuable for its discussion of the problems arising out of the international trade between several socialist communities. An English translation is now reproduced in the next section in the volume and we need therefore say no more about its argument.

All the further discussions of the economic problems of socialism which appeared before the War confined themselves more or less to the demonstration that the main categories of prices, as wages, rent and interest, would have to figure at least in the calculations of the planning authority in the same way in which they appear to-day and would be determined by essentially the same factors. The modern development of the theory of interest played a particularly important rôle in this connection, and after Böhm-Bawerk [1] it was particularly Professor Cassel who showed convincingly that interest would have to form an important element in the rational calculation of economic activity. But none of these authors even attempted to show how these essential magnitudes could be arrived at in practice. The one author who at least approached the problem was the Italian economist Enrico Barone who in 1908 in an article on the Ministry of Production in the Col-

---

[4] In addition to his general work on interest, his essay on " Macht und ökonomisches Gesetz " (*Zeitschrift für Volkswirtschaft, Sozialpolitik und Verwaltung*, 1914) should be specially mentioned, which in many ways must be regarded as a direct predecessor of the later critical work.

28

lectivist State developed certain suggestions of Pareto's.[1] This article is of considerable interest as an example of how it was thought that the tools of mathematical analysis of economic problems might be utilized to solve the tasks of the central planning authority. An English translation will be found as an appendix to this volume.

## 9. THE WAR AND ITS EFFECTS ON CONTINENTAL SOCIALISM

When with the end of the Great War socialist parties came into power in most of the states of Central and Eastern Europe, the discussion on all these problems necessarily entered a new and decisive phase. The victorious socialist parties had now to think of a definite programme of action and the socialist literature of the years immediately following the War was for the first time largely concerned with the practical question how to organize production on socialist lines. These discussions were very much under the influence of the experience of the war years when the states had set up food and raw material administrations to deal with the serious shortage of the most essential commodities. It was generally assumed that this had shown that not only was central direction of economic activity practicable and even superior to a system of competition, but also that the special technique of planning developed to cope with the problems of war economics might be equally applied to the permanent administration of a socialist economy.

[1] V. Pareto, *Cours d'Economie Politique*, Vol. II, Lausanne, 1897, pp. 364 *et seq.*

Apart from Russia, where the rapidity of change in the years immediately following the revolution left little time for quiet reflection, it was mainly in Germany and even more so in Austria that these questions were most seriously debated. Particularly in the latter. country whose socialists had always played a leading rôle in the intellectual development of socialism, and where a strong and undivided socialist party had probably exercised a greater influence on its economic policy than in any other country outside of Russia, the problems of socialism had assumed enormous practical importance. It may perhaps be mentioned in passing that it is rather curious how little serious study has been devoted to the economic experiences of this country in the decade after the War, although they are probably more relevant to the problems of a socialist policy in the Western world than anything that has happened in Russia. But whatever one may think about the importance of the actual experiments made in Austria, there can be little doubt that the theoretical contributions made there to the understanding of the problems will prove to be a considerable force in the intellectual history of our time.

Among these early socialist contributions to the discussions, in many ways the most interesting and in any case the most representative for the still very limited recognition of the nature of the economic problems involved, is a book by Dr. O. Neurath which appeared in 1919, in which the author tried to show that war experiences had shown that it was possible to dispense with any considerations of value in the administration of the supply of commodities and that all the calculations of the central planning authorities should and could be carried out *in natura*, i.e. that the calculations need not be carried through in terms of some common unit of value but that they could be made in kind.[1]  Neurath was quite oblivious of the insuperable difficulties which the absence of value calculations would put in the way of any rational economic use of the resources and even seemed to consider it as an advantage.  Similar structures apply to the works published about the same time by one of the leading spirits of the Austrian social-democratic party, Dr. O. Bauer.[2]  It is impossible here to give any detailed account of the argument of these and a number of other related publications of that time.  They have to be mentioned, however, because they are important as representative expression of socialist thought just before the impact of the new criticism and because much of this criticism is naturally directly or implicitly concerned with these works.

In Germany discussion centred round the proposals of the " socialization commission " set up to discuss the possibilities of the transfer of individual industries to the ownership and control of the State.  It was this commission or in connection with its deliberations that economists like Professor E. Lederer and Professor E. Heimann and the ill-fated W. Rathenau developed plans for socialization which became the main topic of discussion among economists.  For our purpose, however, these proposals are less interesting than their Austrian counterparts because they did not contemplate a completely socialized system but were mainly concerned with the problem of the organization of individual socialized industries in an otherwise competitive system.

---

[1] O. Neurath, *Durch die Kriegswirtschaft zur Naturalwirtschaft*, München, 1919.

[2] O. Bauer, *Der Weg zum Sozialismus*, Wien, 1919.

For this reason their authors did not have to confront the main problems of a really socialist system. They are important, nevertheless, as symptoms of the state of public opinion at the time and in the nation where the more scientific examination of these problems began. One of the projects of this period deserves perhaps special mention not only because its authors are the inventors of the now fashionable term " planned economy ", but also because it so closely resembles the proposals for planning now so prevalent in this country. This is the plan developed in 1919 by the Reichswirtschaftsminister R. Wissel and his under-secretary of state W. v. Moellendorf.[1] But interesting as their proposals of organization of individual industries are and relevant as is the discussion to which they gave rise to many of the problems discussed in England at the present moment, they cannot be regarded as socialist proposals of the kind discussed here, but belong to the halfway house between capitalism and socialism, discussion of which for reasons mentioned above has been deliberately excluded from the present work.

## 10. MISES, MAX WEBER AND BRUTZKUS

The distinction of having first formulated the central problem of socialist economics in such a form as to make it impossible that it should ever again disappear from the discussion belongs to the Austrian economist Professor Ludwig von Mises. In an article on *Economic*

---

[1] This plan was originally developed in a memorandum submitted to the Cabinet of the Reich on May 7, 1919, and later developed by R. Wissel in two pamphlets, *Die Planwirtschaft*, Hamburg, 1920, and *Praktische Wirtschaftspolitik*, Berlin, 1919.

*Calculation in a Socialist Community*, which appeared in the spring of 1920,[1] he demonstrated that the possibility of rational calculation in our present economic system was based on the fact that prices expressed in money provided the essential condition which made such reckoning possible. The essential point where Professor Mises went far beyond anything done by his predecessors was the detailed demonstration that an economic use of the available resources was only possible if this pricing was applied not only to the final product but also to all the intermediate products and factors of production, and that no other process was conceivable which would take in the same way account of all the relevant facts as did the pricing process of the competitive market. A translation of this article is contained in the present volume and it is hoped that the larger work in which it was later incorporated will also soon be available in an English edition. Together the two works represent the starting-point from which all the discussions of the economic problems of socialism, whether constructive or critical, which aspire to be taken seriously must necessarily proceed. As the main argument is contained in the article reproduced later in this volume, nothing further need to be said about it at this point.

While Professor Mises' writings contain beyond doubt the most complete and successful exposition of what from then onwards became the central problem, and while they had by far the greatest influence on all further

---

[1] Die Wirtschaftsrechnung im sozialistischen Gemeinwesen, *Archiv für Sozialwissenschaften und Sozialpolitik*, Vol. 47/1, April, 1920. Most of this article has been embodied in the more elaborate discussion of the economic problems of a socialist community in Part II of Professor Mises' *Gemeinwirtschaft*, Jena, 1922, 2nd ed., 1932.

discussions, it is an interesting coincidence that about the same time two other distinguished authors arrived independently at very similar conclusions. The first was the great German sociologist Max Weber, who in his posthumous *magnum opus*, *Wirtschaft und Gesellschaft*, which appeared in 1921, dealt expressly with the conditions which in a complex economic system made rational decisions possible. Like Professor Mises (whose article he quotes as having come to his notice only when his own discussion was already set up in print), he insisted that the *in natura* calculations proposed by the leading advocates of a planned economy could not provide a rational solution of the problems which the authorities in such a system would have to solve. He emphasized in particular that the rational use and the preservation of capital could be secured only in a system based on exchange and the use of money, and that the wastes due to the impossibility of rational calculation in a completely socialized system might be serious enough to make it impossible to maintain alive the present populations of the more densely inhabited countries.

> The assumption that some system of accounting would in time be found or invented if one only tried seriously to tackle the problem of a moneyless economy does not help here : the problem is the fundamental problem of any complete socialization and it is certainly impossible to talk of a *rationally* " planned economy " while in so far as the all-decisive point is concerned no means for the construction of a " plan " is known.[1]

A practically simultaneous development of the same ideas is to be found in Russia. Here in the summer of 1920 in the short interval after the first military

[1] Max Weber, *Wirtschaft und Gesellschaft* (Grundriss der Sozial-ökonomik, Vol. III), Tübingen, 1921, pp. 55–6.

successes of the new system, when it had for once become possible to utter criticisms in public, Professor Boris Brutzkus, a distinguished economist mainly known for his studies in the agricultural problems of Russia, subjected to a searching criticism in a series of lectures the doctrines governing the action of the communist rulers. These lectures, which appeared under the title " The Problems of Social Economy under Socialism " in a Russian journal and were only many years later made accessible to a wider public in a German translation,[1] show in their main conclusion a remarkable resemblance to the doctrines of Mises and Max Weber, although they arose out of the study of the concrete problems which Russia had to face at that time, and although they were written at a time when their author, cut off from all communication with the outside world, could not have known of the similar efforts of the Austrian and German scholars. Like Professor Mises and Max Weber his criticism centres round the impossibility of a rational calculation in a centrally directed economy from which prices are necessarily absent. An English translation of this essay, together with discussion of the development of economic planning in Russia which conforms in a remarkable way to the expectations which could be based on such theories, will appear simultaneously with the present book as a companion volume to it.

[1] The original title under which these lectures appeared in the winter 1921–2 in the Russian journal *Ekonomist* was the *Problems of Social Economy under Socialism*. They were later reprinted in Russian as a pamphlet which appeared in Berlin, 1923, and a German translation under the title *Die Lehren des Marxismus im Lichte der russischen Revolution* was published in Berlin, 1928.

## 11. More Recent Continental Discussion

Although to some extent Max Weber and Professor Brutzkus share the credit of having pointed out independently the central problem of the economics of socialism, it was the more complete and systematic exposition of Professor Mises, particularly in his larger work on *Die Gemeinwirtschaft*, which has mainly influenced the trend of further discussion on the Continent. In the years immediately succeeding its publication a number of attempts were made to meet his challenge directly and to show that he was wrong in his main thesis, and that even in a strictly centrally directed economic system values could be exactly determined without any serious difficulties. But although the discussion on this point dragged on for several years, in the course of which Mises twice replied to his critics, it became more and more clear that in so far as a strictly centrally directed planned system of the type originally proposed by most socialists was concerned, his central thesis could not be refuted. Much of the objections made at first were really more a quibbling about words caused by the fact that Mises had occasionally used the somewhat loose statement that socialism was impossible, while what he meant was that socialism made rational calculation impossible. Of course any proposed course of action, if the proposal has any meaning at all, is possible in the strict sense of the word, i.e. it may be tried. The question can only be whether it will lead to the expected results, that is whether the proposed course of action is consistent with the aims which it is intended to serve. And in so far as it had been hoped to achieve by means of central direction of all economic activity *at one and the same time* a distribution of income independent of private property in the means of production and a volume of output which was at least approximately the same or even greater than that procured under free competition, it was more and more generally admitted that this was not a practicable way to achieve these ends.

But it was only natural that even where Professor Mises' main thesis was conceded this did not mean an abandonment of the search for a way to realize the socialist ideals. Its main effect was to divert attention from what had so far been universally considered as the most practicable forms of socialist organization to the exploration of alternative schemes. It is possible to distinguish two main types of reaction among those who conceded his central argument. In the first place there were those who thought that the loss of efficiency, the decline in general wealth which will be the effect of the absence of a means of rational calculation, would not be too high a price for the realization of a more just distribution of this wealth. Of course if this attitude is based on a clear realization of what this choice implies there is no more to be said about it, except that it seems doubtful whether those who maintain it would find many who will agree with their idea. The real difficulty here is, of course, that for most people the decision on this point will depend on the extent to which the impossibility of rational calculation would lead to a reduction of output in a centrally directed economy compared with that of a competitive system. And although in the opinion of the present writer it seems that careful study can leave no doubt about the enormous magnitude of that difference, it must be admitted that there is no simple way to prove how great that difference would be. The answer here cannot be derived from general considerations but will have to be based on a careful comparative study of the working of the two alternative systems, and presupposes a much greater knowledge of the problems involved than can possibly be acquired in any other way but by a systematic study of economics.[1]

The second type of reaction to Professor Mises' criticism was to regard it as valid only as regards the particular form of socialism against which it was mainly directed, and to try to construct other schemes that would be immune against that criticism. A very considerable and probably the more interesting part of the later discussions on the Continent tended to move in that direction. There are two main tendencies of speculation. On the one hand it was attempted to overcome the difficulties in question by extending the element of planning even further than had been contemplated before, so as to abolish completely the free choice of the consumer and the free choice of occupation. Or on the other hand it was attempted to introduce various elements of competition. To what extent these proposals really overcome any of the difficulties and to what extent they are practical will be considered in later sections of this volume. In so far as the result of the German dis-

[1] It is perhaps necessary in this connection to state explicitly that it would be wholly inconclusive if such a comparison were made between capitalism as it exists (or is supposed still to exist) and socialism as it might work under ideal assumptions—or between capitalism as it might be in its ideal form and socialism in some imperfect form. If the comparison is to be of any value for the question of principle, it has to be made on the assumption that either system is realized in the form which is most rational under the given condition of human nature and external circumstances which must of course be accepted.

cussions are concerned, Professor G. Halm, who has taken a very active part in these debates, summarizes in his contribution to the present volume, the present state of opinion among those who take a critical attitude to the present. A list of all the more important contributions made in this debate from both sides will be found in the appendix.

## 12. The Purpose of the Present Volume

In the English-speaking world the discussion of these problems began at a considerably later date than on the Continent, and, although it probably began on a somewhat higher level, thus avoiding many of the more elementary mistakes, and has in the last few years produced a number of important studies (also listed in the Appendix just referred to), it has made little use of the results of the discussions on the Continent.[1] Yet clearly it is wasted effort to disregard these precedents. It is the purpose of this volume therefore to present within two covers the main results of the critical analysis of socialist planning attempted by Continental scholars. Together with the translation of Professor Mises' major work and the companion volume containing Professor Brutzkus' studies on Russia it should give a fairly comprehensive survey of the problems raised by any kind of planning.

The present volume, accordingly, is a collection of

[1] A noteworthy early and independent exposition of the way in which the problem of value will make itself felt in a socialist society and of the difficulties which would impede the rational distribution of resources in such a society occurs in a little known small book by John Bowen, *Conditions of Social Welfare*, London, 1926, particularly pp. 23 *et seq.*

material, which may serve as a basis for further discussion, rather than a systematic or connected exposition of a single point of view. The individual essays here collected were not intended for publication in a single volume, but were written at different times and for different purposes. In nearly all cases the later articles were written in ignorance of the earlier ones. The inevitable effect of this is some degree of repetition and occasional differences of opinion between the authors represented. The arrangement follows the chronological order of appearance of the original essays, excepting that of Barone, which is relegated to an appendix only because it is decidedly more technical than the rest of the book. The second appendix contains a bibliography of the more important works on the same subject, which have been published since 1920.

In a concluding essay the editor has attempted to follow up some of these lines of thought and to examine in their light some of the more recent developments of English speculation. It is in this connection also that an attempt is made to assess the importance of the conclusions so far arrived at and to judge their relevance to the practical problems of our day.

## II

# THE PROBLEM OF VALUE IN THE SOCIALIST COMMUNITY [1]

By N. G. PIERSON

(*Translated by* G. GARDINER.)

A STRIKING and somewhat disquieting characteristic of our time is the fact that so little attention is paid, particularly by the younger generation, to problems of theoretical economics. It is the more striking because, in view of the present enthusiasm for social legislation, just the contrary might have been expected. As long as things are permitted to take their own course and the activity of the State is restricted to the maintenance of· order—apart from the provision of education, the execution of public works, and so on—then only scientific interest will provide a stimulus to theoretical economic research. A practical stimulus only appears when people begin to have doubts as to the usefulness of the *laissez-faire* principle. Then they must know, if they are to avoid fundamental errors in their plans for improving conditions, what effect may be expected to result from a given action under given circumstances ; in other

[1] [This article appeared originally under the title " Het waarde-problem in een socialistische Maatschappij " in the Dutch periodical *De Economist* (Vol. 41, s'Gravenhage, 1902, pp. 423–56), and was later reprinted in N. G. Pierson's *Verspreide Economische Geschriften*, edited by C. A. Verrijn Stuart (Haarlem, 1910, Vol. 1, pp. 333–77).—*Ed.*]

words, they must know the significance of the most important economic laws and how these laws operate. Any innovation which was not based upon such knowledge would be a leap in the dark ; and it is the aim of theoretical economics to provide us with this knowledge. The workman who does not wish to improve his tools need not concern himself with mechanics, and the landlord who is content to leave his house as it stands need not study architecture. But the present generation desires radically to improve the social mechanism and is at least far from satisfied with its structure. How, then, may we explain the fact that, with certain exceptions, so little attention is paid to economic theory ?

In order to give a complete answer to this question, various circumstances would have to be considered. It appears to me, however, that the explanation lies principally in the growing sympathy with socialism which is displayed by the younger generation. Theoretical economics seeks to elucidate the construction of society, but present society, in the opinion of many, is doomed ; and whoever believes this cannot be attracted to the scientific study of something whose early disappearance is certain. Who will look for the connection between the wages of labour and capital when he regards the wage system as a form of slavery and discovers the source of interest in an injustice ? Who will devote himself to problems which arise out of the free play of supply and demand, when he seeks to place individuals in quite a different economic relationship to each other than that determined by the law of supply and demand ? Who will attempt to unveil the secrets of the exchanges and the money market, when he believes that bill brokerage is a symptom of disease and money an unnecessary evil ? People who profess such opinions believe that more serious questions, matters of more vital interest, claim the attention of thoughtful men ; and if we ask what problems they have in mind we are referred to the works of Karl Marx. Social legislation, according to them, is useful, but only a makeshift. A complete renewal of society must be the goal.

In this essay I hope to show that it is a mistake to believe on these grounds that the efforts of theoretical economics are unnecessary. This branch of knowledge can never be neglected—not even in the event of socialism being carried into practice. As to whether socialism can be carried into practice I shall not decide here. But for the sake of argument let us suppose that it is. In this case, admittedly, many of the problems which now demand our attention would disappear, but this is by no means true of all the problems, nor of the most important ; these would merely assume other forms. It is not to be believed that the best economic writings of our day would in such circumstances become worthless ; they would be referred to, and not in vain, for advice on many important questions. One problem above all would remain and, appearing in the most diverse forms, would call for a practical solution. I mean the problem of value.

The problem of value ? These words will astonish many of my readers ; this will be the last thing they expected. The problem of value in a socialist society ? Surely, if socialism is realized, there will be no value phenomena and therefore no value problem. Then everything will be a mere question of technique. This opinion is, in actual fact, very widely held, but how-

ever popular it is, and however frequently and dogmatically stated, it is nevertheless profoundly erroneous.
And from more than one point of view the error is
grave. There is first of all the scientific aspect of the
matter. If the view which I am opposing were correct,
then everything which has been taught by the foremost
thinkers in recent years on the idea of value would have
to be completely revised. Secondly, there is the objection that this theory obscures any clear understanding
of the conditions of life in any society—makes, in fact,
such an understanding impossible. Whoever believes
that under the regimen of socialism value has no important task to perform fails to apprehend these conditions of life ; he confuses a particular form of social
life with life itself and lacks a sufficiently clear apprecia-
tion of the duties which the government of a socialist
state would have to discharge.

To many readers of this journal all this will appear
self-evident. Others, however, may require a more
detailed elucidation of what has been said, and this I
hope to offer in these pages. A short digression may
first however be permitted. As, in this essay I shall
speak continually of socialism, I should like to explain
what is to be understood by this term.

There are various kinds of socialism. The first, if
I may be permitted the expression, is the *socialism of
hope*. No serious thinker can study our social system
without becoming aware of its defects, and a recognition
of these may make so deep an impression upon him
that he may begin to have doubts as to whether the
existing social structure can last. If in addition he
believes wholeheartedly in the progress of human nature
and in the evolution of altruistic motives, then he may

eventually reach the point of predicting that these motives will one day become dominant ; and to this he may perhaps subjoin a second prediction which says that a renewal of the social order will one day follow of its own accord. The second prediction is not inseparable from the first ; indeed, it is not difficult to adduce reasons for maintaining that the first precludes the second. Let us assume that mankind has attained so high a degree of moral rectitude that social evils which arise out of a defective moral sense have either disappeared or at least considerably diminished. Alcoholic excess has become rare. Among the workers a sense of duty reigns supreme ; everywhere concern is felt for the future, and to-morrow is no longer sacrificed to to-day. The entrepreneurs conduct themselves as only the best of them behave to-day. Poor relief is organized better and provides real assistance for those in need. Social legislation bears the stamp of the higher ethical code which is gradually being enforced. In such circumstances would there be a call for a reorganization of society ? Or would it then be realized—what has so long and so often been pointed out—that the chief cause of poverty lies not in the social organization but in men themselves ; in the fecklessness and thoughtless conduct of some and in the dissipation and indifference to the common good of others ? Is it not further possible that our descendants having attained so lofty an ethical plane, would hesitate to introduce measures which might involve a lower standard of living for the majority ? Admittedly there are perils which threaten morality in the present order of society ; but this is common to any conceivable social order. Communism, for example, might encourage negligence, idleness or

45

even habitual theft, while on the other hand sagacity and the power of organization might be lost under this system. To predict, therefore, that there will be a considerable improvement in moral standards in no way compels us to predict that society will be reorganized on new principles. Logically the two predictions are independent of each other. In actual fact, however, the first is often linked to the second, and thus arises that socialism of hope which, as I have said, attracts so wide a following to-day. Its partisans have no clear conception of what the future will bring forth. If we suggest to them that they should at least give an account of the general.lines upon which they would proceed to a solution of the various practical problems which would confront socialism, then we are regarded with an air of pity ; we have failed to appreciate their point of view. Some vague feeling tells them that the social order in which we live to-day cannot endure, and that there are hidden moral forces in humanity which as they wax stronger will evolve a better system. They make no attempt, however, to expound this better system nor, in their view, should they be asked to do so. Thus it is even possible to describe this form of socialism as *poetical* socialism. Yet the best plan of all is to follow the advice of Cairnes and to deny it the name of socialism altogether. John Stuart Mill, in his autobiography, numbered himself among the socialists, because he believed that certain ideals would be realized in the distant future. In this connection Cairnes pointed out that true socialism does not consist of a body of ideals which can only be realized if human nature and the conditions of human life are radically transformed. Socialism subsists in the recommendation of certain modes of action and in the utilization of the authority of the state for particular purposes.[1] This appears to me also as the correct view. If, for the purposes of this essay, we describe socialism in this way, then no misunderstandings will arise on account of nomenclature.

Pure communism is just as vague in its conception and just as dogmatically presented as the socialism of hope. In so far as it relates to family life, communism must be sharply distinguished from socialism, but its principles as to the division of income have had the full support of certain socialists.

If the rights already acquired in the existing system are left out of consideration, then there remain alternative principles upon which to base the division of income : a division which is independent of services rendered and a division which takes services rendered as its measure. There is no third method ; and whoever calls himself socialist must, if he wishes to avoid confusion, decide for one or the other. This does not mean that a decision for the second principle implies starvation for those who cannot perform services. The implication is rather that those who cannot perform services will receive only the bare means of subsistence. The first principle is that of communism. It dissolves the connection between work performed and income received. That you must work, it says, is one thing ; that you receive food, clothing and the means of subsistence is another. The second principle is that of society as it exists to-day—though it is not confined to such a society.

The first principle presupposes an obligation on the part of everyone to work. In the programme of the

[1] *Some Leading Principles of Political Economy Newly Expounded*, London, 1874, p. 316.

47

disciples of Marx and Lassalle which was laid down in Gotha in 1875 and which demanded a division " according to equal rights and the reasonable requirements of the individual ", there are included the significant words " with the obligation to work ". If the State is to provide us with all our needs, then it must dispose of all labour at its own discretion, otherwise its task will be impossible. It must be in a position to place us where our work is required and it must not be so far influenced by our wishes that they interfere with its plans. Only the second principle is compatible with a free choice of vocation. Whoever does not wish to relinquish this freedom must oppose communism. This is not to say that he must approve of the existing social system. So far as the principles of the division of income are concerned, it is quite possible, assuming certain adaptations, to imagine a social order which lies between the present system and communism, and which is related to both. Indeed, there is room here for several systems, some of which tend towards the left and others towards the right, and all of them being entitled to the name of socialism.

It is this third kind of which I desire to give an account. It is not to be spoken of with too easy a contempt. Let us not allude to deformed and bastard systems. Where has it been laid down that a social order which is not the logical application of an economic doctrine cannot be practicable ? Why should we not take over from communism and the existing social order just what we choose, if in this way we can attain the system we desire ? I am not suggesting that such a course of action would be wise or good ; I merely affirm that it should not be condemned *a priori*. I do not doubt that in practice this procedure might meet with insuperable difficulties, but I believe we can only be certain of this when we have decided what features of each system are to be appropriated. Many of them will be compatible with one another, many will not ; others will only adjust themselves with difficulty. Socialists of the third group will have to enlighten us on this point. As long as they fail to do this completely we shall have to reserve our judgment on their system as a whole and confine our criticism to such of the parts as have been more or less clearly elaborated.

We are, however, entitled to insist that socialists shall be consistent ; that is to say, when they are put to the question, they must not take up the standpoint first of one group of socialists and then of another ; this would make any fruitful discussion impossible.

Now in what follows let me make certain assumptions. Let me assume that you, reader, are an energetic propagandist and that you are doing your best to secure for socialism a position of influence in the State. You are foremost in prosecuting the class-war. This war is based upon Marx' doctrine that capital receives a share of the product which is not due to it and that it exists therefore at the expense of the worker. When socialists make use of the expression " capitalistically organized society " they mean a society in which all the means of production are in the hands of the capitalists. This state of affairs, they maintain, must be transformed, the lords must be dethroned ; and as those in power are not ordinarily prepared to abdicate of their own free will they must be forcibly deposed in the class-war. Such a war necessarily leads to a political revolution. What must take place then—" on the morrow of the revolution " as Kautsky expressed it briefly in Delft [1]—has in part been communicated to us by this leader of the Marxian school. To know this was even more important than to know the points at which he considered intervention to be desirable.

Now you, reader, are fighting in word and deed on behalf of these ideas, and we therefore ask you a few questions. You are asked to clear up certain very important matters which you and those who think with you have allowed to remain obscure. You are asked how you would propose to order things once it was decided to introduce socialism. That you refuse to answer. You do not accept the notion of introducing socialism. Socialism you say, will come of its own accord in the natural course of evolution, and once this fact is grasped it is clear that difficulties which would otherwise be insuperable will not arise at all. " The uninterrupted evolution of society which makes no sudden jumps, even though it sometimes appears to do so, must itself overcome them. The social democrats proceed upon the assumption that human society, like nature as a whole, is governed by the principle of evolution, of evolution to higher forms. The later stages of society must always be more advanced than those which have preceded them. From this it follows that the intermediate stages and the transitional forms must adjust themselves to the conditions which they find in existence when they arise." [2]

---

[1] [A reference to K. Kautsky's speech made in Delft on April 24, 1902, and later published in an English translation in a pamphlet, *The Social Revolution and on the Morrow of the Revolution*, London, 1907.—*Ed.*]

[2] Loopuet in *Het Volk* of April 20, 1902.

This I find perplexing. Whether evolution never "makes jumps" is a problem in itself upon which the most recent researches of Professor Hugo de Vries have thrown much light ; but it is certain that the socialists who talk in this way are "making jumps" day by day as they participate in the class-war, and their intention that society shall do the same is as clear as possible. Why do they devote themselves so ardently to propaganda if their work will in any case be done for them by the evolution of society ? And why is a Kautsky called into being to tell us what will happen "on the morrow of the revolution" ? If nature is working on our behalf even to the extent of removing "obstacles" which would otherwise be "insuperable", then the life of the socialist must be easy indeed. Yet you, reader, as a socialist, do not seem to conceive it as such.

Before making my second assumption, let me say a few words by way of introduction. Much ill is spoken of communism, and not without reason : few people, I believe, take it altogether seriously to-day. But we must grant it one thing : for the grave problem of unemployment it offers something more than a solution ; for in a communist society the problem cannot arise. If the enjoyment of income is entirely divorced from any rendering of services, it is quite true that great poverty and even starvation may occur ; but this distress will be common to all and will not be confined to those whose work has become temporarily superfluous. Unemployment—I use the word in its technical sense— can only arise in a society in which income depends on service of one sort or another ; and that precisely is what is absent from communism.

This system therefore deals finally with the problem

of unemployment ; but—and let us mark this fact—this is true of no other system than communism. The unemployment problem is not solved merely by placing the means of production in the hands of the State. In the State factory there will not always be employment for the same number of workers. Seasonal variations, changes in taste and fashion, temporary shortages of raw material and excessive stocks due to overestimating the requirements of consumption and export—all these circumstances must arise in any society, however it may be constructed. It may indeed be established that workers who are discharged in such cases shall continue to receive a certain income. Such an income, however, cannot in principle be distinguished in any way from relief, and it is possible without the aid of socialism to mitigate the hardships of unemployment by means of public assistance, labour exchanges and unemployment insurance. Only under communism is it impossible for unemployment—again in its technical sense—to arise.[1]

Then what shall we say of socialists who, proving with every utterance that pure communism is not their objective, nevertheless include among the advantages of their system the disappearance of unemployment. Surely they are decking themselves out in other people's finery ! Their behaviour is comparable to that of people who appeal to the continuity of evolution while pressing on

[1] W. D. P. Bliss, in *A Handbook of Socialism* (London, 1895, p. 197) says explicitly : " if any man refused to work he would be left to starve ". As a palliative he adds : " yet with no one to blame but himself, for *every man would then have an opportunity to work*. By simply doing a few hours of honest work each day for a few years of his life . . . every man would be sure of an honest competence." I doubt, however, whether Bliss was in a position to prove this last statement.

to the greatest of all revolutions. If this continues, the last trace of clarity will vanish from the dispute ; nothing will remain about which argument is possible. To-day the disputant will champion the class-war ; to-morrow (when he has realized to what this war must lead) he will support the socialism of hope ; the day after to-morrow (when he wants to make converts) he will advocate communism ; and so at last (when the absurdities of communism and its demoralizing effects have been demonstrated) he will return to his original position. But this will not do. It is not only essential to know what aim one is pursuing, but also to make it possible for others to know as well.

I have permitted myself this lengthy digression before proceeding to my main study, in order to show that socialism is not to be regarded as a single whole. Even if we ignore " poetical " socialism there still remain the other two, and the distinction between these will have to be kept clearly in mind when we are discussing a socialist society. Such a society may, so far as the division of income is concerned, rest upon a strictly communist foundation ; but it may also retain the principle of the division according to work done, even though it may not recognize as work done all that the existing system understands by these words. In other directions also the socialist society may be in part similar and in part dissimilar to the existing order—may be, in fact, a mixture of various elements. How closely this mixture can resemble the existing system has been indicated in the discussion of Kautsky's speech at Delft in the May number of this journal.[1]

It should not be thought that in demanding con-

---

[1] [*De Economist*, Vol. 41.—*Ed.*]

sistency from socialists I am accusing them of insincerity. Their fault is that they have not always made themselves sufficiently clear as to their own ideals. Thus a certain nonchalance, which is often a peculiarity of their expositional writings, also appears in their polemics. For example, Herr Troelstra, in his *Theorie en Beweging*, ascribes the rejection by the bourgeoisie of the surplus value theory to the fact that this theory is " a standing protest against the ethical feelings of which the bourgeoisie delights to boast " : yet he surely cannot mean this statement to be taken literally. He knows as well as anyone with what weighty arguments—though he may refuse to recognize them—the surplus value theory has been assailed, and he knows how entirely genuine are the ethical feelings of many of those to whom he refers. When he speaks, a few pages later, of the " bourgeois economic doctrine " which " sees the harmony of all interests as a consequence of free competition ", here, again, we are not to take his words literally. He must be quite well aware that the doctrine of Bastiat, which he has in mind, was not approved of by a single writer of repute among the " bourgeois " economists, but that it has in fact been most energetically contested by many of them. Accurate thinking is by no means one of the principal virtues of the social democrats and thus they are guilty of a certain negligence in the exposition of their system. They are not always clear themselves as to what it permits and what it most rigorously excludes. It is possible for them to jump from one point of view to another without themselves being conscious of the change. Onlookers, however, cannot help wishing that they were conscious of it, in order that a considered utterance as to principle might be possible.

We economists—I would add : of the school of Alfred Marshall, as there is no one in the field of thought or endeavour whom we would more willingly recognize as our master and leader—we economists keep an open mind with regard to socialism. Of those who profess that faith we ask only one thing : persuade us ! Yet we cannot be persuaded as to the practicability of any system unless we are first made aware of what it involves and are then given an opportunity of judging whether it would function properly. Do the protagonists of socialism wish to persuade us that the system would work, or do they not ? If they do not, then why all this literature and agitation ? If they do, why do they not grasp the weapons which lie at hand ? That they fail to do so I can only ascribe to the fact that their system has not been thoroughly thought out. Their point of view with regard to the value problem, which I referred to above, and which I have never seen contradicted from socialist sources, makes this appear very probable. The proof that this point of view cannot be maintained may serve to clear up certain points, and it may provide some socialists with a clearer idea of what is demanded of them by a serious student of their opinions.

## I

It is international trade which must first of all claim our attention. This, as is well known, is governed under the present system—and so long as the State does not interfere—by the reciprocal relations of various value phenomena. International trade as it is carried on to-day automatically provides the solutions to a number of practical problems of value. It is now my task to show that some of these problems would persist in the event of the means of production, or at least the more important of them, falling into the hands of the various States. In this case it would be the task of the governments concerned to maintain such trade either on the basis of an agreed code or by negotiation.

Here is one problem of value : who shall furnish the capital necessary for such trade ? Let us state the problem in more detail. If the Netherlands send manufactured goods to Java, and receive in exchange coffee and rice, this business can be transacted in three ways : (1) Java first sends us the coffee and rice, and only when these goods have been received, perhaps only when they have been partly consumed, do we consign the equivalent. (2) The Netherlands first export manufactured goods to Java and await the arrival of the equivalent. (3) Both countries ship their products at approximately the same time, so that they meet half-way. In the first case Java furnishes the capital, in the second the Netherlands, while in the third each does its share. From the point of view of mankind in general there is no doubt as to the proper solution of this problem. There are peoples who could take no part whatever in international trade if they had to supply the necessary capital, because they do not possess it. Others might be in a position to put up the capital, but only by withdrawing it from other purposes from which it could not well be spared. They possess capital, but not nearly enough, and this expresses itself in the rate of interest which is higher with them than elsewhere. A third group of nations, on the other hand, possesses an abundance of available capital, and here the rate of interest is low, sometimes very low. In such countries it is possible for many entrepreneurs to produce commodities and to wait months for payment, while in the meantime their employees' wages have to be paid ; and if in the meantime one of them comes to need capital, there are always persons willing to lend it. Divers credit institutions make a regular business out of the provision of such credits. It is clear that it is the third group of peoples which must provide the capital necessary for international trade, and that the free play of supply and demand will determine automatically to what extent they shall do so.

The manner in which supply and demand perform their task is perhaps not clear to everyone ; many years ago I explained the matter in these columns, and I will now offer a very abridged version of what I then said.[1]

There exists, as is well known, a difference between the value of long- and short-term bills ; this difference is determined by the rate of interest ruling in the domicile of the drawee and not of the drawer, though the latter, in special cases, may exert a certain influence. From this it follows that it cannot as a general rule be profitable to draw bills from a place with a low rate of interest on a place with a high rate. Anyone who is acquainted with exchange business knows also that when the rates of interest in two places are generally different then the long-term bills always run in one direction, namely, from the place with the high rate on the place with the low rate. One never finds a regular quotation for long-term bills in the opposite direction, as there is no regular supply of these. When we consign goods to a place

[1] See *De Economist* of 1867, Part I, pp. 1–19.

with a higher rate of interest we do not draw a bill, but wait for the remittance. When we consign goods to a place with a lower rate of interest we are glad to draw a bill against them. Now let us consider what this means. A merchant in Batavia exports coffee to the Netherlands and draws a long-term bill in settlement of the amount. For this bill he finds a buyer, either another merchant or a banking institution. If it be a merchant, then he buys it because he has to remit money ; and why has he to remit money, if not for goods which he has received ? If, however, he has received goods, then the capital which has to serve as the equivalent of the coffee has gone to Java before the coffee has left it. And this is equally true if the bill has been purchased by a banking institution ; for how can the banking institution pay for the bill if it has no capital, and from what other source can it have obtained the largest part of its capital if not from the payments of share- and bondholders in Europe ? I believe that we need have no hesitation in designating as *active* the trade of peoples who await the receipt of remittances and who therefore commence the export ; while the trade of the others may be described as *passive*. Peoples with abundant capital resources do active business, peoples with limited capital resources do passive business. This arrangement is to the advantage of both parties, since capital will be less useful in places where it is abundant than in places where it is scarce. It is clear that a problem of value has to be solved here. We must avoid employing capital in commerce when its services would be more productive in other directions. We must avoid employing capital for purposes in which it would be less productive than in commerce. And we have seen the mechanism of which society avails itself in regard to these two aspects of the problem.

But this mechanism would not require further consideration in these pages if its expedience and its implications did not claim our attention. We have to investigate not so much the manner in which the problem is solved as its content and practical significance in the widest sense. These will remain the same even if international exchange becomes commerce between States. Then no less than now will the general interest of mankind demand that only such capital be applied to international trade as cannot be more productively employed in other branches of earning ; only such capital in fact as would not perform services of greater value elsewhere. We value things by considering the advantages which, because they are scarce already, would arise if they were not present. The value of the function of capital in every country and in every branch of earning depends therefore upon the degree in which the country or the branch of earning are in need of capital. The various governments will have to look for a measure which will enable them to form a judgment as to this, and such a judgment will be in substance a determination of value. This is what I wished to prove. It is not a purely technical problem which is here in question, but rather a decision as to the most profitable way of employing material things ; and the rightness of such a decision must depend upon the rightness of the evaluation which preceded it.

What has been said of trade is equally true of the means of transport without which no trade is possible ; especially of shipping. These also should be furnished by the peoples who—so far as their character, their situation and other circumstances permit—possess the most capital in relation to their needs. And so it happens to-day. The entrepreneurs seek out the most profitable branches of earning and unless legislation brings about an artificial change capital and labour flow to where, in relation to other branches of business, they will receive the greatest reward for their services. There are peoples who, if possible, leave the business of shipping to others ; and they have good reasons for doing so as they would only be able to carry on a shipping business if they withdrew capital from more profitable employment. The conduct of such States as encourage the building and running of ships by means of subsidies is therefore absurd ; they are forcing production into the wrong channels. A people does not necessarily make a bad bargain if it exports goods and so pays for the services of foreign ships. Where this is not to be ascribed to a lack of knowledge or enterprise it is both a proof and a consequence of a wise assessment of the means by which the greatest income may be obtained with the least exertion.

European capital, as is known, has another rôle outside Europe besides that which has just been discussed ; it is employed in building railways and in establishing and operating agricultural and industrial undertakings. The interests of the capitalists provide the stimulus ; but from the point of view of humanity the useful consequences are what we have just indicated. If on account of a reconstruction of society the forces which to-day transport capital into distant parts should disappear, then something else will have to take their place. The practical problem of value which is automatically solved in these cases would not disappear if its automatic solution were made impossible ; it would remain in its entirety. Then no less, it would subsist in the question : how is the necessary capital to be brought to those places where its functions are of especial value ? I describe this as a value problem because such a movement of capital should not be of a magnitude greater than the purpose demands. The movement itself would be pure technique ; but the movement to an extent necessitated by the occasion, such that the interests of the one party are not sacrificed to those of the other, this is much more than technique. To-day these movements are controlled automatically ; excessive efflux of capital from Europe causes the rate of interest to rise and thus restricts the flow. It would be the duty of the socialist State to find a criterion which in this respect would provide the necessary guidance.

Hitherto I have spoken exclusively of capital whose function is international over a period of years. Capital which is invested in commerce, in shipping, or in foreign enterprise as a rule retains its character for an extensive period, even though its owners may frequently and its component parts may continuously change. In international trade, however, capital also renders temporary services. From the numerous examples which might be adduced I select the most striking : I will assume that in a country which is not among the grain-exporting lands there is a failure of crops.

Here it is important to examine with proper care what difficulties would arise in such a case and what twofold task international trade would have to fulfil.

I say *twofold* task. Any text-book will tell us that in the case of a harvest failure prices will rise, while every country which is in a position to deliver grain will exert itself to consign part of its stocks to the State in which the shortage has occurred. The significance of this phenomenon should not be underestimated ; in such cases international trade performs invaluable services. But if it did no more than this it would only have done half of its work ; it would supply the means of subsistence to those who could purchase grain, but that would not be enough. What is chiefly to be feared in the case of a failure of crops ? The danger is that productive work will slacken and unemployment will increase, so that the poor will be unable to buy grain. In what countries are the effects of famine most severe ? In those countries in which labour for wages is the exception and labour for the immediate satisfaction of the workers' needs is the rule. If in a particular year such labour is insufficiently productive, then only charity can help ; for stocks are usually inadequate. In such regions our much reviled capitalism is insufficiently developed. Yet even in countries where capitalism is advanced a serious situation would arise—at any rate for a section of the populace—if in the event of a harvest failure overseas countries did nothing more than export grain. It is no paradox to maintain that the actual import of grain, while on the one hand it prevents great suffering, on the other hand sows the seed of trouble. For this grain is not given away ; it must be paid for. Capital of equal value must leave the country, and in this way the wages fund may be considerably diminished. The course of events will be as follows. As a result of the heavy withdrawals of capital the rate of interest rises and consequently a number of undertakings become temporarily unprofitable. A slump occurs in the building trade and certain factories go on half time. The

construction of new works is abnormally slack and improvements of land are suspended. It should, however,
be noted that the cause of the slump is not the raising
of the rate of interest but the diminution of capital
resources. Raising the rate of interest only determines
what branches of industry will be injuriously affected
by the diminution ; and we shall see that it provides a
very salutary corrective. This corrective will never be
altogether sufficient, but thanks to international exchange
trade it can accomplish much.

The immediate effect of raising the rate of interest is
that the means of exchange is more economically used ;
thus money becomes available. If, moreover, the bank
is well supplied with gold, so that it may increase its
note issue without difficulty, then this also may help to
overcome the embarrassments which have arisen. But
in the acute case which we have assumed more is required ;
foreign countries must assist. They send grain ; but
they must also help in the matter of payment so that the
wages fund is not drawn upon too heavily. In a country
which possesses many saleable foreign securities the
raising of the rate of interest will depress their price
and this will cause an export of securities. This means
that a part of the grain will be paid for with securities.
For the same reason the quotations of the long-term
bills drawn on the country in question will be lowered,
so that foreigners who have claims on the country which
are not yet due will have an interest in retaining such
bills so far as possible ; and where they are unable to
retain them the long-term bills will be bought by foreign
bankers as investments. The trade of the country will
become temporarily less *active* and more *passive*. If the
rise in the rate of interest is considerable, then capital

may even be imported from abroad. Thus, though the serious consequences of the harvest failure may not be avoided, in one way or another they may be spread over a longer period, so that they are more easily borne.

A socialistically organized society will at times be confronted with the same difficulties and it will only be able to overcome them if it follows the example (*mutatis mutandis*) which the existing society has given in such cases. Through its government it will have to borrow capital and pay interest on this capital. An offer to pay interest would certainly be preferable to an appeal to the good will of neighbours. It would then be possible to approach all States without distinction and without having to beg a favour from any of them ; and what is still more important, the necessary capital would be obtained from those who could best spare it at the moment. The only question is whether the demand for, and payment of, interest is compatible with socialist principles. The same question, however, will arise in all the cases which have already been discussed, and probably the opinion will long have been reached that when in international trade one people renders services of the sort described, a settlement by means of interest is warranted by the most elementary principles of justice. Where goods are delivered and the equivalent is not received until months after, then the full equivalent is not recovered unless interest is paid. Where ships are built and put to sea in the service of others, freight may be claimed which includes the payment of interest on the value of the ships. He who puts capital at the disposal of agricultural and industrial undertakings is entitled to demand a reward. He is entitled to demand a reward because he offers something that has value.

Or is it of no value if a man who is only in a position to trade " passively " is given the opportunity of doing business ?  If, seeking to exchange foreign goods for his own products and unable to build ships himself, others provide him with the transport ?  If, wishing to undertake some new enterprise and lacking the necessary means, others put them at his disposal ?  In such ways as these he may win substantial profits, earnings which he would not willingly forgo, and it is only just that he should give up a part of such income to those who have made it possible.  The socialist States would recognize this ;  probably the first to do so would be those who found themselves compelled to draw upon the capital resources of others.  It would soon become clear to them that in their own interest they would have to offer interest payments ;  while the governments to whom these offers were made would realize that, acting in the interests of those whom they represented, they could not refuse to accept them.  Here the fixing of the rate of interest would in any case imply the solution of a value problem ;  the rate would always be based, on the side of the one party, on an evaluation of the services rendered and, on the side of the other party, on the advantages which would be derived from employing the capital at home.

Enough has been said on this subject ; let us turn our attention to another question.  *Under what conditions would the socialist States trade with one another ?*  Some will probably be inclined to reply that the amount of labour expended on each product should serve as a measure for the quantities to be delivered.  But this answer would not get us much further.  In passing I may remark that the selection of this measure of exchange would imply the solution of a value problem—though to be sure a false solution. It would regard all work—industrious and indolent, efficient and inefficient—as of equal value ; the work of a Chinese coolie, for example, would be regarded as the equivalent of the work of a skilled craftsman. In any case the selection of this measure could hardly come seriously into question, as the amount of work required in the production of any article depends on the circumstances in which it is produced. Less work is required on fertile soil than on unfertile soil ; less in a factory furnished with the most up-to-date machines than in one which is not so well equipped. If it is objected that by " work expended " is meant *average* expenditure, then I reply that this would entitle any country to increase arbitrarily the quantity of goods which it demanded from others : it would be possible to do this by producing on less fruitful ground and by less suitable methods. In this way a higher average expenditure would be attained.

Moreover, it may be questioned whether it would promote the general good if a tariff were established according to which every country could exchange with every other country *ad libitum*. Would such an arrangement give general satisfaction ? Let us suppose that in Java the rice harvest has failed and that there is hardly sufficient rice for the inhabitants ; should every other country be permitted to demand as much rice from Java as they thought fit ? Or, vice versa, let us suppose that we in Holland are well supplied with textile products and that in Java, a tropical country where the demand for such articles is not unlimited, there is at the moment a greater need of iron products. Would Java be forbidden to say : I will gladly exchange my products for

66

European articles ; not however for textiles but for iron goods. Or we may consider the matter from the point of view of our own country. Let us assume that we are abundantly supplied with coffee, having recently received large quantities from Brazil ; but that we would willingly increase our stock of other East Indian products. Should we then be prepared to allow Java to take in exchange for coffee as much of our products as they required ? I need not adduce further examples to prove that unlimited exchange according to a fixed tariff could not be permitted, and that international trade between socialistic States could only be maintained according to the principles which govern international trade to-day. These principles are as follows : (1) Unconditional recognition of the freedom of everyone to exchange or not to exchange at his own discretion. (2) Exchange on a basis of equivalent services.

If these principles are not maintained, international trade will develop into a sort of international plunder. If a people can be compelled to part with things which they need for things which they do not need at all ; if they can be forced to transact business which results in loss ; and if such compulsion be expressly sanctioned ; then *exploitation* will become a principle of justice.

Further, when any people concludes an exchange agreement it must be at liberty to make such terms as it deems satisfactory ; in one case one condition of exchange may appear advantageous and in another case a different condition ; this will depend upon the harvest, the season, and the fluctuations of demand, while the expansion of the population may also exert some influence. Thus the socialist States will have to negotiate with one another ; and the practical problems of exchange trade which they will have to solve also in this connection will have to be regarded as so many value problems. Trade between nations, even if carried on by different methods from those we know to-day, will still retain its present character. Its aim and its outcome will be the mutual balancing of international demand.

So far as I can see there is nothing which contradicts this in the principles of socialism or even of communism. Moreover, I do not believe that either system precludes the use of money in international trade. The course of events would not be any simpler if the use of money were abandoned ; for bills of exchange, essential to-day, and hardly to be dispensed with in the future, would then cease to exist. The bill, after all, is an international means of exchange, and for so extensive a commerce as trade between nations it is quite indispensable. For if we exclude exchange trade in its narrow sense—that is, with uncivilized or half-civilized peoples—international trade is conducted in such a way that there is an equal balance of payments in respect to *all* the transactions of each country, but not *as between* each country. The goods and services which for any reason a particular country has to demand from foreign countries as a whole will exactly balance the goods and services which it must or wants to provide to foreign countries as a whole ; but the annual settlement with each single country will show a debit or credit balance. If country A sends us coffee and tea, this is no reason why we should be able to dispose of our butter and cheese in that country. If country B sends us coal, this is no reason why the best possible market for our potato flour should be country B. It would be exceedingly difficult if we had always to seek markets for our

68

goods in the countries from which we required goods, and it would result in our having to accept bad prices. And it would be equally difficult if we could only buy in places where we sell. Thanks to exchange trade, which makes possible a sort of international *clearing*, this is not necessary. We can pay for the calico which we have bought in Bombay with the meat and vegetables which we have exported to London. Bombay then draws on us, payable in London, and we settle our debt through the English banker with bills on London which the meat and vegetable exporter has given up. We can buy coal in Germany and send sugar to America in settlement; the Americans give us remittances on England which are easily negotiable in Frankfurt or Berlin. Socialists will not imagine that general welfare will be promoted by so fashioning trade that such settlements are impossible; and thus their system will not be able to dispense with bills or—at least for international exchange—with money. But as soon as money and bills come into question, so also do prices and exchange-rates, that is, value phenomena; and such value phenomena always give rise to problems—problems which have to be solved.

## II

The questions we have considered hitherto have none of them been purely technical; in all of them the value of things has played a part. But perhaps I shall be reproached. "How should it be otherwise," it will be asked, "since up till now only exchange has been discussed? Turn your attention from international trade and you will discover no value problems in the socialist society."

69

Very well, we will turn our attention to another field of inquiry. We will now discuss the division of income and we will assume that this is effected according to the most advanced method, that of communism. We at once discover a problem which is a value problem in the strictest sense of the word. What is to be regarded as income, and what therefore comes into question when considering the division ? Naturally only net income ; but the income of the socialist State will also be gross income. Raw materials will be required for the goods which it manufactures, and in the course of manufacture fuel and other things will be consumed and machines and tools will be wholly or partly worn out. The live stock which has been reared will have consumed fodder. In order to calculate its net income the communist society would therefore have to subtract all this from the gross product. But we cannot subtract cotton, coal and the depreciation of machines from yarns and textiles, we cannot subtract fodder from beast. We can only subtract the value of the one from the value of the other. Thus without evaluation or estimation the communist State is unable to decide what net income is available for division.

The following considerations must not be forgotten. Let us assume that railways have been laid down, houses and factories have been erected and enlarged, and steam engines have been built. Meanwhile the workers who have been engaged on the work have had to live. They have received what they needed as their share of the social income from the State warehouses. But have they received too much ? Have they created at least as much income as they consumed ? If not, then they have received more than was proper, and society has been impoverished. That this may have been the case is very possible. Not all work is productive in the economic sense, not even all work which has as its object the increase or improvement of material things. The planting of trees in a richly wooded area, or the laying on of water where there is already abundance of good drinking water would not be production. Now while it is clearly not probable that such gross errors would be committed, other and less perceptible mistakes might well be made continuously. It is possible, for example, to miscalculate demand, to carry out works at too high a cost, to put up buildings in the wrong places and to design them in a manner inappropriate to their purpose. The question which has just been asked can therefore only be answered after an estimation of what the workers have consumed and what they have produced ; and the material, etc., which was required for the work, must be taken into account in the reckoning. Thus estimations and evaluations remain indispensable in determining what the communistic society may regard as net income.

It may perhaps be objected that they would not be indispensable if an inventory were made regularly at the end of each year. An inventory of all stocks would be prepared annually, and by comparing this with that of the preceding year the position would be ascertained. The making of an inventory would certainly be essential —and also the strict control of its accuracy—but that would not be enough. The condition of the goods would first have to be considered, and that in itself would entail an estimation. If, for example, it was found that some of the goods were in bad condition, this fact would have to be taken into consideration, and the spoilt goods would not have to be entered as equivalent to the others. Further, account would have to be taken of whether the goods on hand still served a useful purpose. Those which were useless would naturally be written off, but one would have to remember that there are degrees of usefulness. There is another reason why the mere making of an inventory would not be sufficient : the property of a nation is subject to continual fluctuation. I have already given examples of this. Houses and factories may take the place of consumption goods, and between things which vary among themselves it is only possible to make a comparison of *value*. Finally, I must draw attention to the goods in the warehouses destined to be exchanged for foreign products. Even if the stock of such goods was just as extensive as formerly, the State would be impoverished if the exchange relation between these goods and those required from abroad had moved unfavourably.

I do not wish to conceal the difficulties of making an estimate. These difficulties often appear under the existing system because money value cannot always be used as a measure. A railway, a canal, a museum, a school, or a hospital may be of great value to the community, yet they would not fetch a comparable money price or even a single florin. In examining new proposals for public works we always ask : Is the undertaking worth the sacrifice ? We do not ask whether, if it were sold, it would bring in as much as it cost. In many cases the answer to the latter question would be in the negative, but the expenditure would nevertheless be entirely justifiable. Nor do we consider in such cases the utility of the class of things involved considered in the abstract. The hospital which people want to build may, as a hospital, be very useful, but in the site which has been selected it may be superfluous ; there may, for example, be sufficient hospitals already. In such cases we consider value in the sense of the significance of *specific* things or numbers of things with respect to the satisfaction of which we are in need. In the case of the large majority of goods this expresses itself fairly accurately in the money value, at least in regions where exchange trade is highly developed. But in the examples which I have adduced this is not so, and that is one of the reasons why a State or community, in projecting public works which will not bring in a net income, will be wise to finance such works out of ordinary revenue, or if a loan is necessary, to repay it in a given time. But what in the existing society is the exception will be the rule in the communistic society from which exchange is absent. A value criterion will be lacking except for goods which are exported to foreign countries. This difficulty will have to be recognized as such and in one way or another it will have to be overcome. Otherwise, I repeat, the communist State will be unable to determine what it may regard as income.

And there is another problem of value which such a State will have to solve. In order to explain this I must make an assumption as to the manner in which, from the point of view of pure administrative technique, income will be divided in a communist society : I will make what appears to me the most reasonable assumption. As it is unthinkable that the needs of every individual will be taken into account, I will assume that the population is divided into groups as follows : (A) Unmarried persons ; (B) Families without children, and so on. The more numerous the groups, the better ;

yet however numerous they may be, there will always be cases of individuals who are not adapted to any particular group ; and conditions fluctuate so continually that no grouping can be perfect. A corrective is therefore indispensable. It may be assumed that each individual will receive certificates good for such things as are deemed necessary for him as a member of his group, these being valid for a definite period (weekly, monthly, yearly certificates, and so on). The corrective will lie in the fact that exchange of certificates will be permitted by the State warehouses. A person who, in his own estimation, has received too few certificates for any particular article will be able to obtain more of them in exchange for certificates for another article. The value problem is already obvious. A person who is willing to part with one thing for the sake of another values the latter more than the former. The value problem is to set up a suitable tariff for such legitimate exchange.

In any case, however, it would not be possible to maintain this tariff. As soon as the value relations between the certificates alter, the tariff would have to be modified accordingly. Such fluctuations must necessarily result from the same causes as alter the value of things in everyday life ; and these causes would not cease to operate even if exchange trade were no longer the basis of the economic life of society. Let us suppose that there has been a failure of certain crops in the chief producing countries. Or that a severe winter impedes import and causes an excessive demand for warm clothing and fuel. As a result it is feared that stocks of certain goods may be insufficient. To-day, under such circumstances, the prices of the goods which have become scarce would rise so that their consumption would be restricted. In the communist society some means will have to be found for attaining the same end. A decree will have to be promulgated enacting that a certificate good for so much of such and such a commodity will henceforward be good for only three-quarters or half as much. By the same decree the exchange tariff will have to be altered.

But when this is done it will be observed that something very remarkable happens. To receive less of a thing than was expected is a disappointment for everyone—but not for everyone in the same degree. If, for example, meat is scarce, this will hardly disturb those for whom vegetarian diet serves almost as well ; but those who are unwilling to restrict their consumption of meat will look for means which will enable them to continue as usual. There exist no greater differences than in the extent to which men value the enjoyment of particular things. As long as the communist State can supply each person with what he wants, no trading will arise as a result of such differences ; but when this is no longer the case trading is inevitable. Then price lists will be circulated which will tell us for how many cigar, tea, or coffee certificates we can buy other certificates. Thus the commercial principle, which such a society sought in vain to abolish, comes once more into the foreground. Profits which the State should have been able to claim for itself fall to individual persons. The phenomenon of value can no more be suppressed than the force of gravity. What is scarce and useful *has value.* It may well be possible, in a communist society, to make value a source of profit to individuals, but to annihilate value is beyond the power of man.

Value is not the effect but the cause of exchange. Things do not have value because they are exchanged ; they are exchanged because they have value—more value for some people than for others.

From the most advanced type of socialism I pass now to the less advanced ; to the socialism which does not dissolve the connection between services rendered and income, but maintains it in one form or another. What measure for the division of income would be regarded as best by those whose socialism is of this kind I should find it difficult to say. I am not sure they are agreed among themselves. Kautsky's remarks on the division of income in his speech at Delft are very incomplete. This speech did not fulfil its promise by a long way. On so fundamental a matter as international trade not one word was said, and when the question of the regulation of the wages of labour came up, we receive little more than the intimation that they would be regulated according to the productivity of the labour. Is this now accepted as general theory among those who regard Kautsky as their leader ? I do not know whether I may assume so much. It will be well to deal here with another doctrine which has found support, namely, that of *labour certificates*. According to this theory all work should be rewarded with certificates representing as many hours of work as have been done, and the prices of the goods in the State warehouses should in the same way be measured in hours of work or parts thereof. I shall not undertake a criticism of this system any more than I have undertaken a criticism of the communist division of income. I shall not ask how this system would be applied to articles like meat or milk, or to the rent of houses or to goods which in themselves or in respect to their raw materials are imported from abroad, perhaps in exchange for goods which are also made of foreign materials ; or how under such a system the depreciation of machines and the consumption of oil, coal, etc., would be taken into account. Let us confine ourselves to the question which we have chosen to discuss ; let us convince ourselves that in the system described the proposition we have just proved is even more clearly illustrated : namely, that it is impossible to prevent the appearance of value phenomena.

The fixing of prices in hours of work would be an *evaluation*. In accepting this system no attempt would have been made to avoid the value problem or the necessity for its solution ; on the contrary, the necessity would have been fully recognized. An estimate in hours of work might be defective, but in any case it would be an estimate. With regard to the mutual co-ordination of all kinds of labour I do not venture to say the same, as in such a society this can only be based upon the notion that higher ability should not be entitled to a higher income ; it must not therefore be conceived as a co-ordination in value. The pricing of goods in hours of work, however, cannot admit of any other interpretation, because it cannot be intended that in the socialist State particular individuals should be favoured. Yet what was not intended would certainly be the result. Reality would make mock of an evaluation in hours of work, and would set another in its place. For the value of things does not depend upon the amount of labour they have cost, but on a number of causes, among which the amount of labour plays a part, but not the only part.

With this assertion do I not come into conflict with

Ricardo ?  Even if I did, it would not be the first time
that I have joined issue with a man who, not less through
his skill than through the weakness of many of his
arguments, has succeeded in bedazzling his readers.
On this point, however, Ricardo has not been rightly
understood.  German writers, and not they alone, persist with obstinate conviction in talking of the Ricardo-
Marxian value theory.  I, however,—no more than Dr.
Verijn Stuart in his fine thesis *Ricardo en Marx*—have
never been able to discover the slightest relationship
between the doctrines of these two men.  They treat of
quite different things.  Marx seeks to explain the origin
of the return to capital ; Ricardo seeks to elucidate the
reciprocal value relations—the *relations*—of goods which
by the expenditure of capital and work can be increased
*ad libitum*.  His theory may be expressed briefly as
follows.  Let us assume that a hundred products, produced with equivalent labour, are sold ; the first for
1 fl:, the second for 2 fl., the third for 3 fl., and the
last for 100 fl.  In each of these prices 60 per cent. is
labour wages and 40 per cent. is interest on capital.  It
will now be possible to express the value relations
between the 100 products in the following manner :
1, 2, 3 . . . 100 or also as : 0·60, 1·20, 1·80 . . . 60 ;
and if the wages of each hour's work are 20 cents, as
3, 6, 9 . . . 300.  In short, where the wages and interest
contained in each price are in the same relation, and
each hour of labour is paid for at the same rate, then
the relation between the values of the products will
agree with the relation between the number of hours
of work necessary to produce them.

This simple theory, whose correctness is self-evident
to any one who can multiply and divide, enables Ricardo

to arrive at a principle which has only been fully developed by W. C. Mees in his *Overzicht van eenige Hoofdstukker der Staatshuishoudkunde.* In the case assumed above, the price relations undergo no change if the wages rise at the cost of the interest or if the interest rises at the cost of the wages. Such a rise or fall has an influence on the division of income between capital and labour, but on nothing else. That is what Ricardo wishes to emphasize. If, however, we eliminate this general equality of the relation in which wages and interest make up each price, whatever this relation may be ; if, that is, we consider goods in the production of which capital and labour co-operate in very unequal proportions, then the amount of the wages and interest must have a pronounced influence on the value relation of the goods among themselves. The calculation can easily be made ; and whoever follows out the lead of Mees may arrive at the most significant conclusions. Yet, what has all this to do with the doctrine of Marx ? It always appears to me that those who seek to link the two doctrines misapprehend either the one or the other.

I revert to the system of estimation in hours of labour. What effects would it have ? It is not necessary to quote examples of harvest failures, interruptions of trade and other causes of the normal increase of demand for certain goods, in order to show that this method of value determination would lead to the same phenomenon as we saw emerging earlier on : namely, trading. Things which on account of their intrinsic or superficial qualities are more in accordance with taste would have more value than other things which may have cost just as much in labour and they would naturally be in greater demand in exchange for certificates.

Those who applied for such goods after the stock was disposed of would have to be satisfied with less valuable articles ; many would therefore be prepared to offer more for the goods they wanted. Some might receive furniture produced by unskilled cabinet-makers, or pictures of less merit than those acquired by their neighbours. A farmer might receive an unsatisfactory horse. As long as men are prepared to give a higher price for more suitable and beautiful things than for things which are less suitable and beautiful, then the former will be regarded as more valuable than the latter ; and out of this, exchange trade emerges automatically. The state, if it supplied both at the same price, would unintentionally favour certain individuals. And this would also be true if, in the event of a shortage of stocks which could not be rectified in time, the price tariff were left unchanged : speculators would then earn considerable profits by buying up large quantities of the goods in question. That would certainly have its useful side, as it would result in a timely restriction of consumption ; but it would be so little in accordance with socialist ideals that a system that had such consequences would not, in the long run, satisfy a socialist community. Thus it would eventually be recognized that Schäffle was right when he recommended in *The Quintessence of Socialism* that what he (all too briefly) expressed as the " urgency of demand " should be taken into account when determining the value of goods. Socialism of the kind we are discussing would be sufficiently adaptable to enable us to follow his advice ; but it will never come to this without strife. The solution of the " value problem " will probably long remain the problem of the day.

Let us now turn to Kautsky's formula. This socialist

leader, as far as I remember, did not tell us at Delft
how he conceived that prices would be regulated. Nor
did he acquaint us with the principles according to
which the *productivity of labour* would serve as a measure
for wages. One would naturally like to believe that he
had not overlooked the necessity of distinguishing between gross and net income—in which process, as we
have seen, evaluations are inevitable ; but he did not
tell us how these evaluations are to be made. In order
to avoid repetition I will ignore this important point,
though it will have to be cleared up eventually. I will
turn to another matter. We will assume that the net
product has been ascertained. From this is now deducted
what is needed for the various duties of the State, as
enumerated by Kautsky. There is also deducted what
is required to form new capital—a requirement which
Kautsky clearly recognized. In passing I may remark
that he laid great emphasis on this point. He remembered that the profits and rents which are now gained
by entrepreneurs and capitalists remain to a large extent
unconsumed, thus forming capital, and he pointed out
that in a socialist society the same thing must happen
if the society is to endure. But let us proceed. Let us
suppose that the necessary deductions have been made :
does the worker receive the full balance ? If he does,
then he receives more than the formula meant to imply,
for the productivity of the manual labour, which is only
one of the factors of production, is not equivalent to
the product of all the factors of production working
together. A and B do certain work in common ; in this
case the productivity of A's contribution can certainly
never be equal to the product of the combined work of
both of them, and this remains true when A's contri-

bution is not manual labour, but consists of managerial functions, of finding the necessary resources, or of providing the means of subsistence during the period of the work.

Let us suppose that twenty or thirty workers have combined to form a productive association. Their output is very limited because they are not aware of the newest technical inventions and because they do not know how to seize the most favourable opportunities for the purchase of raw materials or for the disposal of their products. Then someone who possesses this knowledge joins them and their enterprise is forthwith more successful ; is the work of this man not productive ?

Or suppose that the association lacks machines. Someone places machines at its disposal, and its income is increased ; has he who provided the machines not contributed to the productivity of the association ?

Or, finally, let us assume that the members of the association are without the means of support, and cannot therefore venture upon lengthy and protracted undertakings or works whose fruits they will only receive after considerable delay. They cannot, for example, send their goods to India or China, but must confine themselves to working for their own market ; moreover, they must demand payment in cash, and this makes sales difficult. Now someone advances them a loan which enables them to seek markets where they will, and to offer long-term credits. This also has a favourable effect on the income of the association. Has the loan not been productive ?

Thus the productivity of labour can only be ascertained, even if the net product is known, by means of a calculation ; and in this calculation evaluation will have to play its part. For experience does not help us to find this out ; we cannot afford, by way of experiment, temporarily to deprive labour of direction and capital. The productivity of the manual work is the value of such work, as opposed to the value of the managerial ability, to the value of the various functions of capital and also, in the case of agriculture, to the value of the advantages which the more fruitful and more favourably situated land offers over and above the worst land in cultivation. Kautsky's formula, quite scientifically interpreted, will be subscribed to by every economist. No one will object to the worker being assured of the full value of his work : that indeed is the aim of all legislation which seeks to prevent derelictions of justice.

For us economists of the old school, this formula provides the starting-point for much research into the social question. If the value of labour determines its reward, then not only the workers themselves, but all who wish to see an improvement in the workers' position must strive to raise this value. Here philanthropy and legislation may find a wide sphere of activity. The economic value of labour is very closely related to the moral and intellectual qualities of mankind, and it will be enhanced by all that improves these qualities. It will be enhanced by an increase in the number of efficient entrepreneurs and, gradually, by the growth of capital. When people talk of the increasing oppression which results from the vigorous growth of capital, we may be sure that they have not given sufficient attention to the value problem. Great numbers may mean power in the sphere of political strategy, but with regard to the division of income they are a source of weakness. This the workers are continually discovering to their own cost.

The magnitude of the population is the reason why agriculture is extended to unfertile lands and why goods have to be exported at low prices (as otherwise sufficient foreign grain would not be obtained). But the same economic law governs the services of the entrepreneurs and the functions of capital. The more abundantly these services and functions are available, the less will be the profits of the entrepreneurs and the interest on capital, while the value of labour will rise. That the value of labour must also be raised by an economic policy which tends to increase the total income follows from what has just been said, as an increase of the total income of a country always leads, in the long run, to an increase of capital.

I would not venture to assert that Kautsky would admit all this. With some points he would certainly disagree, while to others he would give his hearty support. It is comforting to think that, whatever one's point of view in social questions, agreement may be reached on at least many of the important constituent problems.

So I reach the end of my study ; I hope it will be interpreted as such and not as polemics. Whether the socialists are able to solve the value problems I have put to them may soon be proved. But they will certainly not be successful as long as they fail to appreciate the character and the significance of the problems. And these problems must be solved if we are to be in a position to judge whether the ideas which the socialists are now propagating deserve our support.

On this last point I must insist, while rejecting any appeal to evolution. It is true that no great reform has been undertaken in full knowledge of the difficulties which it might meet and that caution can be carried too far. But no reform will be recommended by serious men as long as they are unable to demonstrate its essential practicability and the probable usefulness of its effects. The same must be demanded of socialists. They recommend, as a first step, the transference of the means of production, or at least the most important of them, to the State. What does this mean ? How will the condition of society be affected ? Will it be led gradually to higher forms of life or will it meet obstacles which hinder its further development and even prevent it from procuring the necessities of its existence ? Will what is proposed bring harmony or chaos ? It must be possible to give a satisfactory answer to these questions ; and those who cannot do so should abstain from propaganda. They should refrain from provoking a class-war, the aim of which is to bring about the fateful step whose utility is in question. Let such people take their place among the poetical socialists ; let them restrict themselves to prophecies and the propagation of moral ideas with which every good-hearted man will agree.

I do not desire to see the debate on socialism closed, but rather to see it grow in significance. With this paper I have sought to contribute something to this end. Continued research is called for and I have indicated certain points to which it should be directed.

# III

# ECONOMIC CALCULATION IN THE SOCIALIST COMMONWEALTH[1]

## By LUDWIG von MISES

### (*Translated from the German by* S. ADLER)

## INTRODUCTION

THERE are many socialists who have never come to grips in any way with the problems of economics, and who have made no attempt at all to form for themselves any clear conception of the conditions which determine the character of human society. There are others, who have probed deeply into the economic history of the past and present, and striven, on this basis, to construct a theory of economics of the " bourgeois " society. They have criticized freely enough the economic structure of " free " society, but have consistently neglected to apply to the

[1] [This article appeared originally under the title " Die Wirtschafts-rechnung im sozialistischen Gemeinwesen " in the *Archiv für Sozialwissenschaften*, vol. 47, 1920.—*Ed.*]

economics of the disputed socialist state the same caustic acumen, which they have revealed elsewhere, not always with success. Economics, as such, figures all too sparsely in the glamorous pictures painted by the Utopians. They invariably explain how, in the cloud-cuckoo lands of their fancy, roast pigeons will in some way fly into the mouths of the comrades, but they omit to show how this miracle is to take place. Wherever they do in fact commence to be more explicit in the domain of economics, they soon find themselves at a loss—one remembers, for instance, Proudhon's fantastic dreams of an " exchange-bank "—so that it is not difficult to point out their logical fallacies. When Marxism solemnly forbids its adherents to concern themselves with economic problems beyond the expropriation of the expropriators, it adopts no new principle, since the Utopians throughout their descriptions have also. neglected all economic consider-ations, and concentrated attention solely upon painting lurid pictures of existing conditions and glowing pictures of that golden age which is the natural consequence of the New Dispensation.

Whether one regards the coming of socialism as an unavoidable result of human evolution, or considers the socialization of the means of production as the greatest blessing or the worst disaster that can befall mankind, one must at least concede, that investigation into the conditions of society organized upon a socialist basis is of value as something more than " a good mental exercise, and a means of promoting political clearness and con-sistency of thought ".[1] In an age in which we are approaching nearer and nearer to socialism, and even,

[1] *v.* Kautsky, *The Social Revolution and on the Morrow of the Social Revolution*, London, 1907, Part II, p. 1.

in a certain sense, are dominated by it, research into the problems of the socialist state acquires added significance for the explanation of what is going on around us. Previous analyses of the exchange economy no longer suffice for a proper understanding of social phenomena in Germany and its eastern neighbours to-day. Our task in this connection is to embrace within a fairly wide range the elements of socialistic society. Attempts to achieve clarity on this subject need no further justification.

## 1. The Distribution of Consumption-goods in the Socialist Commonwealth.

Under socialism all the means of production are the property of the community. It is the community alone which can dispose of them and which determines their use in production. It goes without saying that the community will only be in a position to employ its powers of disposal through the setting up of a special body for the purpose. The structure of this body and the question of how it will articulate and represent the communal will is for us of subsidiary importance. One may assume that this last will depend upon the choice of personnel, and in cases where the power is not vested in a dictatorship, upon the majority vote of the members of the corporation.

The owner of production-goods, who has manufactured consumption-goods and thus becomes their owner, now has the choice of either consuming them himself or of having them consumed by others. But where the community becomes the owner of consumption-goods, which it has acquired in production, such a choice will no longer obtain. It cannot itself consume ; it has perforce to

89

allow others to do so. Who is to do the consuming and what is to be consumed by each is the crux of the problem of socialist distribution.

It is characteristic of socialism that the distribution of consumption-goods must be independent of the question of production and of its economic conditions. It is irreconcilable with the nature of the communal ownership of production-goods that it should rely even for a part of its distribution upon the economic imputation of the yield to the particular factors of production. It is logically absurd to speak of the worker's enjoying the " full yield " of his work, and then to subject to a separate distribution the shares of the material factors of production. For, as we shall show, it lies in the very nature of socialist production that the shares of the particular factors of production in the national dividend cannot be ascertained, and that it is impossible in fact to gauge the relationship between expenditure and income.

What basis will be chosen for the distribution of consumption-goods among the individual comrades is for us a consideration of more or less secondary importance. Whether they will be apportioned according to individual needs, so that he gets most who needs most, or whether the superior man is to receive more than the inferior, or whether a strictly equal distribution is envisaged as the ideal, or whether service to the State is to be the criterion, is immaterial to the fact that, in any event, the portions will be meted out by the State.

Let us assume the simple proposition that distribution will be determined upon the principle that the State treats all its members alike ; it is not difficult to conceive of a number of peculiarities such as age, sex, health, occupation, etc., according to which what each receives will be graded. Each comrade receives a bundle of coupons, redeemable within a certain period against a definite quantity of certain specified goods. And so he can eat several times a day, find permanent lodgings, occasional amusements and a new suit every now and again. Whether such provision for these needs is ample or not, will depend on the productivity of social labour.

Moreover, it is not necessary that every man should consume the whole of his portion. He may let some of it perish without consuming it ; he may give it away in presents ; he may even in so far as the nature of the goods permit, hoard it for future use. He can, however, also exchange some of them. The beer-tippler will gladly dispose of non-alcoholic drinks allotted to him, if he can get more beer in exchange, whilst the teetotaller will be ready to give up his portion of drink if he can get other goods for it. The art-lover will be willing to dispose of his cinema-tickets in order the more often to hear good music ; the Philistine will be quite prepared to give up the tickets which admit him to art exhibitions in return for opportunities for pleasure he more readily understands. They will all welcome exchanges. But the material of these exchanges will always be consumption-goods. Production-goods in a socialist commonwealth are exclusively communal ; they are an inalienable property of the community, and thus *res extra commercium.*

The principle of exchange can thus operate freely in a socialist state within the narrow limits permitted. It need not always develop in the form of direct exchanges. The same grounds which have always existed for the building-up of indirect exchange will continue in a socialist state, to place advantages in the way of those who indulge in it. It follows that the socialist state will thus also afford room for the use of a universal medium of exchange—that is, of Money. Its rôle will be fundamentally the same in a socialist as in a competitive society ; in both it serves as the universal medium of exchange. Yet the significance of Money in a society where the means of production are State-controlled will be different from that which attaches to it in one where they are privately owned. It will be, in fact, incomparably narrower, since the material available for exchange will be narrower, inasmuch as it will be confined to consumption-goods. Moreover, just because no production-good will ever become the object of exchange, it will be impossible to determine its monetary value. Money could never fill in a socialist state the rôle it fills in a competitive society in determining the value of production-goods. Calculation in terms of money will here be impossible.

The relationships which result from this system of exchange between comrades cannot be disregarded by those responsible for the administration and distribution of products. They must take these relationships as their basis, when they seek to distribute goods per head in accordance with their exchange value. If, for instance 1 cigar becomes equal to 5 cigarettes, it will be impossible for the administration to fix the arbitrary value of 1 cigar = 3 cigarettes as a basis for the equal distribution of cigars and cigarettes respectively. If the tobacco coupons are not to be redeemed uniformly for each individual, partly against cigars, partly against cigarettes, and if some receive only cigars and others only cigarettes, either because that is their wish or because the coupon office cannot do anything else at the moment, the market conditions of exchange would then have to be observed. Otherwise everybody getting cigarettes would suffer as against those getting cigars. For the man who gets one cigar can exchange it for five cigarettes, and he is only marked down with three cigarettes.

Variations in exchange relations in the dealings between comrades will therefore entail corresponding variations in the administrations' estimates of the representative character of the different consumption-goods. Every such variation shows that a gap has appeared between the particular needs of comrades and their satisfactions because in fact, some one commodity is more strongly desired than another.

The administration will indeed take pains to bear this point in mind also as regards production. Articles in greater demand will have to be produced in greater quantities while production of those which are less demanded will have to suffer a curtailment Such control may be possible, but one thing it will not be free to do ; it must not leave it to the individual comrade to ask the value of his tobacco ticket either in cigars or cigarettes at will. If the comrade were to have the right of choice, then it might well be that the demand for cigars and cigarettes would exceed the supply, or vice versa, that cigars or cigarettes pile up in the distributing offices because no one will take them.

If one adopts the standpoint of the labour theory of value, the problem freely admits of a simple solution. The comrade is then marked up for every hour's work put in, and this entitles him to receive the product of one hour's labour, less the amount deducted for meeting such obligations of the community as a whole as maintenance of the unfit, education, etc.

Taking the amount deducted for covering communal expenses as one half of the labour product, each worker who had worked a full hour would be entitled only to obtain such amount of the product as really answered to half an hour's work. Accordingly, anybody who is in a position to offer twice the labour-time taken in manufacturing an article, could take it from the market and transfer to his own use or consumption. For the clarification of our problem it will be better to assume that the State does not in fact deduct anything from the workers towards meeting its obligations, but instead imposes an income tax upon its working members. In that way every hour of work put in would carry with it the right of taking for oneself such amount of goods as entailed an hour's work.

Yet such a manner of regulating distribution would be unworkable, since labour is not a uniform and homogeneous quantity. Between various types of labour there is necessarily a qualitative difference, which leads to a different valuation according to the difference in the conditions of demand for and supply of their products. For instance, the supply of pictures cannot be increased, *ceteris paribus*, without damage to the quality of the product. Yet one cannot allow the labourer who had put in an hour of the most simple type of labour to be entitled to the product of an hour's higher type of labour. Hence, it becomes utterly impossible in any socialist community to posit a connection between the significance to the community of any type of labour and the apportionment of the yield of the communal process of production. The remuneration of labour cannot but proceed upon an arbitrary basis ; it cannot be based upon the economic valuation of the yield as in a competitive state of society, where the means of production are in private hands, since—as we have seen—any such valuation is impossible in a socialist community. Economic realities impose clear limits to the community's power of fixing the remuneration of labour on an arbitrary basis : in no circumstances can the sum expended on wages exceed the income for any length of time.

Within these limits it can do as it will. It can rule forthwith that all labour is to be reckoned of equal worth, so that every hour of work, whatever its quality, entails the same reward ; it can equally well make a distinction in regard to the quality of work done. Yet in both cases it must reserve the power to control the particular distribution of the labour product. It will never be able to arrange that he who has put in an hour's labour shall also have the right to consume the product of an hour's labour, even leaving aside the question of differences in the quality of the labour and the products, and assuming moreover that it would be possible to gauge the amount of labour represented by any given article. For, over and above the actual labour, the production of all economic goods entails also the cost of materials. An article in which more raw material is used can never be reckoned of equal value with one in which less is used.

## 2. The Nature of Economic Calculation

Every man who, in the course of economic life, takes a choice between the satisfaction of one need as against another, *eo ipso* makes a judgment of value. Such judgments of value at once include only the very satisfaction of the need itself ; and from this they reflect back upon the goods of a lower, and then further upon goods of a higher order. As a rule, the man who knows his own mind is in a position to value goods of a lower order. Under simple conditions it is also possible for him without much ado to form some judgment of the significance to him of goods of a higher order. But where the state of affairs is more involved and their interconnections not so easily discernible, subtler means must be employed to accomplish a correct [1] valuation of the means of production. It would not be difficult for a farmer in economic isolation to come by a distinction between the expansion of pasture-farming and the development of activity in the hunting field. In such a case the processes of production involved are relatively short and the expense and income entailed can be easily gauged. But it is quite a different matter when the choice lies between the utilization of a water-course for the manufacture of electricity or the extension of a coal-mine or the drawing up of plans for the better employment of the energies latent in raw coal. Here the roundabout processes of production are many and each is very lengthy ; here the conditions necessary for the success of the enterprises which are to be initiated are diverse, so that one cannot apply merely vague valuations, but requires rather more exact estimates and some judgment of the economic issues actually involved.

Valuation can only take place in terms of units, yet it is impossible that there should ever be a unit of subjective use-value for goods. Marginal utility does not posit any unit of value, since it is obvious that the value of two units of a given stock is necessarily greater than, but less than double, the value of a single unit. Judgments

---

[1] Using that term, of course, in the sense only of the valuating subject, and not in an objective and universally applicable sense.

of value do not measure ; they merely establish grades and scales.[1] Even Robinson Crusoe, when he has to make a decision where no ready judgment of value appears and where he has to construct one upon the basis of a more or less exact estimate, cannot operate solely with subjective use-value, but must take into consideration the intersubstitutability of goods on the basis of which he can then form his estimates. In such circumstances it will be impossible for him to refer all things back to one unit. Rather will he, so far as he can, refer all the elements which have to be taken into account in forming his estimate to those economic goods which can be apprehended by an obvious judgment of value—that is to say, to goods of a lower order and to pain-cost. That this is only possible in very simple conditions is obvious. In the case of more complicated and more lengthy processes of production it will, plainly, not answer.

In an exchange economy the objective exchange-value of commodities enters as the unit of economic calculation. This entails a threefold advantage. In the first place, it renders it possible to base the calculation upon the valuations of all participants in trade. The subjective use-value of each is not immediately comparable as a purely individual phenomenon with the subjective use-value of other men. It only becomes so in exchange-value, which arises out of the interplay of the subjective valuations of all who take part in exchange. But in that case calculation by exchange-value furnishes a control over the appropriate employment of goods. Anyone who wishes to make calculations in regard to a complicated process of production will immediately notice whether he has worked more economically than others

[1] Čuhel, *Zur Lehre von den Bedürfnissen*, Innsbruck, 1907, pp. 198 ff.

or not ; if he finds, from reference to the exchange-relations obtaining in the market, that he will not be able to produce profitably, this shows that others understand how to make a better use of the goods of a higher order in question. Lastly, calculation by exchange-value makes it possible to refer values back to a unit. For this purpose, since goods are mutually substitutable in accordance with the exchange-relations obtaining in the market, any possible good can be chosen. In a monetary economy it is money that is so chosen.

Monetary calculation has its limits. Money is no yard-stick of value, nor yet of price. Value is not indeed *measured* in money, nor is price. They merely consist in money. Money as an economic good is not of stable value as has been naïvely, but wrongly, assumed in using it as a " standard of deferred payments ". The exchange-relationship which obtains between money and goods is subjected to constant, if (as a rule) not too violent, fluctuations originating not only from the side of other economic goods, but also from the side of money. However, these fluctuations disturb value calculations only in the slightest degree, since usually, in view of the ceaseless alternations in other economic data—these calculations will refer only to comparatively short periods of time—periods in which " good " money, at least normally, undergoes comparatively trivial fluctuations in regard to its exchange-relations. The inadequacy of the monetary calculation of value does not have its mainspring in the fact that value is then calculated in terms of a universal medium of exchange, namely money, but rather in the fact that in this system it is exchange-value and not sub-jective use-value on which the calculation is based. It can never obtain as a measure for the calculation of those value-determining elements which stand outside the domain of exchange transactions. If, for example, a man were to calculate the profitability of erecting a waterworks, he would not be able to include in his calculation the beauty of the waterfall which the scheme might impair, except that he may pay attention to the diminution of tourist traffic or similar changes, which may be valued in terms of money. Yet these considerations might well prove one of the factors in deciding whether or no the building is to go up at all.

It is customary to term such elements " extra-economic ". This perhaps is appropriate ; we are not concerned with disputes over terminology ; yet the considerations themselves can scarcely be termed irrational. In any place where men regard as significant the beauty of a neighbourhood or of a building, the health, happiness and contentment of mankind, the honour of individuals or nations, they are just as much motive-forces of rational conduct as are economic factors in the proper sense of the word, even where they are not substitutable against each other on the market and therefore do not enter into exchange-relationships.

That monetary calculation cannot embrace these factors lies in its very nature ; but for the purposes of our every-day economic life this does not detract from the significance of monetary calculation. For all those ideal goods are goods of a lower order, and can hence be embraced straightway within the ambit of our judgment of values. There is therefore no difficulty in taking them into account, even though they must remain outside the sphere of monetary value. That they do not admit of such computation renders their consideration in the affairs of life easier and not harder. Once we see clearly how highly we value beauty, health, honour and pride, surely nothing can prevent us from paying a corresponding regard to them. It may seem painful to any sensitive spirit to have to balance spiritual goods against material. But that is not the fault of monetary calculation ; it lies in the very nature of things themselves. Even where judgments of value can be established directly without computation in value or in money, the necessity of choosing between material and spiritual satisfaction cannot be evaded. Robinson Crusoe and the socialist state have an equal obligation to make the choice.

Anyone with a genuine sense of moral values experiences no hardship in deciding between honour and livelihood. He knows his plain duty. If a man cannot make honour his bread, yet can he renounce his bread for honour's sake. Only they who prefer to be relieved of the agony of this decision, because they cannot bring themselves to renounce material comfort for the sake of spiritual advantage, see in the choice a profanation of true values.

Monetary calculation only has meaning within the sphere of economic organization. It is a system whereby the rules of economics may be applied in the disposition of economic goods. Economic goods only have part in this system in proportion to the extent to which they may be exchanged for money. Any extension of the sphere of monetary calculation causes misunderstanding. It cannot be regarded as constituting a kind of yardstick for the valuation of goods, and cannot be so treated in historical investigations into the development of social relationships ; it cannot be used as a criterion of national wealth and income, nor as a means of gauging the value of goods which stand outside the sphere of exchange, as who should seek to estimate the extent of human losses through emigrations or wars in terms of money?[1] This is mere sciolistic tomfoolery, however much it may be indulged in by otherwise perspicacious economists.

Nevertheless within these limits, which in economic life it never oversteps, monetary calculation fulfils all the requirements of economic calculation. It affords us a guide through the oppressive plenitude of economic potentialities. It enables us to extend to all goods of a higher order the judgment of value, which is bound up with and clearly evident in, the case of goods ready for consumption, or at best of production-goods of the lowest order. It renders their value capable of computation and thereby gives us the primary basis for all economic operations with goods of a higher order. Without it, all production involving processes stretching well back in time and all the longer roundabout processes of capitalistic production would be gropings in the dark.

There are two conditions governing the possibility of calculating value in terms of money. Firstly, not only must goods of a lower, but also those of a higher, order come within the ambit of exchange, if they are to be included. If they do not do so, exchange relationships would not arise. True enough, the considerations which must obtain in the case of Robinson Crusoe prepared, within the range of his own hearth, to exchange, by production, labour and flour for bread, are indistinguishable from those which obtain when he is prepared to exchange bread for clothes in the open market, and, therefore, it is to some extent true to say that every economic action, including Robinson Crusoe's own production, can be

---

[1] Cf. Wieser, *Über den Ursprung und die Hauptgesetze des wirtschaf-lichen Wertes*, Vienna, 1884, pp. 185 ff.

termed *exchange*.[1] Moreover, the mind of one man alone—be it never so cunning, is too weak to grasp the importance of any single one among the countlessly many goods of a higher order. No single man can ever master all the possibilities of production, innumerable as they are, as to be in a position to make straightway evident judgments of value without the aid of some system of computation. The distribution among a number of individuals of administrative control over economic goods in a community of men who take part in the labour of producing them, and who are economically interested in them, entails a kind of intellectual division of labour, which would not be possible without some system of calculating production and without economy.

The second condition is that there exists in fact a universally employed medium of exchange—namely, money—which plays the same part as a medium, in the exchange of production-goods also. If this were not the case, it would not be possible to reduce all exchange-relationships to a common denominator.

Only under simple conditions can economics dispense with monetary calculation. Within the narrow confines of household economy, for instance, where the father can supervise the entire economic management, it is possible to determine the significance of changes in the processes of production, without such aids to the mind, and yet with more or less of accuracy. In such a case the process develops under a relatively limited use of capital. Few of the capitalistic roundabout processes of production are here introduced : what is manufactured is, as a rule, consumption-goods or at

---

[1] Cf. Mises, *Theorie des Geldes u. der Umlaufsmittel*, Munich and Leipzig, 1912, p. 16, with the references there given.

least such goods of a higher order as stand very near to consumption-goods. The division of labour is in its rudimentary stages : one and the same labourer controls the labour of what is in effect, a complete process of production of goods ready for consumption, from beginning to end. All this is different, however, in developed communal production. The experiences of a remote and bygone period of simple production do not provide any sort of argument for establishing the possibility of an economic system without monetary calculation.

In the narrow confines of a closed household economy, it is possible throughout to review the process of production from beginning to end, and to judge all the time whether one or another mode of procedure yields more consumable goods. This, however, is no longer possible in the incomparably more involved circumstances of our own social economy. It will be evident, even in a socialist society, that 1,000 hectolitres of wine are better than 800, and it is not difficult to decide whether it desires 1,000 hectolitres of wine rather than 500 of oil. There is no need for any system of calculation to establish this fact : the deciding element is the will of the economic subjects involved. But once this decision has been taken, the real task of rational economic direction only commences, i.e. economically, to place the means at the service of the end. That can only be done with some kind of economic calculation. The human mind cannot orientate itself properly among the bewildering mass of intermediate products and potentialities of production without such aid. It would simply stand perplexed before the problems of management and location.[1]

[1] Gottl-Ottlilienfeld, *Wirtschaft u. Technik* (Grundriss d. Sozial-ökonomik, Section II, Tübingen, 1914), p. 216.

It is an illusion to imagine that in a socialist state calculation *in natura* can take the place of monetary calculation. Calculation *in natura*, in an economy without exchange, can embrace consumption-goods only ; it completely fails when it comes to deal with goods of a higher order. And as soon as one gives up the conception of a freely established monetary price for goods of a higher order, rational production becomes completely impossible. Every step that takes us away from private ownership of the means of production and from the use of money also takes us away from rational economics.

It is easy to overlook this fact, considering that the extent to which socialism is in evidence among us constitutes only a socialistic oasis in a society with monetary exchange, which is still a free society to a certain degree. In one sense we may agree with the socialists' assertion which is otherwise entirely untenable and advanced only as a demagogic point, to the effect that the nationalization and municipalization of enterprise is not really socialism, since these concerns in their business organizations are so much dependent upon the environing economic system with its free commerce that they cannot be said to partake to-day of the really essential nature of a socialist economy. In state and municipal undertakings technical improvements are introduced because their effect in similar private enterprises, domestic or foreign, can be noticed, and because those private industries which produce the materials for these improvements give the impulse for their introduction. In these concerns the advantages of reorganization can be established, because they operate within the sphere of a society based upon the private ownership of the means of production and upon the system of monetary exchange, being thus capable of computation and account. This state of affairs, however, could not obtain in the case of socialist concerns operating in a purely socialistic environment.

Without economic calculation there can be no economy. Hence, in a socialist state wherein the pursuit of economic calculation is impossible, there can be—in our sense of the term—no economy whatsoever. In trivial and secondary matters rational conduct might still be possible, but in general it would be impossible to speak of rational production any more. There would be no means of determining what was rational, and hence it is obvious that production could never be directed by economic considerations. What this means is clear enough, apart from its effects on the supply of commodities. Rational conduct would be divorced from the very ground which is its proper domain. Would there, in fact, be any such thing as rational conduct at all, or, indeed, such a thing as rationality and logic in thought itself ? Historically, human rationality is a development of economic life. Could it then obtain when divorced therefrom ?

For a time the remembrance of the experiences gained in a competitive economy, which has obtained for some thousands of years, may provide a check to the complete collapse of the art of economy. The older methods of procedure might be retained not because of their rationality but because they appear to be hallowed by tradition. Actually, they would meanwhile have become irrational, as no longer comporting with the new conditions. Eventually, through the general reconstruction of economic thought, they will experience alterations which will render them in fact uneconomic. The supply of goods will no longer proceed anarchically of its own accord ; that is true. All transactions which serve the purpose of meeting requirements will be subject to the control of a supreme authority. Yet in place of the economy of the " anarchic " method of production, recourse will be had to the senseless output of an absurd apparatus. The wheels will turn, but will run to no effect.

One may anticipate the nature of the future socialist society. There will be hundreds and thousands of factories in operation. Very few of these will be producing wares ready for use ; in the majority of cases what will be manufactured will be unfinished goods and production-goods. All these concerns will be interrelated. Every good will go through a whole series of stages before it is ready for use. In the ceaseless toil and moil of this process, however, the administration will be without any means of testing their bearings. It will never be able to determine whether a given good has not been kept for a superfluous length of time in the necessary processes of production, or whether work and material have not been wasted in its completion. How will it be able to decide whether this or that method of production is the more profitable ? At best it will only be able to compare the quality and quantity of the consumable end-product produced, but will in the rarest cases be in a position to compare the expenses entailed in production. It will know, or think it knows, the ends to be achieved by economic organization, and will have to regulate its activities accordingly, i.e. it will have to attain those ends with the least expense. It will have to make its computations with a view to finding the cheapest way. This computation will naturally have to be a value-computation. It is eminently clear, and requires no further proof, that it cannot be of a technical character, and that it cannot be based upon the objective use-value of goods and services.

Now, in the economic system of private ownership of the means of production, the system of computation by value is necessarily employed by each independent member of society. Everybody participates in its emergence in a double way : on the one hand as a consumer and on the other as a producer. As a consumer he establishes a scale of valuation for goods ready for use and consumption. As a producer he puts goods of a higher order into such use as produces the greatest return. In this way all goods of a higher order receive a position in the scale of valuations in accordance with the immediate state of social conditions of production and of social needs. Through the interplay of these two processes of valuation, means will be afforded for governing both consumption and production by the economic principle throughout. Every graded system of pricing proceeds from the fact that men always and ever harmonize their own requirements with their estimation of economic facts.

All this is necessarily absent from a socialist state. The administration may know exactly what goods are most urgently needed. But in so doing, it has only found what is, in fact, but one of the two necessary prerequisites for economic calculation. In the nature of the case it must, however, dispense with the other—the valuation of the means of production. It may establish the value attained by the totality of the means of production ; this is obviously identical with that of all the needs thereby satisfied. It may also be able to calculate the value of any means of production by calculating the consequence of its withdrawal in relation to the satisfaction of needs. Yet it cannot reduce this value to the uniform expression of a money price, as can a competitive economy, wherein all prices can be referred back to a common expression in terms of money. In a socialist commonwealth which, whilst it need not of necessity dispense with money altogether, yet finds it impossible to use money as an expression of the price of the factors of production (including labour), money can play no role in economic calculation.[1]

Picture the building of a new railroad. Should it be built at all, and if so, which out of a number of conceivable roads should be built ? In a competitive and monetary economy, this question would be answered by monetary calculation. The new road will render less expensive the transport of some goods, and it may be possible to calculate whether this reduction of expense transcends that involved in the building and upkeep of the next line. That can only be calculated in money. It is not possible to attain the desired end merely by counterbalancing the various physical expenses and physical savings. Where one cannot express hours of labour, iron, coal, all kinds of building material, machines and other things necessary for the construction and upkeep of the railroad in a common unit it is not possible to make calculations at all. The drawing up of bills

---

[1] This fact is also recognized by Neurath (*Durch die Kriegswirtschaft zur Naturalwirtschaft*, Munich, 1919, pp. 216 f.). He advances the view that every complete administrative economy is, in the final analysis, a natural economy. " Socialization ", he says, " is thus the pursuit of natural economy." Neurath merely overlooks the insuperable difficulties that would have to develop with economic calculation in the socialist commonwealth.

on an economic basis is only possible where all the goods concerned can be referred back to money. Admittedly, monetary calculation has its inconveniences and serious defects, but we have certainly nothing better to put in its place, and for the practical purposes of life monetary calculation as it exists under a sound monetary system always suffices. Were we to dispense with it, any economic system of calculation would become absolutely impossible.

The socialist society would know how to look after itself. It would issue an edict and decide for or against the projected building. Yet this decision would depend at best upon vague estimates ; it would never be based upon the foundation of an exact calculation of value.

The static state can dispense with economic calculation. For here the same events in economic life are ever recurring ; and if we assume that the first disposition of the static socialist economy follows on the basis of the final state of the competitive economy, we might at all events conceive of a socialist production system which is rationally controlled from an economic point of view. But this is only conceptually possible. For the moment, we leave aside the fact that a static state is impossible in real life, as our economic data are for ever changing, so that the static nature of economic activity is only a theoretical assumption corresponding to no real state of affairs, however necessary it may be for our thinking and for the perfection of our knowledge of economics. Even so, we must assume that the transition to socialism must, as a consequence of the levelling out of the differences in income and the resultant readjustments in consumption, and therefore production, change all economic data in such a way that a connecting link with the final state of affairs in the previously existing competitive economy becomes impossible. But then we have the spectacle of a socialist economic order floundering in the ocean of possible and conceivable economic combinations without the compass of economic calculation.

Thus in the socialist commonwealth every economic change becomes an undertaking whose success can be neither appraised in advance nor later retrospectively determined. There is only groping in the dark. Socialism is the abolition of rational economy.

## 3. Economic Calculation in the Socialist Commonwealth

Are we really dealing with the necessary consequences of common ownership of the means of production ? Is there no way in which some kind of economic calculation might be tied up with a socialist system ?

In every great enterprise, each particular business or branch of business is to some extent independent in its accounting. It reckons the labour and material against each other, and it is always possible for each individual group to strike a particular balance and to approach the economic results of its activities from an accounting point of view. We can thus ascertain with what success each particular section has laboured, and accordingly draw conclusions about the reorganization, curtailment, abandonment, or expansion of existing groups and about the institution of new ones. Admittedly, some mistakes are inevitable in such a calculation. They arise partly from the difficulties consequent upon an allocation of general expenses. Yet other mistakes arise from the necessity of calculating with what are not from many points of view rigorously ascertainable data, e.g. when in the ascertainment of the profitability of a certain method of procedure we compute the amortization of the machines used on the assumption of a given duration for their usefulness. Still, all such mistakes can be confined within certain narrow limits, so that they do not disturb the net result of the calculation. What remains of uncertainty comes into the calculation of the uncertainty of future conditions, which is an inevitable concomitant of the dynamic nature of economic life.

It seems tempting to try to construct by analogy a separate estimation of the particular production groups in the socialist state also. But it is quite impossible. For each separate calculation of the particular branches of one and the same enterprise depends exclusively on the fact that it is precisely in market dealings that market prices to be taken as the bases of calculation are formed for all kinds of goods and labour employed. Where there is no free market, there is no pricing mechanism; without a pricing mechanism, there is no economic calculation.

We might conceive of a situation, in which exchange between particular branches of business is permitted, so as to obtain the mechanism of exchange relations (prices) and thus create a basis for economic calculation even in the socialist commonwealth. Within the framework of a uniform economy knowing not private ownership of the means of production, individual labour groups are constituted independent and authoritative disposers, which have indeed to behave in accordance with the directions of the supreme economic council, but which nevertheless assign each other material goods and services only against a payment, which would have to be made in the general medium of exchange. It is roughly in this way that we conceive of the organization of the socialist running of business when we nowadays talk of complete socialization and the like. But we have still not come to the crucial point. Exchange relations between production-goods can only be established on the basis of private ownership of the means of production. When the " coal syndicate " provides the " iron syndicate " with coal, no price can be formed, except when both syndicates are the owners of the means of production employed in their business. This would not be socialization but workers' capitalism and syndicalism.

The matter is indeed very simple for those socialist theorists who rely on the labour theory of value.

> As soon as society takes possession of the means of production and applies them to production in their directly socialised form, each individual's labour, however different its specific utility may be, becomes *a priori* and directly social labour. The amount of social labour invested in a product need not then be established indirectly ; daily experience immediately tells us how much is necessary on an average. Society can simply calculate how many hours of labour are invested in a steam engine, a quarter of last harvest's wheat, and a 100 yards of linen of given quality. . . . To be sure, society will also have to know how much labour is needed to produce any consumption-good. It will have to arrange its production plan according to its means of production, to which labour especially belongs. The utility yielded by the various consumption-goods, weighted against each other and against the amount of labour required to produce them, will ultimately determine the plan. People will make everything simple without the mediation of the notorious " value ".[1]

Here it is not our task once more to advance critical objections against the labour theory of value. In this

[1] Engels, *Dührings Umwälzung des Wissenschaft*, 7th ed., pp. 335 f.

connection they can only interest us in so far as they are relevant to an assessment of the applicability of labour in the value computations of a socialist community.

On a first impression calculation in terms of labour also takes into consideration the natural non-human conditions of production. The law of diminishing returns is already allowed for in the concept of socially necessary average labour-time to the extent that its operation is due to the variety of the natural conditions of production. If the demand for a commodity increases and worse natural resources must be exploited, then the average socially necessary labour-time required for the production of a unit increases too. If more favourable natural resources are discovered, the amount of socially necessary labour diminishes.[1] The consideration of the natural condition of production suffices only in so far as it is reflected in the amount of labour socially necessary. But it is in this respect that valuation in terms of labour fails. It leaves the employment of material factors of production out of account. Let the amount of socially necessary labour-time required for the production of each of the commodities $P$ and $Q$ be 10 hours. Further, in addition to labour the production of both $P$ and $Q$ requires the raw material $a$, a unit of which is produced by an hour's socially necessary labour ; 2 units of $a$ and 8 hours' labour are used in the production of $P$, and one unit of $a$ and 9 hours' labour in the production of $Q$. In terms of labour $P$ and $Q$ are equivalent, but in value terms $P$ is more valuable than $Q$. The former is false, and only the latter corresponds to the nature and purpose of calculation. True, this surplus, by which according to value calculation $P$ is

[1] Marx, *Capital*, translated by Eden and Cedar Paul, p. 9.

more valuable than $Q$, this material sub-stratum " is given by nature without any addition from man ".[1] Still, the fact that it is only present in such quantities that it becomes an object of economizing, must be taken into account in some form or other in value-calculation.

The second defect in calculation in terms of labour is the ignoring of the different qualities of labour. To Marx all human labour is economically of the same kind, as it is always " the productive expenditure of human brain, brawn, nerve and hand ".[2]

> Skilled labour counts only as intensified, or rather multiplied, simple labour, so that a smaller quantity of skilled labour is equal to a larger quantity of simple labour. Experience shows that skilled labour can always be reduced in this way to the terms of simple labour. No matter that a commodity be the product of the most highly skilled labour, its value can be equated with that of the product of simple labour, so that it represents merely a definite amount of simple labour."

Böhm-Bawerk is not far wrong when he calls this argument " a theoretical juggle of almost stupefying naïveté ".[3] To judge Marx's view we need not ask if it is possible to discover a single uniform physiological measure of all human labour, whether it be physical or " mental ". For it is certain that there exist among men varying degrees of capacity and dexterity, which cause the products and services of labour to have varying qualities. What must be conclusive in deciding the question whether reckoning in terms of labour is applicable or not, is whether it is or is not possible to bring different kinds of labour under a common denominator without the mediation of the economic subject's valuation of their products. The proof Marx attempts to give is

[1] Marx, ibid., p. 12.    [2] Marx, ibid., pp. 13 et seq.
[3] Cf. Böhm-Bawerk, *Capital and Interest*, p. 384.

not successful. Experience indeed shows that goods are consumed under exchange relations without regard of the fact of their being produced by simple or complex labour. But this would only be a proof that given amounts of simple labour are directly made equal to given amounts of complex labour, if it were shown that labour is the source of exchange value. This not only is not demonstrated, but is what Marx is trying to demonstrate by means of these very arguments.

No more is it a proof of this homogeneity that rates of substitution between simple and complex labour are manifested in the wage rate in an exchange economy— a fact to which Marx does not allude in this context. This equalizing process is a result of market transactions and not its antecedent. Calculation in terms of labour would have to set up an arbitrary proportion for the substitution of complex by simple labour, which excludes its employment for purposes of economic administration.

It was long supposed that the labour theory of value was indispensable to socialism, so that the demand for the nationalization of the means of production should have an ethical basis. To-day we know this for the error it is. Although the majority of socialist supporters have thus employed this misconception, and although Marx, however much he fundamentally took another point of view, was not altogether free from it, it is clear that the political call for the introduction of socialized production neither requires nor can obtain the support of the labour theory of value on the one hand, and that on the other those people holding different views on the nature and origin of economic value can be socialists according to their sentiments. Yet the labour theory of value is inherently necessary for the supporters of socialist production in a sense other than that usually intended. In the main socialist production might only appear rationally realizable, if it provided an objectively recognizable unit of value, which would permit of economic calculation in an economy where neither money nor exchange were present. And only labour can conceivably be considered as such.

## 4. RESPONSIBILITY AND INITIATIVE IN COMMUNAL CONCERNS

The problem of responsibility and initiative in socialist enterprises is closely connected with that of economic calculation. It is now universally agreed that the exclusion of free initiative and individual responsibility, on which the successes of private enterprise depend, constitutes the most serious menace to socialist economic organization.[4]

The majority of socialists silently pass this problem by. Others believe they can answer it with an allusion to the directors of companies ; in spite of the fact that they are not the owners of the means of production, enterprises under their control have flourished. If society, instead of company shareholders, becomes the owner of the means of production, nothing will have altered. The directors would not work less satisfactorily for society than for shareholders.

We must distinguish between two groups of joint-stock companies and similar concerns. In the first group, consisting for the large part of smaller companies, a

[4] Cf. *Vorläufiger Bericht der Sozialisierungskommission über die Frage der Sozialisierung des Kohlenbergbaues*, concluded 15th February, 1919 (Berlin, 1919), p. 13.

few individuals unite in a common enterprise in the legal form of a company. They are often the heirs of the founders of the company, or often previous competitors who have amalgamated. Here the actual control and management of business is in the hands of the shareholders themselves or at least of some of the shareholders, who do business in their own interest; or in that of closely related shareholders such as wives, minors, etc. The directors in their capacity as members of the board of management or of the board of control, and sometimes also in an attenuated legal capacity, themselves exercise the decisive influence in the conduct of affairs. Nor is this affected by the circumstance that sometimes part of the share-capital is held by a financial consortium or bank. Here in fact the company is only differentiated from the public commercial company by its legal form.

The situation is quite different in the case of large-scale companies, where only a fraction of the shareholders, i.e. the big shareholders, participate in the actual control of the enterprise. And these usually have the same interest in the firm's prosperity as any property holder. Still, it may well be that they have interests other than those of the vast majority of small shareholders, who are excluded from the management even if they own the larger part of the share-capital. Severe collisions may occur, when the firm's business is so handled on behalf of the directors that the shareholders are injured. But be that as it may, it is clear that the real holders of power in companies run the business in their own interest, whether it coincides with that of the shareholders or not. In the long run it will generally be to the advantage of the solid company administrator, who is not merely bent on making a transient profit, to represent the shareholders' interests only in every case and to avoid manipulations which might damage them. This holds good in the first instance for banks and financial groups, which should not trifle at the public's expense with the credit they enjoy. Thus it is not merely on the prescriptiveness of ethical motives that the success of companies depends.

The situation is completely transformed when an undertaking is nationalized. The motive force disappears with the exclusion of the material interests of private individuals, and if State and municipal enterprises thrive at all, they owe it to the taking over of "management" from private enterprise, or to the fact that they are ever driven to reforms and innovations by the business men from whom they purchase their instruments of production and raw material.

Since we are in a position to survey decades of State and socialist endeavour, it is now generally recognized that there is no internal pressure to reform and improvement of production in socialist undertakings, that they cannot be adjusted to the changing conditions of demand, and that in a word they are a dead limb in the economic organism. All attempts to breathe life into them have so far been in vain. It was supposed that a reform in the system of remuneration might achieve the desired end. If the managers of these enterprises were interested in the yield, it was thought they would be in a position comparable to that of the manager of large-scale companies. This is a fatal error. The managers of large-scale companies are bound up with the interests of the businesses they administer in an entirely different way from what could be the case in public concerns. They

are either already owners of a not inconsiderable fraction
of the share capital, or hope to become so in due course.
Further, they are in a position to obtain profits by
stock-exchange speculation in the company's shares.
They have the prospect of bequeathing their positions
to, or at least securing part of their influence for, their
heirs. The type to which the success of joint-stock
companies is to be attributed, is not that of a com-
placently prosperous managing director resembling the
civil servant in his outlook and experience ; rather it
is precisely the manager, promoter, and man of affairs,
who is himself interested as a shareholder, whom it is the
aim of all nationalization and municipalization to exclude.

It is not generally legitimate to appeal in a socialist
context to such arguments in order to ensure the success
of an economic order built on socialist foundations.
All socialist systems, including that of Karl Marx, and
his orthodox supporters, proceed from the assumption
that in a socialist society a conflict between the interests
of the particular and general could not possibly arise.
Everybody will act in his own interest in giving of his
best because he participates in the product of all economic
activity. The obvious objection that the individual is
very little concerned whether he himself is diligent and
enthusiastic, and that it is of greater moment to him that
everybody else should be, is either completely ignored
or is insufficiently dealt with by them. They believe
they can construct a socialist commonwealth on the
basis of the Categorical Imperative alone. How lightly
it is their wont to proceed in this way is best shown
by Kautsky when he says, " If socialism is a social
necessity, then it would be human nature and not
socialism which would have to readjust itself, if ever the

two clashed." [1]  This is nothing but sheer Utopianism.

But even if we for the moment grant that these Utopian expectations can actually be realized, that each individual in a socialist society will exert himself with the same zeal as he does to-day in a society where he is subjected to the pressure of free competition, there still remains the problem of measuring the result of economic activity in a socialist commonwealth which does not permit of any economic calculation. We cannot act economically if we are not in a position to understand economizing.

A popular slogan affirms that if we think less bureaucratically and more commercially in communal enterprises, they will work just as well as private enterprises. The leading positions must be occupied by merchants, and then income will grow apace. Unfortunately " commercial-mindedness " is not something external, which can be arbitrarily transferred. A merchant's qualities are not the property of a person depending on inborn aptitude, nor are they acquired by studies in a commercial school or by working in a commercial house, or even by having been a business man oneself for some period of time. The entrepreneur's commercial attitude and activity arises from his position in the economic process and is lost with its disappearance. When a successful business man is appointed the manager of a public enterprise, he may still bring with him certain experiences from his previous occupation, and be able to turn them to good account in a routine fashion for some time. Still, with his entry into communal activity he ceases to be a merchant and becomes as much a bureaucrat as any other placeman in the public employ.

[1] Cf. Kautsky, Preface to Atlanticus (Ballod), *Produktion und Konsum im Sozialstaat*, Stuttgart, 1898, p. 14.

It is not a knowledge of bookkeeping, of business organization, or of the style of commercial correspondence, or even a dispensation from a commercial high-school, which makes the merchant, but his characteristic position in the production process, which allows of the identification of the firm's and his own interests. It is no solution of the problem when Otto Bauer in his most recently published work proposes that the directors of the National Central Bank, on whom leadership in the economic process will be conferred, should be nominated by a Collegium, to which representatives of the teaching staff of the commercial high schools would also belong.[1] Like Plato's philosophers, the directors so appointed may well be the wisest and best of their kind, but they cannot be merchants in their posts as leaders of a socialist society, even if they should have been previously.

It is a general complaint that the administration of public undertakings lacks initiative. It is believed that this might be remedied by changes in organization. This also is a grievous mistake. The management of a socialist concern cannot entirely be placed in the hands of a single individual, because there must always be the suspicion that he will permit errors inflicting heavy damages on the community. But if the important conclusions are made dependent on the votes of committees, or on the consent of the relevant government offices, then limitations are imposed on the individual's initiative. Committees are rarely inclined to introduce bold innovations. The lack of free initiative in public business rests not on an absence of organization, it is inherent in the nature of the business itself. One cannot transfer free disposal of the factors of production to an employee,

[1] Cf. Bauer, *Der Weg zum Sozialismus*, Vienna, 1919, p. 25.

however high his rank, and this becomes even less possible, the more strongly he is materially interested in the successful performance of his duties ; for in practice the propertyless manager can only be held morally responsible for losses incurred. And so ethical losses are juxtaposed with opportunities for material gain. The property owner on the other hand himself bears responsibility, as he himself must primarily feel the loss arising from unwisely conducted business. It is precisely in this that there is a characteristic difference between liberal and socialist production.

## 5. The Most Recent Socialist Doctrines and the Problem of Economic Calculation

Since recent events helped socialist parties to obtain power in Russia, Hungary, Germany and Austria, and have thus made the execution of a socialist nationaliza-tion programme a topical issue, Marxist writers have themselves begun to deal more closely with the problems of the regulation of the socialist commonwealth. But even now they still cautiously avoid the crucial question, leaving it to be tackled by the despised " Utopians ". They themselves prefer to confine their attention to what is to be done in the immediate future ; they are for ever drawing up programmes of the path to Socialism and not of Socialism itself. The only possible con-clusion from all these writings is that they are not even conscious of the larger problem of economic calculation in a socialist society.

To Otto Bauer the nationalization of the banks appears the final and decisive step in the carrying through of the socialist nationalization programme. If all banks are

ECONOMIC CALCULATION

nationalized and amalgamated into a single central bank,
then its administrative board becomes "the supreme
economic authority, the chief administrative organ of
the whole economy. Only by nationalization of the
banks does society obtain the power to regulate its
labour according to a plan, and to distribute its resources
rationally among the various branches of production,
so as to adapt them to the nation's needs." [1] Bauer is
not discussing the monetary arrangements which will
prevail in the socialist commonwealth after the completion of the nationalization of the banks. Like other
Marxists he is trying to show how simply and obviously
the future socialist order of society will evolve from the
conditions prevailing in a developed capitalist economy.
"It suffices to transfer to the nation's representatives
the power now exercised by bank shareholders through
the Administrative Boards they elect," [2] in order to
socialize the banks and thus to lay the last brick on the
edifice of socialism. Bauer leaves his readers completely
ignorant of the fact that the nature of the banks is
entirely changed in the process of nationalization and
amalgamation into one central bank. Once the banks
merge into a single bank, their essence is wholly transformed ; they are then in a position to issue credit
without any limitation. [3] In this fashion the monetary
system as we know it to-day disappears of itself. When
in addition the single central bank is nationalized in a
society, which is otherwise already completely socialized,
market dealings disappear and all exchange transactions
are abolished. At the same time the Bank ceases to be
a bank, its specific functions are extinguished, for there

[1] Bauer, op cit., pp. 26 f.     [2] Ibid., p. 25.
[3] Mises, op. cit., pp. 474 ff.

is no longer any place for it in such a society. It may be that the name " Bank " is retained, that the Supreme Economic Council of the socialist community is called the Board of Directors of the Bank, and that they hold their meetings in a building formerly occupied by a bank. But it is no longer a bank, it fulfils none of those functions which a bank fulfils in an economic system resting on the private ownership of the means of production and the use of a general medium of exchange-money. It no longer distributes any credit, for a socialist society makes credit of necessity impossible. Bauer himself does not tell us what a bank is, but he begins his chapter on the nationalization of the banks with the sentence : " All disposable capital flows into a common pool in the banks." [1] As a Marxist must he not raise the question of what the banks' activities will be after the abolition of capitalism ?

All other writers who have grappled with the problems of the organization of the socialist commonwealth are guilty of similar confusions. They do not realize that the bases of economic calculation are removed by the exclusion of exchange and the pricing mechanism, and that something must be substituted in its place, if all economy is not to be abolished and a hopeless chaos is not to result. People believe that socialist institutions might evolve without further ado from those of a capitalist economy. This is not at all the case. And it becomes all the more grotesque when we talk of banks, bank management, etc. in a socialist commonwealth.

Reference to the conditions that have developed in Russia and Hungary under Soviet rule proves nothing. What we have there is nothing but a picture of the

[1] Bauer, op. cit., p. 24.

destruction of an existing order of social production, for which a closed peasant household economy has been substituted. All branches of production depending on social division of labour are in a state of entire dissolution. What is happening under the rule of Lenin and Trotsky is merely destruction and annihilation. Whether, as the liberals hold, socialism must inevitably draw these consequences in its train, or whether, as the socialists retort, this is only a result of the fact that the Soviet Republic is attacked from without, is a question of no interest to us in this context. All that has to be established is the fact that the Soviet socialist commonwealth has not even begun to discuss the problem of economic calculation, nor has it any cause to do so. For where things are still produced for the market in Soviet Russia in spite of governmental prohibitions, they are valued in terms of money, for there exists to that extent private ownership of the means of production, and goods are sold against money. Even the Government cannot deny the necessity, which it confirms by increasing the amount of money in circulation, of retaining a monetary system for at least the transition period.

That the essence of the problem to be faced has not yet come to light in Soviet Russia, Lenin's statements in his essay on *Die nächsten Aufgaben der Sowjetmacht* best show. In the dictator's deliberations there ever recurs the thought that the immediate and most pressing task of Russian Communism is " the organization of bookkeeping and control of those concerns, in which the capitalists have already been expropriated, and of all other economic concerns ".[1] Even so Lenin is far

[1] Cf. Lenin, *Die nächsten Aufgaben der Sowjetmacht*, Berlin, 1918, pp. 12 f., 22 ff.

from realizing that an entirely new problem is here involved which it is impossible to solve with the conceptual instruments of " bourgeois " culture. Like a real politician, he does not bother with issues beyond his nose. He still finds himself surrounded by monetary transactions, and does not notice that with progressive socialization money also necessarily loses its function as the medium of exchange in general use, to the extent that private property and with it exchange disappear. The implication of Lenin's reflections is that he would like to re-introduce into Soviet business " bourgeois " bookkeeping carried on on a monetary basis. Therefore he also desires to restore " bourgeois experts " to a state of grace.[1] For the rest Lenin is as little aware as Bauer of the fact that in a socialist commonwealth the functions of the bank are unthinkable in their existing sense. He wishes to go farther with the " nationalization of the banks " and to proceed " to a transformation of the banks into the nodal point of social bookkeeping under socialism ".[2]

Lenin's ideas on the socialist economic system, to which he is striving to lead his people, are generally obscure.

" The socialist state ", he says " can only arise as a net of producing and consuming communes, which conscientiously record their production and consumption, go about their labour economically, uninterruptedly raise their labour productivity and thus attain the possibility of lowering the working day to seven or six hours or even lower." [3] " Every factory, every village appears as a production and consumption commune having the right and obligation to apply the general Soviet legislation in its own way (' in its own way ' not in the

[1] Op. cit., p. 15.
[2] Ibid., pp. 21 and 26. Compare also Bucharin, *Das Programm der Kommunisten*, Zürich, 1918, pp. 27 ff.
[3] Cf. Lenin, op. cit., pp. 24 f.

sense of its violation but in the sense of the variety of its forms of realisation), and to solve in its own way the problem of calculating the production and distribution of products." [1]

" The chief communes must and will serve the most backward ones as educators, teachers, and stimulating leaders." The successes of the chief communes must be broadcast in all their details in order to provide a good example. The communes " showing good business results " should be immediately rewarded " by a curtailment of the working day and with an increase in wages, and by allowing more attention to be paid to cultural and aesthetic goods and values ".[2]

We can infer that Lenin's ideal is a state of society in which the means of production are not the property of a few districts, municipalities, or even of the workers in the concern, but of the whole community. His ideal is socialist and not syndicalist. This need not be specially stressed for a Marxist such as Lenin. It is not extraordinary of Lenin the theorist, but of Lenin the statesman, who is the leader of the syndicalist and small-holding peasant Russian revolution. However, at the moment we are engaged with the writer Lenin and may consider his ideals separately, without letting ourselves be disturbed by the picture of sober reality. According to Lenin the theorist, every large agricultural and industrial concern is a member of the great commonwealth of labour. Those who are active in this commonwealth have the right of self-government ; they exercise a profound influence on the direction of production and again on the distribution of the goods they are assigned for consumption. Still labour is the property of the whole society, and as its product belongs to society also,

[1] Ibid., p. 32.    [2] Ibid., p. 33.

it therefore disposes of its distribution. How, we must now ask, is calculation in the economy carried on in a socialist commonwealth which is so organized ? Lenin gives us a most inadequate answer by referring us back to statistics. We must

> bring statistics to the masses, make it popular, so that the active population will gradually learn by themselves to understand and realise how much and what kind of work must be done, how much and what kind of recreation should be taken, so that the comparison of the economy's industrial results in the case of individual communes becomes the object of general interest and education.[1]

From these scanty allusions it is impossible to infer what Lenin understands by statistics and whether he is thinking of monetary or *in natura* computation. In any case, we must refer back to what we have said about the impossibility of learning the money prices of production-goods in a socialist commonwealth and about the difficulties standing in the way of *in natura* valuation.[2] Statistics would only be applicable to economic calculation if it could go beyond the *in natura* calculation, whose ill-suitedness for this purpose we have demonstrated. It is naturally impossible where no exchange relations are formed between goods in the process of trade.

## CONCLUSION

It must follow from what we have been able to establish in our previous arguments that the protagonists of a socialist system of production claim preference for it on the ground of greater rationality as against an economy so constituted as to depend on private ownership of the

[1] Op. cit., p. 33.

[2] Neurath, too (cf. op. cit., pp. 212 et seq.), imputes great importance to statistics for the setting up of the socialist economic plan.

means of production. We have no need to consider this opinion within the framework of the present essay, in so far as it falls back on the assertion that rational economic activity necessarily cannot be perfect, because certain forces are operative which hinder its pursuance. In this connection we may only pay attention to the economic and technical reason for this opinion. There hovers before the holders of this tenet a muddled conception of technical rationality, which stands in antithesis to economic rationality, on which also they are not very clear. They are wont to overlook the fact that " all technical rationality of production is identical with a low level of specific expenditure in the processes of production ".[1] They overlook the fact that technical calculation is not enough to realize the " degree of general and teleological expediency "[2] of an event ; that it can only grade individual events according to their significance ; but that it can never guide us in those judgments which are demanded by the economic complex as a whole. Only because of the fact that technical considerations can be based on profitability can we overcome the difficulty arising from the complexity of the relations between the mighty system of present-day production on the one hand and demand and the efficiency of enterprises and economic units on the other ; and can we gain the complete picture of the situation in its totality, which rational economic activity requires.[3]

These theories are dominated by a confused conception of the primacy of objective use-value. In fact, so far as economic administration is concerned, objective use-value can only acquire significance for the economy through the influence it derives from subjective use-value

[1] Cf. Gottl, op. cit., p. 220.    [2] Ibid., p. 219.    [3] Ibid., p. 225.

on the formation of the exchange-relations of economic goods. A second confused idea is inexplicably involved —the observer's personal judgment of the utility of goods as opposed to the judgments of the people participating in economic transactions. If anyone finds it " irrational " to spend as much as is expended in society on smoking, drinking, and similar enjoyments, then doubtless he is right from the point of view of his own personal scale of values. But in so judging, he is ignoring the fact that economy is a means, and that, without prejudice to the rational considerations influencing its pattern, the scale of ultimate ends is a matter for conation and not for cognition.

The knowledge of the fact that rational economic activity is impossible in a socialist commonwealth cannot, of course, be used as an argument either for or against socialism. Whoever is prepared himself to enter upon socialism on ethical grounds on the supposition that the provision of goods of a lower order for human beings under a system of a common ownership of the means of production is diminished, or whoever is guided by ascetic ideals in his desire for socialism, will not allow himself to be influenced in his endeavours by what we have said. Still less will those " culture " socialists be deterred who, like Muckle, expect from socialism primarily " the dissolution of the most frightful of all barbarisms—capitalist rationality ".[1] But he who expects a rational economic system from socialism will be forced to re-examine his views.

[1] Cf. Muckle, *Das Kulturideal des Sozialismus*, Munich and Leipzig, p. 213. On the other hand, Muckle demands the " highest degree of rationalisation of economic life in order to curtail hours of labour, and to permit man to withdraw to an island where he can listen to the melody of his being ".

# IV

# FURTHER CONSIDERATIONS ON THE POSSIBILITY OF ADEQUATE CALCULATION IN A SOCIALIST COMMUNITY

## By GEORG HALM

### (*Translated from the German by* H. E. BATSON)

## CHAPTER I : THE PROBLEM

### § 1

THE question of the possibility of an adequate economic organization can refer only to a social economy. In a self-sufficient individual economy, the problem does not arise. The person at the head of an individual economy is able directly to satisfy his wants or those of the members of his household with the available labour and materials. The Economic Principle is fulfilled. The wants are satisfied equally and the available resources are employed in the most economical manner. So long as matters are on such a small scale that production and consumption can be adjusted to one another from one centre, there are no theoretical difficulties at all.

One consequence of the development of division of labour is that it makes it more and more difficult to deal with things from one centre in this way. The individual economy grows dependent upon the thousands of other individual economies with which it combines in the creation of the social product. It becomes a member of a social economy. Because of the confusing multiplicity of the relationships that division of labour brings in its

132

train, and because cessation of individual self-sufficiency means at the same time cessation of direct correspondence between consumption and production, there arise in the social economy problems that are completely new. Nobody knows the wants of all the individuals composing the economy, nobody has a complete view of all the available means of production or a grasp of the enormous complexity of the technical processes. And consequently nobody is able to adjust his share in production to his wants. But this lack of self-sufficiency on the part of the individual means that he is in need of guidance among the innumerable possibilities that are open to him if his share in the whole process is to be done in the right place and in the right way.

## § 2

According to the way in which the division of labour between individuals is accomplished, it is usual to distinguish between communistic, capitalistic, and socialistic [1] economies. Under communism, the principles that guide isolated individual economies are applied to the social economy, as if the problem to be solved was the same in both cases. A central authority disposes over all the means of production (labour, materials, and capital-goods), determines the direction of production, and regulates consumption. Individuals have certain quantities of consumption goods allotted to them, just

[1] [Because of the somewhat different meaning which the term socialism has assumed in present-day Germany, the author had in his original German manuscript used the terms ' collectivism ' and ' collectivistic ', where in the translation the more familiar ' socialism ' and ' socialistic ' are used. *Ed.*]

as they have certain labour tasks allotted to them. Once a plan of production has been settled upon, its execution can no more allow for freedom of choice in consumption than it can allow private wishes to affect the selection of the kind of work to be done. The desires of consumers can be taken into account when the plan is being constructed, assuming that suitable methods are discovered for determining wants.[1] But freedom of consumers' choice as it is known in the capitalistic economy, the right, within the limits of a given money income, to any desired portion of the social product, according to its money-price, cannot be combined with the communistic method of production. For it lies in the very nature of a social economic plan that no consideration can be paid to the special wishes of individuals except in so far as they have been allowed for in advance.

The question whether communism is economically possible is one that can hardly be formulated, let alone answered with a plain yes or no. The fundamental difficulty about this question lies in the fact that immediate application of the economic principle to the social economy is impossible. The economic principle refers to the individual economy. But if despite this, and with all due reservation, we still wish to form some opinion of the ' economic ' advantages and disadvantages of the communistic economy, we must realize in the very first place that communism makes it impossible for the individual to fulfil the principle of equal satisfaction of

---

[1] In the opinion of the socialist Carl Landauer, this is an inadmissible assumption and all schemes for determining human wants apart from the evidence of an actual demand for goods (whether by statistical estimates or otherwise) are quite impracticable. Cp. *Planwirtschaft und Verkehrswirtschaft*, Munich and Leipzig, 1931, p. 114.

wants ; for the achievement of this result is absolutely impossible if there is not freedom of consumption. The individual alone knows what will satisfy his wants, the individual alone is able to make the choice between the innumerable alternatives, and even then only if he knows how much his total share of the social product is to be. It is obvious that little can be attained with the help of statistics. The only sort of inquiry that would be of any use would involve offering each individual a choice between an infinite number of combinations of goods ; for it is possible for the individual to say what kind and quantity of goods he desires, only when he knows how his choice concerning any one particular good will affect all his other opportunities of satisfying his wants. That it would be possible to distribute the product throughout the community in one way or another is, of course, not open to doubt. But what was to be distributed and what was to be consumed would be determined by what had already been produced, while the question at issue is the adjustment of the product to the desires of the consumers. If the members of the community have simply to accept what has been produced, there remains no criterion of economic behaviour in production. Where, as in Soviet Russia under the Five Year Plan, the State is governed in such a way that the provision of the people with even the necessaries of life becomes almost a matter of in-difference, the purely economic point of view ceases to be relevant.

It can hardly be supposed that it would be possible for one central authority in the communistic economy to direct the process of production in all its immense diversity so that its individual parts worked together without friction. It is of course conceivable that the process of production would not be disturbed by any outward and visible crisis. But that would merely be due to the individual's lack of power to control affairs, and to the power of the central authority, that has already been referred to, of always being able to bring production and consumption into correspondence. But since consumption would be adjusted to a disturbed and therefore diminished production, individuals would be just as hard hit by the losses as in any other economic order. If Pierson's assertion [1] that unemployment could not be conceived of in the communistic economy is to be accepted as correct, it must be interpreted as implying nothing more than that consumption would always be adapted to what is made available by production.

## § 3

The protagonists of socialism reject communism. They wish to retain freedom of consumption and a certain degree of freedom of choice of occupation, but to do this without falling into the mistakes of the capitalistic system. For if the communist system must be criticized on the grounds that it does not provide for the fulfilment of the economic principle inasmuch as it does not provide for the satisfaction of individual needs, the capitalistic system must likewise be criticized on the grounds that, while it certainly allows the individuals composing it to act economically within the limits of their money-incomes, throughout the community as a whole there is great inequality of satisfaction, as might be imagined, because the incomes themselves are so

---

[1] N. G. Pierson, ' The Problem of Value in a Socialist Community '. See above, Part II of the present volume, p. 51.

unequal. (For even if uniform satisfaction of wants throughout the community is an unattainable ideal, owing to the impossibility of comparing the wants of different persons, yet a fairly equal distribution of incomes may be regarded as an *approximation* to the principle of uniform satisfaction of wants.) It has, in fact, always been one of the chief aims of socialism to level out inequalities of incomes, and in particular to prevent the receipt of ' unearned ' interest and rent.[1] It is partly from this that the demand for centralized management of production follows. For the abolition of unearned incomes involves the suppression of private property in the material means of production and as a consequence the renunciation of private economic leadership.

The socialist economy must be thought of as a mixture of capitalistic and communistic elements. Like capitalism, it permits freedom of choice in consumption and occupation. Socialism is to allow everybody, within the limits of his money-income, to choose what he will consume ; and, as far as possible, it is to allow everybody to develop and use his abilities as he sees fit also. But, like communism, socialism envisages the nationalization of capital-goods and land, the elimination of unearned incomes, and the central control of economic life by the State.

This form of social economy seems peculiarly fitted to afford the advantages of both capitalism and communism without imposing their disadvantages into the bargain. It appears to combine in the happiest manner individual

[1] ' The chief aim of Socialism is to equalize people's economic position, not necessarily to establish exact equality of incomes and resources, but to eliminate the causes of those gross inequalities which distinguish the individualist system.' R. G. Hawtrey, *The Economic Problem*, London, 1926, p. 337.

freedom with planned central control. It promises to achieve a considerable step towards equality of incomes without surrendering the inducement of reward in accordance with service, and to permit central regulation of production and the abolition of the ' anarchy ' of the pure market-economy without interfering with freedom of consumption.

It is our task in what follows to investigate whether socialism is economically possible ; to discover if the elements that it seeks to combine really can be combined, or if it is founded upon ignorance of the laws that govern the ways in which social institutions can be combined, and so is self-contradictory and incapable of practical realization.

It might possibly be objected that such a method of investigation is one-sided, that it deals with one particular socialistic system chosen haphazard and that it is consequently quite unable to justify any conclusion as to the impossibility of socialism in general. It is true that there are very many socialisms. This is due to the position of socialism between capitalism and communism ; the various socialistic systems are distinguished from each other by their closer approximation to the one or other extreme. If social institutions can be combined *ad lib.*, then there must be an infinite number of different possible kinds of socialistic economy. But the argument that follows shows that economic laws do not permit the arbitrary combination of what are essentially different elements. The best way of proving this is to examine the practicability of an economy in which there is free choice of consumption and occupation and centralized control of production. It will then be considered whether any change in the assumptions could alter the conclusion.

## Chapter II : The Capitalistic Economy

### § 4

Since a comparison may be the best means of revealing the nature of the socialistic economy, let us begin with a brief consideration of the present capitalistic system.

The capitalistic economy is a pure market-economy ; i.e. it is not under the direction of a central authority like the communistic or the socialistic economy; its sole organization consists in the exchanges undertaken by the individual economies that are made dependent on each other by the division of labour. The individual economies have control of the means of production, the labour, capital, and land, that is in their private possession. By means of temporary transfers of saved portions of income from one person to another, the power of disposal of particular individuals can be temporarily increased, and economic activity made to a certain extent independent of the accidents of personal ownership. Individuals either produce goods and services themselves with the means of production that they own or they transfer these means of production to entrepreneurs who produce goods and services with them to sell in the market. The direction of production is determined by prices : by the prices of the means of production—costs—and the prices of the products. If a new branch of production is to be started or an old one

maintained at its previous level, the prices of the products must be at least high enough to cover their costs.
If the prices of the goods do not cover the costs, a loss
is incurred and production has to be restricted. If the
prices of the products exceed their costs, profits are made
and production is extended. This happens because the
leaders of the capitalistic economy are led by the desire
for profit, and have no alternative to obeying this motive,
in view of the competition that exists between them and
of the impossibility of carrying on production indefinitely
at a loss. Profitability is the sole justification for existence. Thus, from the point of view of social ethics, the
endeavour to attain it is neutral.

From what has been said it is clear that the deciding
factor is the process of price-determination. The pricing
process is based on the circumstance that, in an economy
where there is division of labour without central control,
all the individual economies are dependent upon exchange, and at the same time are concerned to get as
much out of it as they can. Since as a rule there are
always several would-be sellers and several would-be
buyers present, the acquisitive tendency, which aims at the
payment of low prices and the receipt of high prices, is
counteracted by the fear of competition, which produces
a readiness to accept low prices and to pay high prices.
Acquisitiveness and competition together are responsible
for the fact that the conflict of offerers and demanders
among and against each other (for each fights on two
fronts : against the person with whom he is bargaining
and against his competitors) leads to the establishment
of the highest price at which the total supply can just be
sold. In this way the prices of consumption-goods and
the prices of the means of production are determined,

and all the pricing processes in the community are connected with one another.

The demand for consumption-goods is determined by income-levels, which in their turn are determined by the prices of the factors of production. The demand on the part of receivers of incomes for consumption-goods is transformed into a demand on the part of entrepreneurs for means of production. As a rule, the means of production are such as can be employed for the most various products. On that account, there will be competition among entrepreneurs in different lines of production for these means of production, quite apart from the competition among entrepreneurs in any single line of production. Since those who are offering the means of production (labourers, capitalists, and landowners) are desirous of obtaining the highest price possible, the pricing processes in the markets for means of production will tend to bring about the employment of the means of production in those particular channels where they command the highest prices. But only those entrepreneurs can pay this price who obtain a correspondingly high price for their products, i.e. who satisfy an intensive effective demand. Thus the factors of production have no constant or inherent value, but are valuable only in the degree in which they are fitted to satisfy a demand of a particular intensity and purchasing power. Of course, not only does the demand for consumption-goods determine the direction of production and the prices of the means of production, but fluctuations in the prices of the means of production, as a rise or fall of costs, influence the decisions of the entrepreneur from the other side. The margin of profit of the entrepreneur is determined from two directions : by the prices both of the products and of the means of production.

But this by no means exhausts the inter-relationships between the various processes of price-determination. Since, as has already been emphasized, demand depends upon incomes, and incomes are determined by the prices of the means of production, every alteration in the prices of the means of production, which itself has originated in a variation of the demand for commodities, must in its turn influence demand by causing a change in incomes. Furthermore, demand in the commodity markets is dependent on commodity-prices. The demand for a good changes, not only when the price of that particular good changes, but also when the prices of other goods change. Thus, not only does demand determine prices, but prices in turn also affect demand. But since the prices of consumption-goods are also influenced by costs, which are the prices of means of production, there arises a further connexion between the two great divisions of the pricing process. Finally, the supply of means of production is not a fixed quantity. Within certain limits, it may react to changes in prices, and so evoke all the reactions again that have been described.

These reciprocal price relationships have a tendency to bring the economy to a state of rest, in which every means of production is employed where it satisfies the highest effective demand, and therefore obtains the highest price—a state of equilibrium in which further variations of price are inconceivable, because there is no longer any opportunity for any supplier of goods or productive services to get higher prices or more than average profits in any other part of the economy. In this state of the economy, prices can no longer change of themselves, i.e. without a preceding change in supply or demand.

But supply and demand are partly determined by factors that lie outside the pricing process, and that restrict within more or less narrow limits their reactions to variations in prices. Demand is ultimately determined by the primary scales of values of individual human beings, the peculiar characteristics of which are not immediately dependent upon prices and incomes. And supply likewise has ultimate determinants that are largely independent of prices : the supply of means of production (i.e. the size and composition of the population, natural resources, and capital) and the knowledge of processes of production that exists at any given time (i.e. the level of technique). The ultimate causes of all variations in the pure market-economy are therefore human needs (which are measured according to the purchasing power with which they can be endowed) and the scarcity of the means that are available for the satisfaction of these needs. If the determinants of prices alter, then scope is offered for new acquisitive and competitive activities, and there is again a tendency for a state to be reached which represents the new optimum of private activity in the new conditions (and which, of course, must not be confused with any such *social* optimum as would be implied in the idea of an economic harmony between private and social interests).

§ 5

Nevertheless, it may be asserted not only that this organization of social economic activity leads to a rapid and fairly exact accommodation of production to continual changes in effective demand, and thus to an automatic arrangement of the productive forces in the whole economic process so as to achieve this result, but also that it provides individuals at the same time with a motive for fulfilling the economic principle as far as possible, in the sense of using given means to secure the greatest possible results. Since, under competitive conditions, individuals are not free to raise the prices of the goods they sell or to force down the prices of the factors of production they buy, they must take pains to employ in the most advantageous way possible the means of production that are at their disposal. This is particularly true of the entrepreneur, whose function it is to combine the means of production in suitable ways. The entrepreneur will endeavour to reduce costs by using the smallest possible amount of means of production to obtain a given yield, so setting free means of production which become available to society for other productive purposes. Very often this ' rationalization ' of the productive process will consist in an introduction of new productive techniques, for the entrepreneur will constantly endeavour to disturb the state of equilibrium in order to obtain private advantage from a reduction of costs. Under competitive conditions, this advantage must in the long run benefit the consumer; for other entrepreneurs will follow the example of the first and, by increasing supply, will always force prices down to the level of the reduced costs.

But the delicacy of the reaction to technical progress and the complexity of the economic problem would be greatly under-estimated if we assumed that the choice of the most suitable technique of production was never anything more than a purely technical problem, so that the selection of the technically best method of production meant the fulfilment of the economic principle. In choosing the best means of production, the entrepreneur needs in addition the guidance afforded by the pricing process. The best organization of an undertaking from the technical point of view need not always be the best from the economic point of view. That method of production which is technically inferior may be economically superior ; as, for example, when the use of cheaper building material or inferior fuel saves more than is lost by the qualitative or quantitative inferiority of the result. Of course, the technical result is *one* of the factors that determine the choice of methods of production, but the decision is modified by considerations of costs, i.e. by considerations of a question of pure economic fact. Not only for solving the problem of *which* goods are to be produced, but also for answering the question of *how* these goods are to be produced, the guidance afforded by the pricing process cannot be dispensed with. In a communistic economy, as the example of Soviet Russia shows, there would be a tendency to confuse the technical with the economic optimum, because in all probability the absence of any way of discovering the economic value of the means of production would lead to the adoption of the best methods from the technical point of view. It is very significant that socialists are always criticizing the capitalistic economy on the grounds that it only exploits the productive possibilities of modern technique in a very imperfect manner. This objection can be explained in part by a failure to distinguish between social and private considerations, the concept of the technical optimum from the individual point of view being transferred by simple multiplication to the social economy. But in reality it is nothing but the consideration of *other* individual economies and the needs that they have to satisfy that justifies the renunciation of the optimum technical equipment of the individual undertakings ; for this renunciation releases means of production that are wanted more urgently in other branches of production and employs means of production that could not produce an equal product elsewhere. Thus, to take economic considerations into account *along with* technical considerations does not mean paying attention to private profit at the cost of social benefit ; on the contrary, it implies a simultaneous, if unconscious, regard to *all* branches of production, such as, in fact, might be expected from those who advocate central control of the whole social process of production. But the ' technocrats ' of all times have had so little comprehension of the economic principle that they have confused the functioning of the technical apparatus of production with soundness in economic affairs. From the fact that technique is independent of questions of economic organization they draw the comforting conclusion that a disturbance of the organization of production through a change in the social foundations of the economy need not even be considered as a possibility. We shall not go very far wrong if we regard the technocratical attitude of socialist theorists, which is as old as the socialist movement itself, as one of the chief reasons why the problem of the centralized control of economic life, so far from being adequately handled— not to speak of anything like a positive solution,—has until very recently hardly been so much as formulated.

# Chapter III : The Socialistic Economy

## § 6

In what follows we shall have to investigate how production is to be organized in a socialistic economy based on division of labour, and what advantages and disadvantages such a new order would have in comparison with capitalism. Since it has been assumed that there would be free consumers' choice in the socialistic economy, production would have to be accommodated to a demand that was always variable and uncontrolled. Production would not govern consumption, but consumption production. Socialism is not like communism, under which goods are produced arbitrarily and then doled out to the consumers ; but neither is it like capitalism, under which, according to socialist opinion, it is not the consumers who determine the direction of production, but the entrepreneurs, acting for motives of profit ; under which, that is to say, profitability, not productivity, is supposed to be the deciding factor.

The opinion that the socialist economy is peculiarly adapted to the satisfaction of needs, in contrast to the ' anarchistic ' capitalistic economy, which is only focused upon profits and not upon real needs, can hardly be called correct. It is precisely the endeavour to make profits which induces the entrepreneur to turn to those branches of production in which effective demand awaits satisfaction, and to abandon production where a falling demand no longer promises selling-prices that will cover costs. Not even centralized control of production could conform more closely to uncontrolled demand. The immediate object of the entrepreneur may certainly be to attain the greatest possible profit. But it would be a mistake to suppose that profitability and productivity must necessarily diverge. In an economy governed by motives of private gain, when anybody obtains large profits because he has been better able to satisfy the demand than his competitors, or because better organization of production has enabled him to reduce his costs below the average, then private and social advantage coincide and profitability and productivity are identical. It is true that there are many cases in which profitability and productivity are not identical. Protective duties may prove profitable to the protected industries, but they need not be productive if they cripple international division of labour. Or an increase in land-rents, though profitable for land-owners, is, from the social point of view, an indication of increasing scarcity of good land, i.e. an indication of a tendency to decreasing productivity. But neither protection nor the law of diminishing returns to land are characteristically capitalistic.

The oft-repeated argument about the anarchy of the capitalistic economy and its profit-yielding unproductiveness can hardly be explained except by supposing that the existence of certain kinds of luxury-production at the same time as many consumers with low incomes lack even the necessaries of life is regarded by the critics of capitalism as one of its defects, while the real responsibility for this unsatisfactory state of affairs lies with inequality of incomes and the irrationality of certain forms of expenditure.

It is easy to see that socialism, too, would have to provide for just such an adjustment of production to demand as that provided by capitalism ; that socialism, like capitalism, would have to accommodate production to the prices of consumption-goods. If price-movements were not accepted as a guide, then production would have to go on independently of them, according to some universal scale of values or other ; but in that case supply and demand would no longer correspond to each other in such a way that the demand-price was at the same time the price which would cover the cost of production. To accommodate production to the urgency, necessity, or usefulness of the demands that have to be met, as for example Robert Deumer [1] recommends, instead of simply to the criterion of prices, would amount to a systematic disorganization of the economy. For either production is planned, in which case freedom of consumers' choice must be abolished ; or else consumption is left free, in which case production must be accommodated to it. The only way in which freedom of consumption can be interfered with, with even comparative safety, is by the extension of collective demand and the consequent artificial restriction of individual demands. Roads, parks, or playing-fields can be constructed, for instance, and the necessary resources secured by restricting the branches of production that satisfy the demands of individuals ; and this, under capitalism, ultimately means increased taxation, and, under socialism, appropriate central direction. But what is not possible is on the one hand to allow freedom of consumption and on the other hand to produce according to a plan.

[1] In his book *Die Verstaatlichung des Kredits*, Munich and Leipzig, 1927.

Planning and freedom of choice cannot possibly be realized simultaneously. All proposals that aim at accommodating consumption to production are either misconceived or communistic.

## § 7

If freedom of consumers' choice means that production must be guided by the prices of consumption-goods, it remains to be shown how this accommodation of production to demand can be achieved in the socialist economy.

If consumption in the socialistic economy is uncontrolled ; if everybody, so far as his monetary resources permit, is allowed to buy what he likes, then for every product a certain price will be established in the consumption-goods market (for according to our assumptions such a market must exist in the socialist economy too). If we first of all take supply as given, a rising price will indicate an increasing demand, a falling price a decreasing demand. But it would be a great mistake to suppose that these price-movements alone would be a sufficient guide to production ; for the prices of consumption-goods can have no significance for the central authority of the socialistic economy except in relation to costs of production. Even the capitalistic entrepreneur is unable to act in accordance with the economic principle if he only knows about the probable prices that can be obtained and not about the costs of production. Economic management is always based upon a comparison of the prices of the products and their costs of production. Thus, not only have consumption-goods to be valued, but intermediate goods and means of production also.

Only when the values of the means of production can be compared with one another and with the values of their products is economic management possible[1]; for only then is it possible to decide in which branch of production it will be best to employ a certain quantity of scarce means of production (which for purposes of simplification may be assumed to be employable in the production of many different kinds of goods). To employ means of production to the value of 100 monetary units in the production of goods that can only command a price of 80 units, when they might have been used for the production of goods to the value of 100 or more, is uneconomic. For the fact that considerably more would have been offered in the second case for the product of the same quantity of the same kind of means of production shows that this alternative product would have satisfied a greater effective demand. If it were not possible to compare costs and prices, a correct decision could never be arrived at.

Neither could a correct decision be arrived at if identical quantities of means of production were credited with different values in different avenues of employment. If production is to be regulated by the economic principle, a homogeneous pricing process of the means of production is obviously indispensable. A brief description has already been given of the way in which this pricing process works under capitalism. In what may be called the factor markets (e.g. the labour and capital markets), labour and capital are demanded and offered, and if there

---

[1] On this and what follows compare the path-breaking investigations of Ludwig Mises, *Economic Calculation in the Socialist Commonwealth* (see preceding section of the present volume) and *Die Gemeinwirtschaft, Untersuchungen über den Sozialismus*, 2nd edition, Jena, 1932.

is competition on both sides, a price is determined which reaches its normal level when the demand is so limited by it that it can just be satisfied with the available supply. Since local differences are soon reduced to costs of transport, the prices of homogeneous goods are necessarily uniform. For different varieties of a factor of production, which are not interchangeable with one another, the prices will be different, but the proportions between these prices will be determined by the relative scarcities of the various kinds of factor. If certain goods that are in great demand cannot be produced except with the aid of a highly-specialized kind of labour, this labour will command a higher price than labour which is easy to obtain and easy to replace. Thus, here again the deciding point is scarcity in relation to demand. Every change in the supply of the factor in question and every change in the demand for it must exert an influence on its price until the subsequent increase or decrease in its supply or demand leads to the establishment of a new equilibrium.

*If labour were the only factor of production*, then the total wages bill would have to be just sufficient to buy the total product ; for total wages, total incomes (which would consist solely of wages), and total prices, would necessarily be equal. And these totals would have to be distributed according to relative scarcities, on the one hand among the different kinds of goods, and on the other hand among the different kinds of labour, because only such a distribution could adjust supply and demand to one another.

§ 8

Since, *ex hypothesi*, there is to be free choice of occupation in the socialistic economy also, that is to say,
the individual is to be left free to decide what services
he will offer, the relationships that have been described
as existing under capitalism can also be assumed to
exist under socialism. In fact, they appear to be even
more true of the socialistic economy than of the capitalistic; for they were based on the assumption that
labour is the only factor of production. Now under
capitalism this assumption does not hold good ; for
land and capital are also subject to the pricing process
and so enter along with labour into costs of production
and commodity-prices. Furthermore, within this pricing
process, an unearned income is obtained from the ownership of these material means of production. It is quite
otherwise under socialism. For the very purpose of
doing away with this unearned income, the material
means of production are removed from private ownership and transferred to the direct ownership of the
community. According to many socialists, no price at
all need then be paid for these material means of production, for the socialistic economy, being the owner
of them, need no longer stimulate the supply of capital
or land by suitably high prices. Nobody need pay for
the use of means of production if he owns them himself.

Now if wages are the only costs of production that
need be considered, and if there is free choice of occupation and a free market for the determination of wages, the
problem of price-determination and economic calculation
under socialism is well on the way to solution. The
only important point of difference between this case

and the similar case assumed to exist under capitalism is that the present is one not of bilateral, but only of unilateral, competition. And this not only in the market for consumption-goods, but also in the labour market. For in the socialistic economy, the State alone demands labour ; and in the socialistic economy, likewise, the State alone distributes goods. Thus the central authority has a monopoly, both in the labour market and in the commodity market ; that is to say, in the labour market it can arbitrarily determine the demand, in the commodity market the supply, and consequently in both cases the price. Of course, since it may be assumed that the authorities in a socialistic community would not exploit their power to the disadvantage of the labourers or the consumers (who are the same persons), this State monopoly, which would be far greater than any monopoly that has ever been known, could not be objected to on grounds of principle. The question, however, does arise, of whether the lack of competition on the demand side of the labour market and on the supply side of the commodity market would not result in the pricing process becoming too unwieldy, inasmuch as the characteristic under-bidding and out-bidding, that is essential for the rapid determination of prices, would in such circumstances be lacking. But still, perhaps it is justifiable to assume that this unwieldiness might possibly be compensated for by the way in which the socialistic central authority would set itself out as far as possible to meet the wishes of the labourers and con-sumers. And we need not investigate here the possible danger that wages would be raised above the normal level in attempts to shield the labourers from the effects of market fluctuations for which they were not responsible, or that equalitarian ideals would cause certain key-services to be insufficiently rewarded. But it should be remarked that any such utilization of the monopolistic position of the State would mean a departure from the principle of freedom of choice in consumption and occupation.

## § 9

But, these small difficulties pointed out, the problem of the socialistic economy must by no means be regarded as finished with. For the supposition of the socialists, that nothing but labour need have a value in the socialistic economy, that no factors but labour need enter into economic calculation, is entirely unfounded. All that can be said is that the supply of the material means of production would not have to be tempted by the offer of prices as at present under capitalism. But the evocation of supply is not the sole function of the pricing process of the material means of production, even in the capitalistic market-economy. Even if the capitalist agreed to renounce his interest and the landowner his rent, interest and rent would still be paid in the capitalistic economy, because capital and land are scarce. Only by means of suitably high prices could the demand for the means of production be so far restricted as to enable the available quantity to go round. It remains to be seen whether the same is true of the socialistic economy.

It must first be pointed out that a socialistic economy is not an economy that renounces the use of capital-goods in production. Everybody is agreed that the socialistic economy must in *this* sense be capitalistic also. In fact, the extent to which the socialistic economy is to be furnished with capital is often estimated with excessive optimism.

What the socialist means by capitalism is not an economic system in which capital is used, but a social order in which a relationship of exploitation on a class basis exists between those who own the material means of production and those who do not, a sort of monopoly relationship which yields a profit or tribute to the owners in the form of a ' surplus value '. Since the labourers possess no means of production of any sort and yet cannot put their labour to good use without the assistance of land and capital-goods, they are driven to offer their labour to the owners of these means of production with an urgency which the capitalist does not share, and which therefore gives him the power to exploit them. According to socialist opinion, interest arises solely from this kind of exploitation. If the unilateral monopoly position were destroyed by the transference of the material means of production to the ownership of the community, then, it is asserted, surplus value and interest would cease to exist, and the labourer would be able to secure the full product of his labour. If this is true, it is obviously unnecessary to reckon with interest in the socialistic economy.

If it should be objected that interest is a price that has to be paid because of the scarcity of capital-goods, and that it is therefore necessary for restricting the demand in any sort of economic organization that is based upon exchange, it is argued that capital, in fact, is *not* scarce. Capital-goods, it is declared, can be manufactured at any time in any desired quantity, for nothing further is necessary for their production than labour, on the one hand, and materials, on the other hand, which are either obtainable as gifts of nature or else in their turn can be produced by labour. The only primary factor of production, it is said, is thus seen to be labour, for all *produced* means of production can be resolved into the labour necessary for their production. The only scarcity that can be ascribed to capital-goods is therefore the scarcity of the labour that produces them. Any scarcity other than this is inconceivable, if it is true that any desired capital-goods can always be manufactured at any time out of labour and materials.

## § 10

There is, however, a flaw in this argument. It is by no means possible to requisition any desired quantity of labour and materials for the manufacture of capital-goods. If more than a certain proportion of the limited quantity of available labour and materials were devoted to the production of capital-goods, the output of consumption-goods would have to be correspondingly restricted. But the output of consumption-goods cannot be restricted any farther than immediate needs permit. It is true that the output of production-goods is in the last analysis destined to be nothing other than an output of consumption-goods ; it is even true that the ultimate output of consumption-goods may thus be far more abundant than anything that could be obtained in the present. (It is on this account that capital is in universal demand and increased possession of capital means the same thing as increased productivity.) But the increase of productivity does not occur until later, while for the present that amount of satisfaction that might be enjoyed must be forgone, in order to make possible the institu-

tion of what are called ' roundabout ' methods of production, i.e. in order to make possible the production
of capital-goods, the employment of which is to increase
the productivity of labour.

Now in so far as labour and material are at first used
for the manufacture of machines, plant, and so forth, a
period of time must elapse before they are able to satisfy
wants. The satisfaction of the wants must be *waited*
for, and, in every economic order, the possible extent
of this waiting is limited. Even the controlling authority
of a socialistic economy could hardly propose to devote
many more labourers to the production of production-
goods than does the capitalistic economy. The impossibility of unlimited capital-accumulation is particularly obvious if the typical consumer in the capitalistic
economy is borne in mind and it is observed that only
a fraction of his income, and often not even this, can be
spared over and above current expenditure for the
accumulation of savings. And what is true of the
individual is also true of society ; society is equally
obliged to look to current needs before it can think
about a more abundant satisfaction of future needs.
The lower the standard of satisfaction in the present, the
harder it is, of course, to accomplish any restriction of
consumption. Thus, in impoverished countries, the
formation of new capital is a slow process.

§ 11

So, to resume, it can be taken as established that
' saving ', the ' restriction of present needs in the interest
of future needs ', is always—in every economic order
without exception—possible to a limited degree only.

But since the productive effects of capital make the demand for capital-goods insatiable ; since agriculture and industry could go on employing more capital to an unlimited extent ; since innumerable technical inventions that are already known are still awaiting application, while new improvements of the apparatus of production are discovered every day, and there are wide possibilities of extension for those methods that have already been put into operation ; because of all this, the supply of capital must always remain small in comparison with the enormous demand for it, and power of disposal over factors of production for the purpose of producing capital-goods will always have to be restricted. Therefore capital also is a 'primary' factor of production, in the sense that it possesses a value of its own that cannot be ascribed to any other factor of production ; in the sense that it must be dealt with in a particular fashion, on the basis of its own particular price.

This can in no way be altered by the fact that capital in the socialistic economy is owned by the community. In view of the scarcity of capital in relation to the need for it, the socialistic economy like any other must endeavour so to employ its capital as the accommodation of production to the free choice of consumers requires. The capital will have to be employed in those particular branches of production that represent an effective demand sufficient to allow for the inclusion of a payment for interest in the price of the product over and above its labour-cost. Wants that are not backed by sufficient purchasing power to be able to pay this supplement must remain excluded from satisfaction. Goods produced with the aid of capital cannot be sold for their mere labour-cost for the very reason that if they *were* sold at this price the demand for capital-goods would greatly exceed the available supply of them. To illustrate this point it will suffice to imagine the demand for houses that might be expected if rents did not include interest on the capital employed in building, i.e. if they had only to cover the cost of amortization. But in this case the significant thing is not simply that the price exceeds the labour-cost. The price must exceed the labour-cost by an amount just sufficient to cover all other costs, including interest ; and the interest on the capital-sums employed must be just so high that the demand for all consumption-goods produced with the use of capital is sufficiently restricted for the available capital to suffice for their production. Wants that cannot be endowed with enough purchasing power to pay this interest have to go unsatisfied. For the whole meaning of economic calculation, in this case the calculation of interest, is of course simply to employ the scarce means of production so that they are distributed among all the wants in an economic manner. Since *ex hypothesi* each individual's consumption is to be decided quite freely within the limits of his monetary resources, there is no other possibility than to limit it by means of prices. It is obvious that the pricing process for capital must be homogeneous, that interest must be uniformly calculated as a percentage of the amount of capital expended. For only if it has a uniform unit-price is it possible for capital to be distributed among different uses according to their importance. Moreover, it is a peculiarity of capital that so long as it retains its monetary form it is completely fungible and universally applicable, so that a single price is established throughout the capital market, in a different and simpler manner from that in the labour market.[1]

The fact that interest is necessary in the socialistic economy is thus beyond doubt. Given free consumers' choice, some restriction of the indirect demand of the consumers for scarce capital-goods is absolutely essential. But freedom of consumption does not leave the manner in which this comes about open to arbitrary decision (as in the case of rationing), but requires that attention be paid to the relative urgency of the demands. The only way in which this accommodation can be brought about is by establishing a uniform price for the use of capital and satisfying only those demands that are prepared to pay this price. Interest must be high enough to accommodate the total supply of capital and the total demand for it to one another.

## § 12

*Now it is unfortunate that this allowance for interest, the need for which is urgently dictated by economic considerations, cannot be adopted in the socialistic economy. Perhaps this is the most serious objection that can be maintained against socialism.* On this account, it requires closer examination.

When the socialists assert that interest is unnecessary in the socialistic economy because the central

[1] In the capitalistic economy the rate of interest varies according as the capital is lent for a longer or a shorter period. The author's ' Das Zinsproblem am Geld- und Kapitalmarkt ', *Jahrbücher für Nationalökonomie und Statistik*, 133. Bd., 1926, pp. 1 ff. may be consulted upon this special problem, which need not be dealt with in the present place.

authority, which owns all capital-goods, does not find it necessary to pay itself a price for the use of these capital-goods, they unwittingly put their finger on the principal difficulty. Because capital is no longer owned by many private persons, but by the community, which itself disposes of it directly, a rate of interest *can* no longer be determined. A pricing process is always possible only when demand and supply meet in a market, when the competition of many offerers and demanders, the mutual out-bidding on the part of the buyers and under-cutting on the part of the sellers, leads by trial and error to the gradual emergence of a price, which may be called normal because it is that price at which the available supply, no more and no less, can be exactly disposed of. At present, in the capitalistic economy, interest is determined in the capital market, in which the offerers of capital and the demanders of capital meet in free competition. In the socialistic economy such a process of interest-determination would be impossible. There can be no demand and no supply when the capital from the outset is in the possession of its intending user, in this case the socialistic central authority.

Now it might perhaps be suggested that, since the rate of interest cannot be determined automatically, it should be fixed by the central authority. But this likewise would be quite impossible. It is true that the central authority would know quite well how many capital-goods of a given kind it possessed or could procure by means of a compulsory restriction of consumption ; it would know the capacity of the existing plant in the various branches of production ; *but it would not know how scarce capital was.* For the scarcity of means of production must always be related to the demand for them, whose fluctuations give rise to variations in the value of the good in question, in this case capital, even if the supply of it remains constant.

If it should be objected that a price for consumption-goods would be established, and that in consequence the intensity of the demand and so the value of the means of production would be determinate, this would be a further serious mistake. The demand in the commodity market is in the first place only a demand for consumption-goods. The demand for means of production, labour and capital-goods, is only indirect. If there is only one single factor of production that has to be taken into account, as was previously assumed with regard to labour, and if, even under socialism, this factor has its own proper market-price (which is a reasonable assumption to make in view of the freedom of choice of occupation which prevails under socialism), then an adequate determination of prices is conceivable. But not so when *several* factors of production take part in the production of goods and a special price is not determined for each of them in separate factor markets. For, of course, the essential thing is the possibility of establishing a comparison between *known* commodity-prices and *known* costs of production. Any sort of economic calculation that aims at deducing the value of the factors of production from the prices of the commodities is consequently impracticable.

## § 13

If the prices of various products that have been produced with the aid of capital exceed their labour costs, that alone is not sufficient for determining the rate of interest, for the margin may be due to the employment of capital-goods of the most varied kinds.

This brings us to a new difficulty. The central authority can never find out how much capital is being employed ! How can the total plant of one factory be compared with that of another ?   How can a comparison be made between the values of even only two capital-goods ?   The question seems an idle one simply because our experience of the capitalistic economy leads us to assume as self-evident the possibility of a comparative valuation of capital-goods.   In the market for capital-goods, particular capital-goods fetch particular prices, which are determined by supply and demand, and, in the long run, by cost.   The socialistic economy no more provides such a pricing process of capital-goods than it provides a process of interest-determination.   The central authority itself produces the machines it requires and need not buy them in the market for capital-goods. But it is not even possible to determine the costs of production of capital-goods ;  for they themselves are the product of labour and capital, and a value must therefore be ascribed to capital in advance in order to permit the determination of the cost of using capital. Now to use a fictitious rate of interest in order to calculate a value of capital-goods that may be taken as given in determining the rate of interest, is to argue in a circle.

But if the prices of capital-goods cannot be ascertained, it cannot be determined whether given margins between labour-costs and commodity-prices are to be attributed to a greater or smaller quantity of capital.   It is impossible for the central authority to find any standard of comparison for the values of capital-goods of different kinds.   And for this reason, even if it were possible for it to discover the normal rate of interest (although actually this would be quite out of the question), it would still be impossible for it to undertake a process of interest-determination. For interest is a price that is calculated as a certain fraction of a value that is expressed as a sum of money. It is, indeed, on this account that a homogeneous pricing process for all the different kinds of capital-good is possible only in the form of an interest-determining process. If capital-goods cannot be reduced to a common denominator by being stated in terms of money-value, then the process of interest-determination is robbed of its technical basis. But if we are obliged to treat each individual capital-good as a peculiar factor of production that is not comparable with any other, we most seriously offend against the requirement that the pricing process should be homogeneous, without fulfilment of which a rational direction of production in the market economy is inconceivable.

So even if a certain margin could be calculated, by subtracting wage-costs from the prices of consumption-goods, it would still be impossible to direct the use of capital in accordance with it. For the amount of capital employed would still remain unknown, and so the amounts of surplus product *per unit of capital* could not be determined. Apart from this, and even supposing that such a calculation were possible, it still could be used as a basis for the correct organization of production only if it were possible to compare the surplus product so calculated with a normal rate of interest. For only then would it be possible to say in which branches of production an increased investment of capital would be economic (viz. those in which the surplus product exceeded the normal rate of interest) and in which branches an extension of investment must be forgone (because the interest-costs would not be completely covered by the surplus product). But it has already been pointed out that in the socialistic economy the normal rate of interest cannot be ascertained.

## § 14

But in reality it is not possible to calculate interest from the margin between labour-cost and commodity-price, even with the limitations already referred to. For, besides covering labour-costs and capital-costs, commodity-prices usually contain payment for the use of scarce natural forces, or other rents of one sort or another, which cannot be regarded as a price for the use of capital. In a community where land of various qualities has to be taken into use because the land of the best quality is not alone sufficient for all the production that is required, the employment of the superior land yields a rent, inasmuch as a product equal to that of the poorer land can be obtained from it with a smaller outlay of labour and capital. Thus rent is the equivalent of saved labour and capital; or, in other words, it is the extra product of good land compared with poorer when the same quantity of labour and capital is employed on each. Rents also exist in manufacturing industry wherever the conditions of production vary and the scarcity of the products supplied under the more favourable conditions causes their price to rise high enough to cover the costs of production even under the less favourable conditions.

It is obvious that this big differentiation of the costs of production of goods of the same kind introduces additional difficulties into the problem. For even if the attempt were made to avoid this new complication, by reckoning in together all the undertakings producing a given good as if they constituted one undertaking only, and using their average cost to determine market price, so that the rents were passed on to the consumers in the form of lower prices, the results of the attempt, in the absence of adequate knowledge of the costs actually incurred, would necessarily remain extremely dubious.

## § 15

Until now we have made the assumption that, given freedom of choice of occupation, a price would at least be established for labour, so that it would be possible, by comparing labour-costs and commodity-prices, at least to calculate some crude kind of interest, in the form of a price in excess of labour-cost due to the scarcity of the products made with the help of capital-goods. But even this assumption is untenable. The description of the way in which a rate of wages might be determined in the socialistic economy was based on the assumption that labour is the only factor that costs anything. This assumption is essential for establishing a direct relationship between commodity-prices and wages; for unless it is possible to ascertain the product of labour directly, the central authority does not know what wages it can afford to pay to any particular kind of labour, and is therefore unable to direct the available labour-supply into those branches of production in which it can satisfy the highest effective demand and in which on that account the highest wages can be paid.

If capital as well as labour is used in production, it is no longer possible to establish this direct connexion between prices and wages. Since, under modern conditions, practically every kind of good is produced by both labour and capital, it will hardly ever be possible to derive the value of the labour from the value of the product. In normal cases, the attribution of their respective shares to labour and capital will be an insoluble problem. Independent determination of the value of labour, by comparison of the supply of a given type of labour with the demand for it on the part of the central authority, is impossible, because so long as the central authority is ignorant of the value of the product of the labour, its demand for the labour must be unknown or arbitrary. But the product of the labour cannot be separated from the product of the capital, neither can the share attributable to labour be calculated by subtracting the capital-cost from the commodity-price; for the capital-cost, as has been shown already, is also unknown.

## § 16

Thus, in whatever direction the problem of economic calculation in the socialistic economy is investigated, insoluble difficulties are revealed. They are all to be ascribed to the nationalization of the material means of production, which are consequently no longer subject to a free pricing process. Nationalization of the means of production involves the central control of economic activity. The inevitable presence of this centralistic element, which must partake rather of the nature of a planned economy than of an exchange economy, must necessarily disturb the pricing process which, according to our assumption, is still present even under socialism. For the pricing process, as we have attempted to show, is an endless network of exchange-relationships from which individual pieces cannot be arbitrarily torn without injuring the rest. If the threads of these relationships are cut, by making it impossible for all the material means of production to enter into a pricing process based on free individual exchange, then those parts of the pricing process that remain will lack that tautness and interdependence which is the *sine qua non* of an effective exchange economy.

If the absence of an adequate pricing process prevents production from being carried on in such a way that the scarce factors of production are distributed according to the criterion of effective demand, then freedom of choice of consumption does not mean very much. For the freedom of choice would not control production ; it would apply only to goods *that had been produced already*, while what is wanted above all is that demand should control the allocation, not merely of commodities, but also of means of production. But, if this is so, socialism differs from communism only in its allowing the consumer a free selection from among existing consumption-goods and in its achieving the necessary restriction of demand by appropriate price-fixing, while under communism a method of distribution similar to war-time rationing would be adopted. Thus the atrophy of the exchange elements in socialism as compared with its planned elements extends to its solution of the problem of distribution.

§ 17

It might possibly be objected to this criticism of socialism that the way in which it would restrict satisfaction by failing to produce according to needs would be more than compensated by the opportunities for increasing consumption that would be afforded by the abolition of unearned incomes. If the profits of ownership of the material means of production go directly to the central authority, it may be asserted that the central authority will clearly be able to re-distribute this profit. But to argue in this way would obviously be to forget that the socialistic economy, like any other, must take steps to maintain the output of capital-goods. Consumed capital-goods must be re-placed and, in a progressive economy, a steadily increasing stream of new and better capital-goods must be main-tained. This end can be achieved only if fewer con-sumption-goods are produced than could have been produced with the available means ; or, in other words, if those who are employed in the consumption-goods industries obtain less than the full product of their labour, so that a sufficient surplus remains to support those who are employed in the capital-goods industries also. There is no question of everybody receiving the full product of his labour.

Now since the prices of consumption-goods must be higher than the total labour-costs incurred (because of the scarcity of material means of production), and since only wage-incomes affect purchasing power (because *ex hypothesi* there is to be no other sort of personal income), then less goods must be consumed in the social-istic economy than are produced ; i.e. means of production must remain free for the production of capital-goods. It is clear that the central authority's income from material means of production must be put to a very similar use to that which a large part of the unearned income of capitalism is put to at present. It is true that the socialistic authority might decide to accumulate less than its full income from capital and land, and to allow a greater or smaller part of this income to be used for the production of consumption-goods, which would result in a fall in the prices of the consumption-goods in question and thus in an increase in the real incomes of the consumers (since a given income would now command more consumption-goods). It is also conceivable that the central authority might accumulate *more* capital than the margin between total receipts from the sale of final products and total labour-cost. It might employ a greater proportion of labour and other means of production in the production of capital-goods, and then, of course, it would have fewer consumption-goods to sell and would limit the demand by selling them at higher prices. But, in any case, capital could not be accumulated except at the cost of consumption. Thus it would be a mistake to suppose that consumption could be materially increased in the socialistic economy by doing away with the unearned income of the capitalistic economy. If the socialistic economy is to be as productive as the capitalistic economy, then it must maintain as big a capital equipment. Hence, the supply of necessaries could be increased only by directing to their production those resources that are at present used for luxury purposes. If it were possible, after certain transition difficulties had been overcome, to produce necessaries with the means of production

171

that have hitherto been used for producing luxuries, that (according to the principle of uniform satisfaction of wants) would be a step in the right direction. But it must be pointed out, that to imagine that this increase of satisfaction could prove anything like a compensation for the decrease that would inevitably result from the lack of guidance in production, would be to over-estimate its amount considerably.

## § 18

The principal object of the preceding criticism has been to show that, despite freedom of consumers' choice, it would not be possible in the socialistic economy to accommodate production to demand, and that a considerable sacrifice of productivity would therefore be necessitated. For, however great its technical perfection may be, the production of the wrong kinds of things must always be comparatively worthless. Not merely does such production offend against the principle of uniform satisfaction of wants ; at the same time it leaves unfulfilled the requirement that the greatest possible result is to be obtained with a given set of means.

This latter requirement, however, is usually understood in a narrower sense than the above. It is usually understood to mean only that a branch of production is to be conducted in an economic manner, *assuming that it is desirable to engage in it at all*. Thus it still remains to ask, can the socialistic economy produce economically in this narrower sense or has the capitalistic economy an advantage over it in this respect also ? Opinions on this point differ widely. It is those very socialists who see clearly that no considerable advance can be made by a mere change in distribution, who often incline to the view that socialistic methods could greatly increase the total product. But there are others who have very grave doubts whether the socialist economy could even so much as succeed in equalling the capitalistic level of productivity.

It is true that this problem of the rationalization of production under socialism cannot be entirely isolated from the problem, already dealt with, of a correct division of the means of production among the various branches of production. These problems, as has been shown, are connected by the fact that economic decisions must reckon, not with a single branch of production, but with all branches of production, and that from this point of view the means of production that are needed for the technical improvement of a process in one branch of production often prove to be still more urgently required in another branch, while partial substitutes for their products in the former branch are abundant. It is possible to make a satisfactory selection among the infinite possibilities of productive organization only if unequivocal decisions can be arrived at from extremely precise data concerning the costs that would be incurred. Since the socialistic economy cannot command an adequate pricing process, a truly economic organization of individual branches of production under it is fundamentally impossible. In the socialistic economy, as in the communistic, the probable tendency will be to introduce wherever possible those methods that are the best technically, possibly without it ever being realized that the best from the technical point of view need not be the best from the economic point of view.

In this connexion, it must also be remembered that

it is continually asserted and re-asserted by socialists that the anticipated increase in the incomes of the working classes (in consequence of the abolition of unearned incomes) is only the first step towards an enormous increase of productivity which it has never before been possible to attain because there has been insufficient purchasing power to carry off the goods produced. The untenability of this assertion (which, of course, is also put forward in support of claims for constantly increasing wages within the framework of the capitalistic system), is evident from the contradiction that lies in the intention, on the one hand, to devote all unearned income to the extension of consumption and so, of course, to diminish capital accumulation in a corresponding measure, coupled with the belief, on the other hand, that it is possible, despite this diminished capital accumulation, to extend production to any desired extent.

Neither do there seem to be adequate grounds for supposing that new methods of organization and improvements in the technique of production will be discovered in greater number in the socialistic economy than under capitalism. At present there is insufficient experience to go upon. But it should be pointed out that the growth and development of the capitalistic economy was paralleled by an improvement of technique and an increase of productivity of such an astonishing magnitude that it is justifiable to assume a necessary connexion between this advance and the present form of economic organization.

But if capitalism and socialism are compared in regard to productivity, there is one point above all that must not be overlooked : the capitalistic economy is by its very nature a competitive economy. Under capitalism those will secure the greatest profits who are able to draw the custom of buyers from their rivals by offering their goods at lower prices. No other form of social economy can provide in the very principle of its organization so strong an incentive to economic behaviour as the competitive economy, unless mankind changes so much that other motives of human conduct prove to be as effective as the motive of gain is at present.

It would be impossible for the motive of gain to be as effective under socialism as it is under capitalism. The initiative of the private entrepreneur would be lacking. Those who for the sake of principle act economically even when they incur unpopularity by so doing (as, for example, when a public authority in a capitalistic country unselfishly adopts a most difficult policy of economy solely for the purpose of doing its share in relieving the country from an excessive burden of taxation)—such as these would remain exceptional even in the socialistic economy. But what is worst of all is that even those who were willing to act economically would not be able to do so, because they would not have an adequate pricing process to go upon.

# Chapter IV : Some Possible Objections Considered

## § 19

It is not possible to deal with all the objections against the arguments of the preceding chapter that might be based upon alternative assumptions concerning the structure of the socialistic economy. Between free competition and exchange-less communism there are endless conceivable combinations of the various structural elements of the social economy. In fact, it was for this reason that the decision was made to examine the socialistic economy as a type lying between the two extremes. Mixed forms which too nearly approach one or other of the two extremes, capitalism or communism, are not of interest in a theoretical investigation of the possibility of socialistic economic calculation, because the problem to be investigated either does not arise under them or else is already disposed of.

Reference, for example, to the monopolistic combinations of the modern capitalistic economy cannot demonstrate the possibility of a systematic socialistic economy. Whenever allusion is made to present-day evolutionary tendencies as a basis for the argument (as if it were established beyond doubt) that the capitalistic economy is automatically changing into a socialistic, this can only be a consequence of a lack of understanding of the problem of economic calculation under socialism. It must never be forgotten that the economic management of all the monopolistic structures that it is usual to refer to in this connexion—public undertakings, autonomous boards, cartels, pools, trusts, and the like—would be inconceivable without the constant guidance of the pricing process. The fact that such monopolistic organizations are able to influence the pricing process within certain limits in no way affects the fact that they form part of it. And this is what matters, that despite the tendency towards combination there exists an entirely adequate, and in some circumstances even an improved, mechanism of exchange between individual undertakings which provides a foundation for a complete pricing process and hence for economic behaviour. But socialism means nationalization of production and hence the abolition of the exchange relationships that constitute the essence of the market economy. If the independent undertakings as such are done away with, and made by decree dependent members of a planned economy, then an entirely new problem arises, fundamentally different from that of managing the independent undertakings or combinations of them : the problem of directing the whole economic process without pricing, which, as we have attempted to point out, has not yet been solved.

It follows that there is nothing in common between these tendencies in the organization of the members of an individualistic system and any general planning of the whole social economy ; that, in fact, the most definite boundary that can be drawn in economics separates them, the boundary between the individual economy and the social economy. Realization of this would make it impossible to assert that the capitalistic economy is automatically changing into a socialistic economy with free consumers' choice and public ownership of the material means of production ; and even more clearly impossible to assert that this evolutionary tendency has gone so far that ' the outlines of the new economic order ' are already discernible.[1]

Probably the frequent reference to this supposed automatic development results from the same reason that led Marx to restrict himself to criticizing capitalism and describing its inevitable collapse : the fact that it is impossible to make any pronouncement about the form of the socialistic economy of the future. The only difference between the two views is that according to the one the new order is to be heralded by the development and improvement of capitalism and, according to the other, by its complete collapse. We are not free to suppose that it is justifiable for the evolutionary theory (as compared with the collapse theory) to refrain from a more exact description of the practical organization of the socialistic economy on the ground of an expectation that the structure will be transformed bit by bit, without its decay and destruction being waited for. For the mistake in the evolutionary theory lies in its taking tendencies, which are working themselves out without in any way transgressing the conditions of the capitalistic market economy, and making them the basis of the assertion that the market economy might change into a planned economy of an entirely different nature from its own.

§ 20

Other objections may be passed over because they abandon the fundamental assumptions which are the

---

[1] As is asserted in the economic programme of the social-democratic trade unions. Cp. *Wirtschaftsdemokratie : Ihr Wesen, Weg und Ziel.* Pub. for the Allgemeine Deutsche Gewerkschaftsbund by Fritz Naphtali, Berlin, 1928.

source of the difficulties, particularly the assumption of free consumers' choice, and because they consequently approach too closely to the other, communistic, extreme. This is not always obvious, because those who hold such views mostly remain quite unconscious of the fact that they actually would abrogate this freedom. It is all the easier for the true state of affairs to be disguised because projects of the kind referred to here are often intended to be completely restricted to the limits of the pure market economy and to bring about what seem to be only trivial alterations in the organization of production (and not in that of distribution at all). Such, for example, are the multifarious proposals for the socialization of credit and the nationalization of the banks, which have the object of making it possible to influence production in accordance with some scheme or other of economic planning. Such schemes provide that credit would no longer be granted with regard to capacity and willingness to pay a given rate of interest, but allotted, with regard to considerations of economic productivity, to individual branches of production at artificially high or low rates. The decision would be made by the central banking authority ; that is to say, from the consumers' point of view, it would be an arbitrary decision. The fact that the consumer, within the limits of his restricted money-income, would be free to decide what to consume, would clearly no longer be of importance, since a truly free consumers' choice can only be spoken of where the consumers control production by means of their demand prices and not where they merely compete for what has already been produced. Despite their innocuous appearance, such proposals and objections are definitely of a communistic character, and consequently inadmissible in a discussion of the possibilities of the socialistic economy. They settle the problem of adjusting production to demand by giving it up in advance.[1]

## § 21

Thus there remain two groups of objections which are distinguished from one another by the fact that the one group (approaching the communistic ideal of central planning) asserts the possibility of controlling economic life without an effective determination of market prices for the factors of production and that the other (approaching the capitalistic extreme) asserts the possibility of a competitive pricing process within individual factor markets under socialism. But the essential thing is that both groups retain the presuppositions of freedom of consumers' choice and of the socialization of at least the material means of production, and thus hold that competition in the factor markets is reconcilable with public ownership, and that central control of economic life is reconcilable with freedom of consumers' choice.

Some theorists think it possible to overcome the difficulties referred to by reference to the possibility of an ' imputation of quantitative significances '. Eduard Heimann, for example, says [2] that the valuation of consumption-goods is ' reflected ' in the valuation of the

---

[1] Further objections are dealt with in the present writer's article on ' Sozialisierung des Bankwesens ', in the *Handwörterbuch des Bankwesens*, Berlin, 1932.

[2] Eduard Heimann, *Mehrwert und Gemeinwirtschaft : kritische und positive Beiträge zur Theorie des Sozialismus*, Berlin, 1922 ; *Kapitalismus und Sozialismus* (particularly III, ' Zur Kritik des Kapitalismus und der Nationalökonomie '), Potsdam, 1931.

factors of production, that the prices in the markets for consumption-goods are ' transmitted ' through all the stages of production (and apparently without reference to the situation of the parties in the production-goods markets), that the values of consumption-goods and of the factors of production are connected by an ' elastic string ' and that it is consequently possible, even if private property is abolished, to ' calculate the significance of each factor in the manufacture of goods if the prices of the products are given '.

It must be pointed out that of course it is not enough to show that there is some sort of connexion between the value of the product and the value of the total number of units of means of production employed. For this alone will not permit independent determination of the value of the individual factors of production. Since as a rule all three factors share in production, and since the proportions of their shares may vary indefinitely, it is quite impossible to ascribe a particular share of value to labour, capital, and land in any given instance. It is not even correct to say that the value of the whole product is the value of the three combined factors of production. For economic calculation essentially consists in the comparison of known costs of production with known or estimated commodity-prices. The essence of the process lies in ascertaining the existence of a profit or loss, on the basis of which, and not without which, production can be organized efficiently. Thus it is necessary above all that means of production that can be used for many different employments shall be valued individually and independently, quite apart from the accidental circumstances of any particular employment ; for this alone will make possible the comparison of costs and prices that is the foundation of economic calculation. What is wanted is not a postliminious imputation of accidental commodity-prices among the accidental combination of means of production employed (a process that can never give *individual* values for the factors), but immediate light on the question of what costs are *to be incurred*, obtained from an independent valuation of the separate factors of production, taking into consideration the different possibilities of employment that are open to them.

But all the possibilities of employment can be taken into consideration in this way only within a complete pricing process, and not by any such device as *imagining* ' each good changed over from one employment to another until it has actually attained the highest attainable significance '.[1] If factors are experimentally moved about, the total utilities of the products alter, and it is in the highest degree questionable whether the increase in the total utility of a good that results from the addition of a certain unit of a factor should be completely imputed to this particular unit. For the increased yield is the product of the co-operation of all the various factors of production employed. And besides, it is obvious that *imaginary* extensions and contractions of production cannot demonstrate an increase or decrease of total utility. The impossibility of comparing the wants of different persons makes it quite impracticable to express exactly, as changes in quantitative amounts of significance, the reactions of the consumers to such an attempt.

Such singular proposals as these are obviously based upon the supposition that it would be just as possible

[1] Carl Landauer, *Planwirtschaft und Verkehrswirtschaft*, Munich and Leipzig, 1931, p. 119.

for the central authority of the socialistic economy as for the manager of a self-sufficent farm to weigh all the alternative possibilities of production and consumption against one another and so to arrive at a decision about them. But examples of the actual practice of such a method are limited to isolated economies that are small enough for all the conditions of production and demand within it, and so the values to which these give rise, to be surveyed at a glance. When the total demand is built up of innumerable incommensurable scales of valuation ; when the division of labour is carried to the utmost extreme of partition into countless inter-dependent tasks ; when, that is to say, the enormous process of production is beyond the power of appre-hension of any individual, or even of the central authority ; then any ' imputation ' other than through market-pricing is inconceivable. The management of a self-sufficient farmstead and the control of a modern social economy are tasks that differ from one another not merely in degree but in kind. If the assumption of free con-sumers' choice is to mean that individuals' subjective valuations are to be taken account of in the social economy also, they must be translated into sufficiently objective terms by the pricing process to make an ade-quate economic calculation possible. The pricing pro-cesses in the consumption-goods markets are not enough. There must also be a real pricing process in the markets for means of production. No meaning can be assigned to any proposal to replace this pricing process by a process of ' imputation ', which, being a purely individual construction of a scale of values, has no relevance to the objectivized sphere of the social economy.

§ 22

It has been asserted, with no better foundation, that mathematical economics provides us with exact methods ' for determining the equilibrium prices of the means of production without the assistance of the market and its processes '.[1] What is meant here is the systems of equations such as have sometimes been used to demonstrate the functional relationships that we have referred to. If, in particular, Professor Cassel's well-known price formulae have been interpreted as if their assistance would enable the prices of the means of a production in a socialistic economy to be priced without market competition, Professor Cassel himself is partly to blame. For he declares that ' in the centrally and rationally organized socialistic economy, the cost principle would in fact have to be adhered to much more closely than is possible in the existing economic order '.[2]

According to Professor Cassel, the ideal pricing process must be conceived of in the following terms :

> If the quantities of the various factors of production that are available for the production of commodities in any year are given, then, if the prices of the factors are provisionally regarded as known, the prices of the finished commodities can be calculated in accordance with the principle of cost. This makes it possible to calculate the demand for each commodity, and since the principle of cost requires that this demand must be met (and in such a way that each demand bears the full cost of its satisfaction and that the total demand

---

[1] Kläre Tisch, *Wirtschaftsrechnung und Verteilung im zentralisch organisierten sozialistischen Gemeinwesen*, Bonner Dissertation, 1932, p. 24.

[2] Gustav Cassel, *Theoretische Sozialökonomie*, 4th edition, Leipzig, 1927, p. 115.

for each commodity is equal to the total supply), then it is also possible to calculate the quantity of each commodity to be produced. Now, if the technique of production is quite fixed and unalterable, it is possible to calculate the quantities of each factor that are required in production. And since the cost principle demands that these quantities must coincide with the amount available for each factor, an equation can be obtained, which is obviously what is necessary and sufficient for determining the prices of these factors of production.[1]

It is clear that what Professor Cassel provides us with here is not an explanation that will fit actual pricing processes, but an ideal price scheme to which actual pricing processes are to be fitted. Instead of a causal explanation, he gives us rules and principles. He does *not* help us ' to understand the type of connexion between cause and effect that is characteristic of the social economy.'[2] Such an understanding can be attained only by taking account of the acquisitive and competitive impulses and by supposing the means of production to be in private ownership. For only in such circumstances can the existence of adequate pricing processes be assumed. But Cassel thinks that competition should be replaced by the cost principle so as to make the pure theory of the exchange economy applicable to the socialistic economy in which there cannot be an adequate competitive pricing process because the material means of production are to be in the ownership of the community.

Even if Professor Cassel himself does not fall into the crude error of hoping actually to calculate prices with the help of equations established according to this scheme, he

---

[1] Gustav Cassel, ' Der Ausgangspunkt der theoretischen National-ökonomie ', *Zeitschrift für die gesamte Staatswissenschaft*, 58. Jahrg., 1902, pp. 696–7.

[2] Ibid., p. 696.

does nevertheless lend it his support by asserting that prices could be adequately determined in the socialistic economy according to the principle of cost. The pricing process, of course, has not the teleological character, that this implies. But, in any case, prices could not be calculated with the help of the equations, because these equations (or formulae, as it would be more correct to call them) give no expression for the functions connecting the dependent with the independent variables.

§ 23

Many claim to have discovered in the application of the methods of calculation developed by the modern science of business administration what appears to be a staggeringly simple solution of the problem. Such arguments as the following are typical :

> In the manufacture of a given good the department concerned first receives all the materials necessary for that stage of production from the stores manager. Each worker or group of workers has to complete the allotted process in a period of time which is based upon stop-watch readings. Thus the exact amount of time occupied in the manufacture of a good can be determined. Materials are reckoned at cost price and wage costs are calculated at piece-rates or time-rates. The cost of production consists of the costs of materials and labour plus a supplement for general overhead costs. . . . It follows that as far as costs of production are concerned it is completely a matter of indifference whether the factory in question competes with others or works with them as part of a general industrial plan. Costs of production plus marketing costs, together with a margin of profit, are the ultimate data for calculating the price of the commodity.[1]

---

[1] Roderich von Ungern-Sternberg, *Die Planung als Ordnungsprinzip der deutschen Industriewirtschaft*, Stuttgart, 1932, pp. 56–7.

This account is so devoid of meaning that one would hesitate to quote it if it were not unfortunately typical of the common belief that technical data provide a sufficient basis for answering economic questions. Rates of wages, however, cannot be read off from stop-watches, and so they, as well as the prices of the raw materials, are simply assumed as given. Writers in this strain clearly fail to realize that the very point at issue is the manner in which the prices are determined which serve as a basis for comparison of costs and selling prices. Neither are they any more conscious of the fact that without knowledge of these prices it is impossible to decide what processes of production are to be adopted ; for this decision is made not solely by the works manager on technical grounds, but also by the entrepreneur, who is guided by economic considerations.

## § 24

It might perhaps be suggested that prices could simply be fixed by the central authority. This has, in fact, been explicitly demanded as far as the rate of interest is concerned. But if this were done, the case would be one of central planning of production without regard to the controlling element of consumers' choice. All that it would mean would be controlling production through the medium of fictitious prices instead of directly reckoning in units of goods and services. In Soviet Russia, an attempt is being made to employ both kinds of planning side by side. But this method, of course, is practicable only if there is no intention of letting real scarcity prices be determined for the products, which would be expected to coincide with the fictitious cost prices. For this coincidence cannot be achieved if production is directed without regard to scales of wants and yet the final valuation of the product left to uncontrolled demand. Such a policy must necessarily lead to communism, i.e. it must cease to be socialistic, because a pricing process determined by the value-scales of individuals is irreconcilable with an arbitrary programme of production and would have to be abandoned in favour of maximum prices and rationing.

It might be objected that a completely free market is not appropriate to a socialistic economy and that what is lost in this way *should* be replaced by planned elements ; that, in fact, the peculiar characteristic of the centrally-controlled economy is that it is controlled with regard to social interest and without regard to considerations of private profitability. However true this may appear, and however necessary such an attitude may be on the part of those who support socialistic ideals, it remains difficult to see how central control of the economy can be reconciled with the assumption of a really free choice of consumption and occupation. If the want of an adequate pricing process compels the central authority to construct a general economic plan, it will also compel it to dispose of labour as it sees fit. But in that case the labourers can no longer be allowed a free choice of occupation. If the allocation of the labour should be brought about by appropriate wage policies, prices in the labour market would have to vary much more than in the capitalistic economy, since the demands for labour would follow the plan, without regard to the prices that had to be paid, and the freedom of occupation that existed in such circumstances would be as problematic as the freedom of consumption that exists in a commodity market where the only choice offered is that between goods that have already been produced.

## § 25

Whereas the objections that have been dealt with so far attempt to show that economic calculation would be possible in the socialistic economy without competition, and thus imply that an adequate competitive pricing process would not exist, or at least would not be necessary, in another group of objections the greatest stress is laid upon the assertion that exchange relationships would exist even apart from private property, and that an adequate competitive pricing process could therefore be maintained even in a planned economy. Often the same writers who put forward the theory that there would be competition between different branches of the civil service also hold the view already discussed that quantitative significance could be imputed to commodities ; but such an attempt to make assurance doubly sure scarcely carries conviction.

Nothing need be said of the common argument ' that State railways compete with State canals and that State coal mines similarly cannot help coming into competition with State electricity undertakings ',[1] except that it betrays complete ignorance of the fundamental problems of the socialistic economy. Nobody can deny the obvious fact that business relationships do exist between public undertakings or assert that the possibility of exchange

---

[1] Kromphardt in the *Zeitschrift für Nationalökonomie*, Bd. I, Vienna, 1930 (review of the present writer's book *Die Konkurrenz*, Munich and Leipzig, 1929).

relationships in the present economic order is bound up with the existence of private property—*in individual cases.* But this in no way affects the fact that the pricing process *as a whole*, the foundation of the present economic order, is based upon private property, and that public undertakings only participate in normal business relationships and compete with other undertakings (among which are other public undertakings) because they are run, *not* on administrative, but on business, lines, and above all because their pricing processes conform to the general pricing process. As is well known, this is what also constitutes the distinction between partial and complete socialization, of which Liefmann says that ' what is called partial socialization is no socialization at all in the true sense, because it in no way alters the present-day economic order ',[1] and of which Mises rightly observes that all partial socialization is only made possible by ' the actions of the undertakings in question being so far supported by the uncontrolled commercial organism that surrounds them that the essential characteristics of the socialistic economy cannot appear in them at all '.[2]

Heimann [3] is somewhat more penetrating, although it is unfortunate that he should restrict himself to mere sug-

[1] Robert Liefmann, *Geschichte und Kritik des Sozialismus*, Leipzig, 1922, p. 165.

[2] Ludwig Mises, *Die Gemeinwirtschaft*, 2nd ed. Jena, 1932, p. 98.

[3] Eduard Heimann, *Kapitalismus und Sozialismus* (especially II. ' Ueber Konkurrenz, Monopol und sozialistische Wirtschaft '), Potsdam, 1931. My references to Dr. Heimann are not intended to provoke a re-discussion of a long-standing difference of opinion between us, but merely to provide an independent statement of the objections with which I am concerned without laying myself under the obligation to outline the concept of fictitious competition in the socialistic economy and so exposing myself to the charge of having deliberately chosen an unfavourable example.

gestions and leave the constructive work to the critic, as is the common practice of socialistic theorists. For the establishment of competition (which he himself, it is true, puts in inverted commas), it is enough for Heimann that supply and demand should emanate from different public authorities which ' have a different personnel and an ideal and material interest in the results of their work '. According to Heimann, everything would then go on ' just as under present conditions. . . . Consumers' demands for products would be transformed into the demands for means of production on the part of the producing undertakings—whether communistic or capitalistic makes no difference—and interest and wages would be determined exactly as hitherto. . . . Both the form and the content of economic calculation would therefore be retained. Nothing is altered in the economic constitution of this form of organization, and consequently it would function in the old manner '. And, despite all this, the decisive step into socialism would have been taken, private ownership of the means of production have been abolished, and ' personal ' distribution separated from ' functional '. There would be no more unearned incomes, for rent and interest would go directly to the central authority.

Thus, apparently, the only change is that the managers of the individual public undertakings are no longer the owners of the means of production over which they have power of disposal, and no longer receive the profits or have to bear the losses. Any participation in the profits would have to be restricted within the narrowest limits if all considerable private accumulation of capital had to be prevented in order to preserve the public ownership of the means of production. That the socialistic economy is to this extent psychologically inferior to the capitalistic is admitted by many socialistic theorists. It forgoes 'the stimulus to good service which lies in the capitalistic connexion between economic calculation and income' (Heimann). The importance of this statement can only be gauged after an investigation into the degree in which the profit-making tendency is the indispensable motive force of the capitalistic economy and into the question of whether an adequate substitute for it could be found in the socialistic economy. Those who advocate economic planning are at this point in the position of having to count upon a change of the general attitude towards economic life without being able to educe any presumption of its reliability or any reason why it should come about at all.

The manager of a planned economic undertaking holds a monopoly position in the market. There is no supply except by the public authorities and it may be supposed that all the production in any one branch of industry is comprised within a single undertaking, at least for accounting purposes. That is the least that may be expected from planned control of production. And as has already been pointed out, the elimination of rent demands a similar unification. It follows that the manager of such a branch of industry will possess, according to capitalistic standards, an unusual amount of power, and that precautions will have to be taken to see that he does not abuse it. In a communistic economy the necessity for absolute subordination to the general plan would, in theory, prevent any arbitrary exercise of power on the part of individuals. But in a socialistic economy, which is to be controlled by the competition of public authorities, the managers of the individual monopolies would have to be given a certain amount of freedom.  If they were furthermore required to make profits, the danger of monopolistic abuses would be extraordinarily great.

Heimann attempts to avoid this danger by demanding ' complete restraint ' on the part of the monopolists.[1] The monopolists are to see that prices cover costs ; they are simply to follow demand schedules instead of themselves initiating supply schedules, thus ' ceasing to act as independent parties and leaving the mechanism of the market in free operation '.

It is clear that such a restriction as this of the use of monopoly power cannot prove very reassuring.  Since the monopolists no longer bear any risks and are able to compensate any loss by raising prices, provision must be made for strict control.  And the question of an adequate check leads us back to the question with which we started : whether it is possible under socialism to have a competitive pricing process in the factor markets and so a genuine calculation of profits in individual undertakings.

The various public authorities ' compete ' in the factor markets.  According to our assumptions, the

[1] In a similar fashion the guild socialists demand a control of production by guilds, neither in their own interests alone nor solely in that of the consumer,' but in the common interest.  The guilds, however, are not to work for profit at all, but only to meet demand. There is to be no competition, and the State is only quite occasionally to fix prices.  It is absolutely impossible to discover the principles according to which such a society could be governed.  Since there is, however, no way in which prices could be determined otherwise, the State would after all be responsible for apportioning the work of production among the different guilds.  And thus guild socialism would relapse into communism, although the freedom which the guilds would enjoy is supposed to give it an advantage even over socialism.

demand for capital and labour is dependent upon changes in the prices of the products and in the profits which arise in consequence of these changes. Capital is exclusively owned by the community, which receives all interest-payments and all the profits of the individual undertakings. The demand for capital in the individual industries is restricted by a uniform rate of interest that is just high enough to restrict the total demand to the level of the available resources. Under communism, credit is allotted arbitrarily, but under our present assumptions this must be avoided. But there cannot be a genuine pricing process in the credit market because of the monopoly which is enjoyed by the central authority. The rate of interest must be fixed experimentally. And so all the objections that have already been considered arise again.

Obviously the central authority cannot be satisfied with the simple promise that the branches of industry that are demanding capital will pay a certain rate of interest. In any case, all interest and profit goes to the central authority; and, in the absence of personal responsibility, promises of payment have a very different character from that which they bear in the capitalistic economy, and one that makes much stricter control necessary. What is necessary is to determine whether the industries in question can be expected to be able to pay a given sum of interest out of their gross profits and to yield a net profit in addition; but, of course, not at the expense of a sufficiently monopolistic treatment of the consumers.

Unified accounting in all branches of industry would necessarily be a task so difficult as to be practically insoluble, if only because the enterprises concerned would be so extremely numerous and the different kinds of organization and production technique so varied. It is certain that this task would be incomparably more difficult to perform than the similar task in the communistic economy, which would only involve a comparison of the actual figures with those of the general plan; for under socialism, each figure would have to be checked with regard to the efficiency of the whole undertaking, which in its turn could only be determined by comparison with the figures of all the other enterprises according to the principle of homogeneous price determination.

Thus the decisive question is whether it is possible to determine net profits at all within individual branches of industry. The problem is one of comparing commodity-prices with costs. The difficulty arises from the reciprocal monopoly relationships. Even in the commodity markets, real competition prevails only on the demand side ; supplies are in the hands of monopolists who determine the extent of production and so the level of prices. In these circumstances, even if costs could be assumed as known, it would be uncommonly difficult to decide whether profits were due to an efficient organization of production, a correct estimate of demand, or a monopolistic exploitation of consumers. In the capitalistic economy, uncertainties of this kind cannot arise, so far as there is competition within the individual branches of production. Thus the problem of competition in the socialistic economy is already involved in the fact that the monopolistic difficulties which appear here and there in the capitalistic economy extend throughout the whole of the socialistic economy. Even in the markets for consumption-goods there are *only* monopoly prices.

But the monopoly problem becomes considerably more complicated when we turn to the markets for the means of production. It has already been pointed out that there would be an absolute monopoly of supply in the capital market. But the demanders too would be monopolists. It is true that they would ' compete ' with one another for the available supply, but only in regard to profits the calculation of which is the very point at issue, especially considering the ease with which true profits may be confused with monopoly profits. It is not conceivable that a normal rate of interest would be arrived at in these circumstances, because the monopolists would always be able to raise the rate they were paying. All they need do would be to restrict production accordingly. Within the industry there would be no such competition as would prevent such action on the part of a private entrepreneur. Thus it is quite conceivable that the individual monopolists would exploit their monopoly position to raise the rate of interest. Neither would such a tendency be at all surprising, seeing that there would be an absolute monopoly on the supply side, and that the position of the suppliers would therefore be incomparably more powerful than that of the demanders. There would be no force that could be relied upon to reduce the rate of interest to normal.

If we assume, however, that in spite of all these difficulties capital is distributed among the individual branches of industry in correspondence with the demand for it, then primary products, capital-goods, and labour will be demanded with this purchasing power. On the markets for raw materials and capital-goods, monopolists are opposed to one another ; it is difficult to see how a market-price can be established. If it should be suggested that all intermediate products should be supplied to the next stage of production at prime cost, the questions would arise of how the prime cost could be calculated, and of how the capital could be distributed in accordance with profits if *ex definitione* there are to be no profits in the production of raw materials and the manufacture of capital-goods.

As for the determination of the price of labour, it must be repeated that the apparent precision of the process, even with a free choice of occupation, would be destroyed by the lack of precision of the process of interest-determination. And furthermore, all the objections that arise from the monopolistic position of the employers, in both the labour and the commodity markets, and that have already been touched upon in connexion with the question of interest, are equally valid in the present connexion.

But the problem becomes still more complicated if, as many socialistic theorists advocate, we separate personal from functional distribution here also. How are we to conceive of the determination of wages in a labour market co-existing with an arbitrary allocation of incomes ? It might perhaps be suggested that a central labour office could supply labour at the existing ' market-price ' and then proceed to *pay* an entirely different wage based upon some ethical criterion or other. But in such circumstances it is difficult to see, not only how the total supply of labour is to be distributed among individual industries in the first place, that is to say, how the choice of occupation on the part of new recruits is to be regulated, but also how a given supply of each kind of labour is to be distributed among the individual branches of a particular industry. A further difficulty, that does not arise in regard to capital, springs from the fact that the labour must have many different prices, and not one uniform price, because of its heterogeneous nature. Probably demand, and so a tendency towards low wages, would be in the stronger position in the case of such labour as had relatively few uses, and supply, and so a tendency towards high wages, in the case of such labour as had relatively many uses. This would therefore mean a tendency for highly specialized labour to be underpaid and for relatively unspecialized labour to be overpaid ; a consequence that gives food for thought.

This examination of the conditions that would prevail in the ' markets ' for means of production should have made it clear that it would be entirely correct to say that real competition would exist only in the markets for consumption-goods, and that the competition between public authorities for the means of production would be competition in inverted commas only. All that those in charge of economic activity have ostensibly to do is to transform the consumers' demand for products into a demand for means of production. They are supposed to play no active role at all, but passively to set the mechanism of the free market in motion. But it is important to remember in this connexion that, in the first place, the competition in the markets for consumption-goods is only unilateral, and that, in the second place, there cannot be markets for the means of production at all if there is an absolute monopoly on their supply side and *ex hypothesi* no active demand at all.

Of course it will be said that it would be the function of the managers of the socialistic economy, by trans-forming the demand for products into a demand for means of production, to bring the competition of the consumers into immediate contact with the scarce means of production. But this is to forget that an *independent* pricing process of the factors of production is just as necessary for economic calculation as is the pricing process of the product ; and that such a pricing process cannot be brought about by attempting to breathe some of the life of the *genuine* competition of the commodity-market into the socialistic industrial scheme. Consumers' demand alone is not a sufficient basis for a genuine pricing process in the markets for means of production. For this, although ultimately the decisive side, is nevertheless only *one* side of the general pricing process. Supply (as reflecting the scarcity of means of production in relation to unlimited needs) must also be taken account of. The laws of price cannot be fulfilled without it. But on the supply side the socialization of the means of production does away with all real competition. It is not a question of transferring competition on the demand side, in however artificial a manner, but of securing competition on the *supply* side. Socialistic theorists make the mistake of imagining it possible to replace competition on both the demand and supply sides by an actual and a fictitious competition, both on the demand side. At a pinch it is conceivable that individual public authorities might compete with one another on the demand side ; with a centralized supply of capital (and labour), competition on the supply side is necessarily out of the question. But even if the labourers competed among themselves, the situation, as has been shown, would not be materially improved.

Thus there results a graduated monopoly : free competition among consumers, and monopoly on the part of those who supply consumption-goods ; fictitious competition among those who demand means of production, and absolute monopoly among those who supply labour and capital. Demand is restricted, not by a pricing *process*, but by experimental price-*fixing*. Instead of the means of production being distributed automatically they are allocated according to estimates of results, which, in the absence of exact cost accounting, would not really be feasible at all. Thus, an automatic grouping of the factors of production will, in all probability, also be replaced by arbitrary allocation as a necessary counterpart to the arbitrary allocation of incomes (which, it must be admitted, the pricing of the factors of production would render impossible). With all this, exact calculation of profit and loss would be more necessary in the socialistic economy than in the capitalistic, for where all calculations are recognized as fictitious (and there would be no genuine counting of costs), and where the struggle for existence does not compel adequate recognition of the economic principle, negligence increases, and with it the need for safeguards along purely accounting lines. A decline in individual responsibility means an inevitable expansion of the central auditing apparatus.

# V

# THE PRESENT STATE OF THE DEBATE

By F. A. HAYEK

## 1. THE EFFECTS OF CRITICISM

In spite of a natural tendency on the part of socialists to belittle its importance, it is clear that the criticism of socialism epitomized in the foregoing chapters has already had a very profound effect on the direction of socialist thought. The great majority of " planners " are, of course, still unaffected by it : the great mass of the hangers-on of any popular movement are always unconscious of the intellectual currents which produce a change of direction.[1] Moreover, the actual existence

---

[1] This applies, unfortunately, also to most of the organized collective efforts which profess to be devoted to the scientific study of the problem of planning. Anyone who studies such publications as the *Annales de l'economie collective*, or the material contributed to the " World

in Russia of a system, which professes to be planned, has led many of those who know nothing of its development to suppose that the main problems are solved ; in fact, as we shall see, Russian experience provides abundant confirmation of the doubts already stated. But among the leaders of socialist thought not only is the nature of the central problem more and more recognized, but the force of the objections raised against the types of socialism, which in the past used to be considered as most practicable, is also increasingly admitted. It is now rarely denied that, in a society which is to preserve freedom of choice of the consumer and free choice of occupation, central direction of all economic activity presents a task which cannot be rationally solved under the complex conditions of modern life. It is true, as we shall see, that even among those who see the problem, this position is not yet completely abandoned ; but its defence is more or less of the nature of a rearguard action where all that is attempted is to prove that " in principle " a solution is conceivable. Little or no claim is made that such a solution is practicable. We shall later have occasion to discuss some of these attempts. But the great majority of the more recent schemes try to get around the difficulties by the construction of alternative socialist systems which differ more or less fundamentally from the traditional types against which the criticism was directed in the first instance and which are supposed to be immune against the objections to which the latter are subject.

Social Economic Congress, Amsterdam, 1931 ", and published by the " International Relations Institute " under the title *World Social Economic Planning* (The Hague, 2 vols., 1931–2), will search in vain for any sign that the problems are even recognized.

In the preceding section, Professor Halm has examined some of the solutions proposed by Continental writers. In this concluding essay, the recent English literature of the subject will be considered and an attempt will be made to evaluate the recent proposals which have been devised to overcome the difficulties which have now been recognized. Before we enter into this discussion, however, a few words on the relevance of the Russian experiment to the problems under discussion may be useful.

## 2. The Lessons of the Russian Experiment

It is of course neither possible nor desirable to enter at this point into an examination of the concrete results of this experiment. In this respect it is necessary to refer to detailed special investigations, particularly to that of Professor Brutzkus, which will appear simultaneously with the present volume and which forms an essential complement to the more abstract considerations presented here.[1] At this moment we are only concerned with the more general question of how the established results of such an examination of the concrete experiences fit in with the more theoretical argument, and how far the conclusions reached by *a priori* reasoning are confirmed or contradicted by empirical evidence.

It is perhaps not unnecessary to remind the reader at this point that it was not the possibility of planning as such which has been questioned on the grounds of general considerations, but the possibility of successful planning, of achieving the ends for which planning was undertaken. Therefore we must first be clear as to the tests by which we are to judge success, or the forms in

[1] B. Brutzkus, *Economic Planning in Russia*, London (Routledge), 1935.

which we should expect failure to manifest itself. There is no reason to expect that production would stop, or that the authorities would find difficulty in using all the available resources somehow, or even that output would be permanently lower than it had been before planning started. What we should anticipate is that output, where the use of the available resources was determined by some central authority, would be lower than if the price mechanism of a market operated freely under otherwise similar circumstances. This would be due to the excessive development of some lines of production at the expense of others, and the use of methods which are inappropriate under the circumstances. We should expect to find over-development of some industries at a cost which was not justified by the importance of their increased output, and to see unchecked the ambition of the engineer to apply the latest developments made elsewhere, without considering whether they were economically suited in the situation. In many cases the use of the latest methods of production, which could not have been applied without central planning, would then be a symptom of a misuse of resources rather than a proof of success.

It follows therefore that the excellence, from a technological point of view, of some parts of the Russian industrial equipment, which most strikes the casual observer and which is commonly regarded as evidence of success, has little significance in so far as the answer to the central question is concerned. Whether the new plant will prove to be a useful link in the industrial structure for increasing output depends not only on technological considerations, but even more on the general economic situation. The best tractor factory may not be an asset, and the capital invested in it is a sheer loss, if the labour which the tractor replaces is cheaper than the cost of the material and labour, which goes to make a tractor, *plus* interest.

But once we have freed ourselves from the misleading fascination of the existence of colossal instruments of production, which is likely to captivate the uncritical observer, only two legitimate tests of success remain : the goods which the system actually delivers to the consumer, and the rationality or irrationality of the decisions of the central authority. There can be no doubt that the first test would lead to a negative result, for the present, at any rate, or if applied to the whole population and not to a small privileged group. Practically all observers seem to agree that even compared with pre-war Russia the position of the great masses has deteriorated. Yet such a comparison still makes the results appear too favourable. It is admitted that Tsarist Russia did not offer conditions very favourable to capitalist industry, and that under a more modern régime capitalism would have brought about rapid progress. It must also be taken into account that the suffering in the past fifteen years, that " starving to greatness " which was supposed to be in the interest of later progress, should by now have borne some fruits. It would provide a more appropriate basis of comparison if we assumed that the same restriction of consumption, which has actually taken place, had been caused by taxation, the proceeds of which had been lent to competitive industry for investment purposes. It can hardly be denied that this would have brought about a rapid and enormous increase of the general standard of life beyond anything which is at present even remotely possible.

There only remains, then, the task of actually examining the principles on which the planning authority has acted. And although it is impossible to trace here, even shortly, the varied course of that experiment, all we know about it, particularly from Professor Brutzkus' study referred to above, fully entitles us to say that the anticipations based on general reasoning have been thoroughly confirmed. The breakdown of " war-communism " occurred for exactly the same reasons, the impossibility of rational calculation in a moneyless economy, which Professor Mises and Professor Brutzkus had foreseen. The development since, with its repeated reversals of policy, has only shown that the rulers of Russia had to learn by experience all the obstacles which a systematic analysis of the problem reveals. But it has raised no important new problems, still less has it suggested any solutions. Officially the blame for nearly all the difficulties is still put on the unfortunate individuals who are persecuted for obstructing the plan by not obeying the orders of the central authority or by carrying them too literally. But although this means that the authorities only admit the obvious difficulty of making people follow out the plan loyally, there can be no doubt that the more serious disappointments are really due to the inherent difficulties of any central planning. In fact, from accounts such as that of Professor Brutzkus, we gather that, far from advancing towards more rational methods of planning, the present tendency is to cut the knot by abandoning the comparatively scientific methods employed in the past. Instead are substituted more and more arbitrary and uncorrelated decisions of particular problems as they are suggested by the contingencies of the day. In so far as political or psychological problems are concerned Russian experience may be very instructive. But to the student of economic problems of socialism it does little more than furnish illustrations of well-established conclusions. It gives us no help towards an answer to the intellectual problem which the desire for a rational reconstruction of society raises. To this end we shall have to proceed with our systematic survey of the different conceivable systems which are no less important for only existing so far as theoretical suggestions.

## 3. The Mathematical Solution

As has been pointed out in the Introduction, discussion of these questions in the English literature began relatively late and at a comparatively high level. Yet it can hardly be said that the first attempts really met any of the main points. Two Americans, Professor F. M. Taylor and Mr. W. C. Roper, were first in the field. Their analyses, and to some extent also that of Mr. H. D. Dickinson in this country [1] were directed to show that on the assumption of a complete knowledge of all relevant data, the values and the quantities of the different commodities to be produced might be determined by the application of the apparatus by which theoretical economics explains the formation of prices and the direction of production in a competitive system. Now it must be admitted that this is not an impossibility in the sense that it is logically contradictory. But to argue that a determination of prices by such a procedure being logically conceivable in any way invalidates the contention that it is not a possible solution, only proves

[1] For exact references to the writings of these authors, see the bibliography in Appendix B.

that the real nature of the problem has not been perceived. It is only necessary to attempt to visualize what
the application of this method would imply in practice
in order to rule it out as humanly impracticable and
impossible. It is clear that any such solution would have
to be based on the solution of some such system of
equations as that developed in Barone's article in the
Appendix. But what is practically relevant here is not
the formal structure of this system, but the nature and
amount of concrete information required if a numerical
solution is to be attempted and the magnitude of the
task which this numerical solution must involve in any
modern community. The problem here is, of course,
not how detailed this information and how exact the
calculation would have to be in order to make the solution
perfectly exact, but only how far one would have to go
to make the result at least comparable with that which
the competitive system provides. Let us look into this
a little further.

In the first place it is clear that if central direction is
really to take the place of the initiative of the manager of
the individual enterprise and is not simply to be a most
irrational limitation of his discretion in some particular
respect, it will not be sufficient that it takes the form of
mere general direction, but it will have to include and be·
intimately responsible for details of the most minute
description. It is impossible to decide rationally how
much material or new machinery should be assigned to
any one enterprise and at what price (in an accounting
sense) it will be rational to do so, without also deciding at
the same time whether and in which way the machinery
and tools already in use should continue to be used or
be disposed of. It is matters of this sort, details of

technique, the saving of one material rather than the other or any other of the small economies which cumulatively decide the success or failure of a firm, and in any central plan which is not to be hopelessly wasteful, they must be taken account of. In order to be able to do so it will be necessary to treat every machine, tool, or building not just as one of a class of physically similar objects, but as an individual whose usefulness is determined by its particular state of wear and tear, its location, and so on. The same applies to every batch of commodities which is situated at a different spot or which differs in any other respect from other batches. This means that in order to achieve that degree of economy in this respect which is secured by the competitive system, the calculations of the central planning authority would have to treat the existing body of instrumental goods as being constituted of almost as many different types of goods as there are individual units. And so far as ordinary commodities, i.e. non-durable semi-finished or finished goods are concerned, it is clear that there would be many times more different types of such commodities to consider than we should imagine if they were classified only by their technical characteristics. Two technically similar goods in different places or in different packings or of a different age cannot possibly be treated as equal in usefulness for most purposes if even a minimum of efficient use is to be secured.

Now since in a centrally directed economy the manager of the individual plant would be deprived of the discretion of substituting at will one kind of commodity for another, all this immense mass of different units would necessarily have to enter *separately* into the calculations of the planning authority. It is obvious that the mere statistical task of enumeration exceeds anything of this sort hitherto undertaken. But that is not all. The information which the central planning authority would need, would also include a complete description of all the relevant technical properties of every one of these goods, including costs of movement to any other place where it might possibly be used with greater advantage, cost of eventual repair or changes, etc. etc.

But this leads to another problem of even greater importance. The usual theoretical abstractions used in the explanation of equilibrium in a competitive system include the assumption that a certain range of technical knowledge is " given ". This, of course, does not mean that all the best technical knowledge is concentrated anywhere in a single head, but that people with all kinds of knowledge will be available and that among those competing in a particular job, speaking broadly, those that make the most appropriate use of the technical knowledge will succeed. In a centrally planned society this selection of the most appropriate among the known technical methods will only be possible if all this knowledge can be used in the calculations of the central authority. This means in practice that this knowledge will have to be concentrated in the heads of one or at best a very few people who actually formulate the equations to be worked out. It is hardly necessary to emphasize that this is an absurd idea even in so far as that knowledge is concerned which can properly be said to " exist " at any moment of time. But much of the knowledge that is actually utilized is by no means " in existence " in this ready-made form. Most of it consists in a technique of thought which enables the individual engineer to find new solutions rapidly as soon as he is confronted with new constellations of circumstances. To assume the practicability of these mathematical solutions, we should have to assume that the concentration of knowledge at the central authority would also include a capacity to discover any improvement of detail of this sort.[1]

There is a third set of data which would have to be available before the actual operation of working out the appropriate method of production and quantities to be produced could be undertaken, data relative to importance of the different kinds and quantities of consumers' goods. In a society where the consumer was free to spend his income as he liked, these data would have to take the form of complete lists of the different quantities of all commodities which would be bought at any possible combination of prices of the different commodities which might be available. These figures would inevitably be of the nature of estimates for a future period based upon past experience. But past experience cannot provide the range of knowledge necessary. And as tastes change from moment to moment, the lists would have to be in process of continuous revision.

It is probably evident that the mere assembly of these data is a task beyond human capacity. Yet if the centrally run society were to work as efficiently as the competitive society, which as it were decentralizes the task of collecting them, they would have to be present. But let us assume for the moment that this difficulty, the " mere difficulty of statistical technique ", as it is contemptuously referred to by most planners, is actually overcome. This would be only the first step in the

[1] On the more general problem of experimentation and the utilization of really new inventions, etc., see below, p. 223 *et seq.*

solution of the main task. Once the material is collected it would still be necessary to work out the concrete decisions which it implies. Now the magnitude of this essential mathematical operation will depend on the number of unknowns to be determined. The number of these unknowns will be equal to the number of commodities which are to be produced. As we have seen already, we have to take as different commodities all the final products to be completed at different moments, whose production has to be started or to be continued at present. At present we can hardly say what their number is, but it is hardly an exaggeration to assume that in a fairly advanced society, the order of magnitude would be at least in the hundreds of thousands. This means that, at each successive moment, every one of the decisions would have to be based on the solution of an equal number of simultaneous differential equations, a task which, with any of the means known at present, could not be carried out in a lifetime. And yet these decisions would not only have to be made continuously, but they would also have to be conveyed continuously to those who had to execute them.

It will probably be said that such a degree of exactitude would not be necessary, since the working of the present economic system itself does not come anywhere near it. But this is not quite true. It is clear that we never come near the state of equilibrium described by the solution of such a system of equations. But that is not the point. We should not expect equilibrium to exist unless all external change had ceased. The essential thing about the present economic system is that it does react to some extent to all those small changes and differences which would have to be deliberately disregarded under the system we are discussing if the calculations were to be manageable. In this way rational decision would be impossible in all these questions of detail, which in the aggregate decide the success of productive effort.

It is improbable that any one who has realized the magnitude of the task involved has seriously proposed a system of planning based on comprehensive systems of equations. What has actually been in the minds of those who have mooted this kind of analysis has been the belief that, starting from a given situation, which was presumably to be that of the pre-existing capitalistic society, the adaptation to the minor changes which occur from day to day could be gradually brought about by a method of trial and error. This suggestion suffers, however, from two fundamental mistakes. In the first instance, as has been pointed out many times, it is inadmissible to assume that the changes in relative values brought about by the transition from capitalism to socialism would be of a minor order, so permitting the prices of the pre-existing capitalistic system to be used as a starting-point, and making it possible to avoid a complete re-arrangement of the price-system. But even if we neglect this very serious objection, there is not the slightest reason to assume that the task could be solved in this way. We need only to remember the difficulties experienced with the fixing of prices, even when applied to a few commodities only, and to contemplate further that, in such a system, price-fixing would have to be applied not to a few but to all commodities, finished or unfinished, and that it would have to bring about as frequent and as varied price-changes as those which occur in a capitalistic society every day and every hour, in order to see that this is not a way in which the solution provided by competition can even be approximately achieved. Almost every change of any single price would make changes of hundreds of other prices necessary and most of these other changes would by no means be proportional but would be affected by the different degrees of elasticity of demand, by the possibilities of substitution and other changes in the method of production. To imagine that all this adjustment could be brought about by successive orders by the central authority when the necessity is noticed, and that then every price is fixed and changed until some degree of equilibrium is obtained is certainly an absurd idea. That prices may be fixed on the basis of a total view of the situation is at least conceivable, although utterly impracticable; but to base authoritative price-fixing on the observation of a small section of the economic system is a task which cannot be rationally executed under any circumstances. An attempt in this direction will either have to be made on the lines of the mathematical solution discussed before, or else entirely abandoned.

## 4. ABROGATION OF THE SOVEREIGNTY OF THE CONSUMER

In view of these difficulties, it is not surprising that practically all, who have really tried to think through the problem of central planning, have despaired of the possibility of solving it in a world in which every passing whim of the consumer is likely to upset completely the carefully worked out plans. It is more or less agreed now that free choice of the consumer (and presumably also free choice of occupation) and planning from the centre are incompatible aims. But this has given the impression that the unpredictable nature of the tastes of the consumers is the only or the main obstacle to successful planning. Dr. Maurice Dobb [1] has recently followed this to its logical conclusion by asserting that it would be worth the price of abandoning the freedom of the consumer if by the sacrifice socialism could be made possible. This is undoubtedly a very courageous step. In the past, socialists have consistently protested against any suggestion that life under socialism would be like life in a barracks, subject to regimentation of every detail. Dr. Dobb considers these views as obsolete. Whether he would find many followers if he professed these views to the socialist masses is not a question which need concern us here. The question is, would it provide a solution to our problem?

Dr. Dobb openly admits that he has abandoned the view, now held by Mr. H. D. Dickinson and others, that the problem could or should be solved by a kind of pricing system under which the prices of the final products and the prices of the original agents would be determined in some kind of a market while the prices of all other products would be derived from these by some system of calculation. But he seems to suffer from the curious delusion that the necessity of any pricing is only due to the prejudice that consumers' preferences should be respected, and that in consequence the categories of economic theory and apparently all problems of value would cease to have significance in a socialist society. " If equality of reward prevailed, market valuations would *ipso facto* lose their alleged significance, since money cost would have no meaning."

Now it is not to be denied that the abolition of free consumers' choice would simplify the problem in some

[1] See the article in the *Economic Journal* quoted in Appendix B.

respects. One of the unpredictable variables would be eliminated and in this way the frequency of the necessary readjustments would be somewhat reduced. But to believe, as Dr. Dobb does, that in this way the necessity of some form of pricing, of an exact comparison between costs and results, would be eliminated, surely indicates a complete unawareness of the real problem. Prices would only cease to be necessary, if one could assume that in the socialist state production would have no definite aim whatever—that it would not be directed according to some well-defined order of preferences, however arbitrarily fixed, but that the State would simply proceed to produce something and consumers would then have to take what had been produced. Dr. Dobb asks what would be the loss. The answer is : almost everything. His attitude would only be tenable if costs determined value, so that so long as the available resources were used somehow, the way in which they were used would not affect our well-being, since the very fact that they had been used would confer value on the product. But the question whether we have more or less to consume, whether we are to maintain or to raise our standard of life, or whether we are to sink back to the state of savages always on the edge of starvation, depends mainly on how we use our resources. The difference between an economic and an uneconomic distribution and combination of resources among the different industries is the difference between scarcity and plenty. The dictator, who himself ranges in order the different needs of the members of the society according to his views about their merits, has saved himself the trouble of finding out what people really prefer and avoided the impossible task of combining the individual scales into an agreed common scale which expresses the general ideas of justice. But if he wants to follow this norm with any degree of rationality or consistency, if he wants to realize what he considers to be the ends of the community, he will have to solve all the problems which we have discussed already. He will not even find that his plans are not upset by unforeseen changes, since the changes in tastes are by no means the only, and perhaps not even the most important, changes that cannot be foreseen. Changes in the weather, changes in the numbers or the state of health of the population, a breakdown of machinery, the discovery or the sudden exhaustion of a mineral deposit, and hundreds of other constant changes will make it no less necessary for him to reconstruct his plans from moment to moment. The distance to the really practicable and the obstacles to rational action will have been only slightly reduced at the sacrifice of an ideal which few who realized what it meant would readily abandon.

## 5. Pseudo-Competition

In these circumstances it is easy to understand that Dr. Dobb's radical solution has not had many followers and that many of the younger socialists seek for a solution in quite the opposite direction. While Dr. Dobb wants to suppress the remnants of freedom or competition which are still assumed in the traditional socialist schemes, much of the more recent discussion aims at a complete reintroduction of competition. In Germany such proposals have actually been published and discussed. But in this country thought on these lines is still in a very embryonic stage. Mr. Dickinson's suggestions are a slight step in this direction. But it is known that some of the younger economists, who have given thought to these problems, have gone much farther and are prepared to go the whole hog and to restore competition completely, at least so far as in their view this is compatible with the State retaining the ownership of all the material means of production. Although it is not yet possible to refer to published work on these lines, what one has learnt about them in conversations and discussions is probably sufficient to make worth while some examination of their content.

In many respects these plans are very interesting. The common fundamental idea is that there should be markets and competition between independent entrepreneurs or managers of individual firms, and that in consequence there should be money prices, as in the present society, for all goods, intermediate or finished, but that these entrepreneurs should not be owners of the means of production used by them but salaried officials of the State, acting under State instructions and producing, not for profit, but so as to be able to sell at prices which will just cover costs.

It is idle to ask whether such a scheme still falls under what is usually considered as socialism. On the whole, it seems it should be included under that heading. More serious is the question whether it still deserves the designation of planning. It certainly does not involve much more planning than the construction of a rational legal framework for capitalism. If it could be realized in a pure form in which the direction of economic activity would be wholly left to competition, the planning would also be confined to the provision of a permanent framework within which concrete action would be left to individual initiative. And the kind of planning or central organization of production which is supposed to lead to organization of human activity more rational than " chaotic " competition would be completely absent. But how far this would be really true would depend of course on the extent to which competition was reintroduced—that is to say, on the crucial question which is here crucial in every respect, namely of what is to be the independent unit, the element which buys and sells on the markets. At first sight there seem to be two main types of such systems. We may assume either that there will be competition between industries only, and that each industry is represented as it were by one enterprise, or that within each industry there are many independent firms which compete with each other. It is only in this latter form that this proposal really evades most of the objections to central planning as such and raises problems of its own. These problems are of an extremely interesting nature. In their pure form they raise the question of the *rationale* of private property in its most general and fundamental aspect. The question, then, is not whether all problems of production and distribution can be rationally decided by one central authority but whether decisions and responsibility can be successfully left to competing individuals who are not owners or are otherwise directly interested in the means of production under their charge. Is there any decisive reason why the responsibility for the use made of any part of the existing productive equipment should always be coupled with a personal interest in the profits or losses realized on them, or would it really be only a question whether the individual managers, who deputize for the community in the exercise of its property rights under the scheme in question, served the common ends loyally and to the best of their capacity ?

## 6. A WORLD OF COMPETING MONOPOLIES

We may best discuss this question when we come to deal with the schemes in detail. Before we can do that, however, it is necessary to show why, if competition is to function satisfactorily, it will be necessary to go all the way and not to stop at a partial reintroduction of competition. The case which we have therefore to consider next is that of completely integrated industries standing under a central direction but competing with other industries for the custom of the consumer and for the factors of production. This case is of some importance beyond the problems of socialism which we are here chiefly concerned with, since it is by means of creating such monopolies for particular products that those who advocate planning within the framework of capitalism hope to " rationalize " the so-called chaos of free competition. This raises the general problem, whether it is ever in the general interest to plan or rationalize individual industries where this is only possible through the creation of a monopoly, or whether, on the contrary, we must not assume that this will lead to an uneconomic use of resources and that the supposed economies are really diseconomies from the point of view of society.

The theoretical argument which shows that under conditions of widespread monopoly there is no determinate equilibrium position and that in consequence under such conditions there is no reason to assume that resources would be used to best advantage, is now fairly well accepted. It is perhaps not inappropriate to open the discussion of what this would mean in practice by a quotation from the work of the great scholar who has been mainly responsible for establishing it.

It has been proposed as an economic ideal [wrote the late F. Y. Edgeworth [1]] that every branch of trade and industry should be formed into a separate union. The picture has some attractions. Nor is it at first sight morally repulsive ; since, where all are monopolists, no one will be the victim of monopoly. But an attentive consideration will disclose an incident very prejudicial to industry—instability in the value of all those articles the demand for which is influenced by the prices of other articles, a class which is probably very extensive.

Among those who would suffer by the new régime there would be one class which particularly interests readers of this Journal, namely abstract economists, who would be deprived of their occupation, the investigation of the conditions which determine value. There would survive only the empirical school, flourishing in the chaos congenial to their mentality.

Now the mere fact that the abstract economists would be deprived of their occupation would probably be only a matter of gratification to most advocates of planning if it were not that at the same time the order which they study would also cease to exist. The instability of values, of which Edgeworth speaks, or the indeterminateness of equilibrium, as the same fact can be described in more general terms, is by no means a possibility only to disturb theoretical economists. It means in effect that in such a system there will be no tendency to use the available factors to the greatest advantage, to combine them in every industry in such a way that the contribution which every factor makes is not appreciably smaller than that which it might have made if used elsewhere. The actual

[1] Cf. *Collected Papers*, Vol. I, p. 138.

tendency prevailing would be to adjust output in such a way, not that the greatest return is obtained from every kind of available resources, but so that the difference between the value of factors which can be used elsewhere and the value of the product is maximized. This concentration on maximum monopoly profits rather than on making the best use of the available factors is the necessary consequence of making the right to produce a good itself a " scarce factor of production ". In a world of such monopolies this may not have the effect of reducing production all around in the sense that some of the factors of production will remain unemployed, but it will certainly have the effect of reducing output by bringing about an uneconomic distribution of factors between industries. This will remain true even if the instability feared by Edgeworth should prove to be of a minor order. The equilibrium that would be reached would be one in which the best use would have been made only of one scarce factor : the possibility of exploiting consumers.

## 7. The " Economies " of Rationalization

This is not the only disadvantage of a general reorganization of industry on monopolistic lines. The so-called economies which it is claimed would be made possible if industry were " reorganized " on monopolistic lines prove on closer examination to be sheer waste. In practically all the cases where the planning of individual industries is advocated at present, the object is to deal with the effects of technical progress.[1] Sometimes it is

---

[1] On these problems cf. A. C. Pigou, *Economics of Welfare*, 4th ed., 1932, p. 188, and F. A. Hayek, " The Trend of Economic Thinking ", *Economica*, May, 1933, p. 132.

claimed that the desirable introduction of a technical innovation is made impossible by competition. On other occasions it is objected against competition that it causes waste by forcing the adoption of new machines, etc. when producers would prefer to continue using the old ones. But in both cases, as can be easily shown, planning which aims to prevent what would happen under competition would lead to social waste.

Once productive equipment of any kind is already in existence it is desirable that it should be used so long as the costs of using it (the " prime costs ") are lower than the total cost of providing the same service in an alternative way. If its existence prevents the introduction of more modern equipment this means that the resources which are necessary to produce the same product with more modern methods can be used with greater advantage in some other connection. If older and more modern plants exist side by side and the more modern firms are threatened by the " cut-throat competition " of the more obsolete works, this may mean either of two things. Either the newer method is not really better, i.e. its introduction has been based on a miscalculation and should never have taken place. In such a case, where operating costs under the new method are actually higher than under the old the remedy is, of course, to shut down the new plant, even if it is in some sense " technically " superior. Or—and this is the more probable case—the situation will be that while operating costs under the new method are lower than under the old, they are not sufficiently lower to leave at a price which covers the operating costs of the old plant, a margin sufficient to pay interest and amortization on the new plant. In this case, too, miscalculation has taken place. The new plant should

223

never have been built. But once it exists the only way in which the public can derive at least some benefit from the capital which has been misdirected is for prices to be allowed to fall to the competitive level and part of the capital value of the new firms to be written off. Artificially to maintain capital values of the new plant by compulsory shutting down the old would simply mean to tax the consumer in the interest of the owner of the new plants without any compensating benefit in the form of increased or improved production.

All this is even clearer in the not infrequent case where the new plant is really superior in the sense that if it had not already been built it would be advantageous to build it now, but where the firms using it are in financial difficulties because it has been erected at a time of inflated values they are in consequence loaded with an excessive debt. Instances like this, where the technically really most efficient firms are at the same time the financially most unsound, are said to be not infrequent in some English industries. But here again any attempt to preserve capital values by suppressing competition from the less modern firms can only have the effect of enabling producers to keep prices higher than they otherwise would be, solely in the interests of the bondholders. The right course from the social point of view is to write down the inflated capital to a more appropriate level, and potential competition from the less modern concerns has therefore the beneficial effect of bringing prices down to a level appropriate to present costs of production. The capitalists who have invested at an unfortunate moment may not like this, but it is clearly in the social interest.

The effects of planning in order to preserve capital

values are perhaps even more harmful when it takes the form of retarding the introduction of new inventions. If we abstract, as we are probably entitled to do, from the case where there is reason to assume that the planning authority possesses greater foresight and is better qualified to judge the probability of further technical progress than the individual entrepreneur, it should be clear that any attempt in this direction must have the effect that that which is supposed to eliminate waste is in fact the cause of waste. Given reasonable foresight on the part of the entrepreneur, a new invention will only be introduced if it makes it either possible to provide the same services as were available before at a smaller expenditure of current resources (i.e. at a smaller sacrifice of other possible uses of these resources) or to provide better services at an expenditure which is not proportionately greater. The fall in the capital values of existing instruments which will undoubtedly follow is in no way a social loss. If they can be used for other purposes, a fall of their value in their present use below that which they would attain elsewhere is a distinct indication that they should be transferred. And if they have no other use but their present one their former value is of interest only as an indication how much cost of production must be lowered by the new invention before it becomes rational to abandon them entirely. The only persons who are interested in the maintenance of the value of already invested capital are its owners. But the only way this can be done in these circumstances is by withholding from the other members of society the advantages of the new invention.

## 8. THE CRITERION OF MARGINAL COSTS

It will probably be objected that these strictures may be true of capitalist monopolies aiming at maximum profits, but that they would certainly not be true of the integrated industries in a socialist state whose managers would have instructions to charge prices which just covered costs. And it is true that the last section has been essentially a digression into the problem of planning under capitalism. But it has enabled us not only to examine some of the supposed advantages which are commonly associated with any form of planning but also to indicate certain problems which will necessarily accompany planning under socialism. We shall meet some of these problems again at a later stage. For the moment, however, we must once more concentrate upon the case where the monopolized industries are conducted not so as to make the greatest profit but where it is attempted to make them act as if competition existed. Does the instruction that they should aim at prices which will just cover their (marginal) cost really provide a clear criterion of action ?

It is in this connection that it almost seems as if perhaps excessive preoccupation with the conditions of a hypothetical state of stationary equilibrium has led modern economists in general, and especially those who propose this particular solution, to attribute to the notion of costs in general a much greater precision and definiteness than can be attached to any cost phenomenon in real life. Under conditions of widespread competition the term cost of production has indeed a very precise meaning. But as soon as we leave the realm of extensive competition and a stationary state and consider a world where most of the existing means of production are the product of particular processes that will probably never be repeated ; where, in consequence of incessant change, the value of most of the more durable instruments of production has little or no connection with the costs which have been incurred in their production but depends only on the services which they are expected to render in the future, the question of what exactly are the costs of production of a given product is a question of extreme difficulty which cannot be answered definitely on the basis of any processes which take place inside the individual firm or industry. It is a question which cannot be answered without first making some assumption as regards the prices of the products in the manufacture of which the same instruments will be used. Much of what is usually termed cost of production is not really a cost element that is given independently of the price of the product but a quasi-rent, or a depreciation quota which has to be allowed on the capitalized value of expected quasi-rents, and is therefore dependent on the prices which are expected to prevail.

For every single firm in a competitive industry these quasi-rents, although dependent on price, are not a less reliable and indispensáble guide for the determination of the appropriate volume of production than true cost. On the contrary, it is only in this way that some of the alternative ends which are affected by the decision can be taken into account. Take the case of some unique instrument of production which will never be replaced and which cannot be used outside the monopolized industry and which therefore has no market price. Its use does not involve any costs which can be determined independent from the price of its product. Yet if it is at all durable and may be used up either more or less rapidly, its wear and tear must be counted as true cost if the appropriate volume of production at any one moment is to be rationally determined. And this is not only true because its possible services in the future have to be compared with the results of a more intensive use at present, but also because while it exists it saves the services of some other factor which would be needed to replace it and which can meanwhile be used for other purposes. The value of the services of this instrument is here determined by the sacrifices involved in the next best way of producing the same product; and these services have therefore to be economized because some alternative satisfactions depend on them in an indirect way. But their value can only be determined if the real or potential competition of the other possible methods of producing the same product is allowed to influence its price.

The problem which arises here is well known from the field of public utility regulation. The problem how, in the absence of real competition, the effects of competition could be simulated and the monopolistic bodies be made to charge prices equivalent to competitive prices, has been widely discussed in this connection. But all attempts at a solution have failed, and as has recently been demonstrated by Mr. R. F. Fowler,[1] they were bound to fail because fixed plant is extensively used and one of the most important cost elements, interest and depreciation on such plant can only be determined after the price which will be obtained for the product is known.

Again it may be objected that this is a consideration

[1] R. F. Fowler, *The Depreciation of Capital, Analytically Considered*, London, 1934, pp. 74 *et seq.*

which may be relevant in a capitalistic society, but that since even in a capitalistic society fixed costs are disregarded in determining the short run volume of production, they might also with much more reason be disregarded in a socialist society. But this is not so. If rational disposition of resources is to be attempted, and particularly if decisions of this sort are to be left to the managers of the individual industry, it is certainly necessary to provide for the replacement of the capital out of the gross proceeds of the industry, and it will also be necessary that the returns from this reinvested capital should be at least as high as they would be elsewhere. And it would be as misleading under socialism as it is in a capitalistic society to determine the value of the capital which has thus to be recouped on some historic basis such as the past cost of production of the instruments concerned. The value of any particular instrument and therefore the value of its services which have to be counted as cost must be determined from a consideration of the returns expected, having regard to all the alternative ways in which the same result may be obtained and to all the alternative uses to which it may be put. All those questions of obsolescence due to technical progress or change of needs, which were discussed in the last section, enter here into the problem. To make a monopolist charge the price that would rule under competition, or a price that is equal to the necessary cost, is impossible, because the competitive or necessary cost cannot be known unless there is competition. This does not mean that the manager of the monopolized industry under socialism will go on, against his instructions, to make monopoly profits. But it does mean that since there is no way of testing the economic advantages of one method of production as compared with another, the place of monopoly profits will be taken by uneconomic waste.

There is also the further question whether under dynamic conditions profits do not serve a necessary function, whether they are not the main equilibrating force which brings about the adaptation to any change. Certainly when there is competition within the industry the question whether it is advisable to start a new firm or not can only be decided on the basis of the profits made by the already existing industries. At least in the case of the more complete competition which we have yet to discuss, profits as an inducement to change cannot be dispensed with. But one might conceive that where any one product is manufactured only by one single concern it will adapt the volume of its output to the demand without varying the price of the product except in so far as cost changes. But how is it then to be decided who is to get the products before supply has caught up with an increased demand ? And even more important, how is the concern to decide whether it is justified in incurring the initial cost of bringing additional factors to the place of production ? Much of the cost of movement of transfer of labour and of other factors is of the nature of a non-recurrent investment of capital which is only justified if interest at the market rate can permanently be earned on the sums involved. The interest on such non-tangible investments connected with the establishment or expansion of a plant (the " goodwill ", which is not only a question of popularity with the buyers but equally one of having all the required factors assembled in the proper place) is certainly a very essential factor in such calculations. But once these investments have been made it cannot in any sense be regarded as cost but will appear as profit which shows that the original investment was justified.

And these are by no means all the difficulties which arise in connection with the idea of an organization of production on State monopolistic lines. We have said nothing about the problem of the delimitation of the individual industries, the problem of the status of a firm providing equipment needed in many different lines of production, nor of the criteria on which the success or failure of any of the managers would be judged. Is an " industry " to include all processes that lead up to any single final product or is it to comprise all plants which turn out the same immediate product, in whatever further process it is used ? In either case the decision will involve also a decision on the methods of production to be adopted. Whether every industry is to produce its own tools or whether it has to buy them from another industry which produces them at large scale will essentially affect the question whether it will be advantageous to use a particular instrument at all. But these or very similar problems will have to be discussed in some detail in connection with proposals for readmitting competition in a much more complete form. What has been said here seems however sufficient to show that if one wants to preserve competition in the socialist state in order to solve the economic problem, it would not really help to get a satisfactory solution to go only half-way. Only if competition exists not only *between* but also *within* the different industries can we expect it to serve its purpose. It is to the examination of such a more completely competitive system that we have now to turn.

## 9. The Possibility of Real Competition under Socialism

At first sight it is not evident why such a socialist system with competition within industries as well as between them should not work as well or as badly as competitive capitalism. All the difficulties one might expect to arise seem likely to be only of that psychological or moral character about which so little definite can be said. And it is true that the problems which arise in connection with such a system are of a somewhat different nature from those arising in a " planned " system, although on examination they prove not to be so different as may appear at first.

The crucial questions in this case are, What is to be the independent business unit ? Who is to be the manager ? What resources are to be entrusted to him and how his success or failure is to be tested ? As we shall see, these are by no means only minor administrative problems, questions of personnel such as those which have to be solved in any large organization to-day, but major problems whose solution will affect the structure of industry almost as much as the decisions of a real planning authority.

To begin with, it must be clear that the need for some central economic authority will not greatly diminish. It is clear, too, that this authority will have to be almost as powerful as in a planned system. If the community is the owner of all material resources of production, somebody will have to exercise this right for it, at least in so far as the distribution and the control of the use of these resources is concerned. It is not possible to conceive of this central authority simply as a kind of super-bank which lends the available funds to the highest bidder. It would lend to persons who have no property of their own. It would therefore bear all the risk and would have no claim for a definite amount of money as a bank has. It would simply have rights of ownership of all real resources. Nor can its decisions be confined to the redistribution of free capital in the form of money, and perhaps of land. It would also have to decide whether a particular plant or piece of machinery should be left further to the entrepreneur who has used it in the past, at his valuation, or whether it should be transferred to another who promises a higher return from it.

In imagining a system of this sort it is most charitable to assume that the initial distribution of resources between individual firms will be made on the basis of the historically given structure of industry and that the selection of the managers is made on the basis of some efficiency test and of previous experience. If the existing organization of industry were not accepted it could be improved or rationally changed only on the basis of very extensive central planning, and this would land us back with the systems which the competitive system is an attempt to replace. But acceptance of the existing organization would solve the difficulties only for the moment. Every change in circumstance will necessitate changes in this organization and in the course of a comparatively short space of time the central authority will have to effect a complete reorganization.

On what principles will it act ?

It is clear that in such a society change will be quite as frequent as under capitalism. It will also be quite as unpredictable. All action will have to be based on anticipation of future events and the expectations on the part of different entrepreneurs will naturally differ. The decision to whom to entrust a given amount of resources will have to be made on the basis of individual promises of future return. Or, rather, it will have to be made on the statement that a certain return is to be expected with a certain degree of probability. There will, of course, be no objective test of the magnitude of the risk. But who is then to decide whether the risk is worth taking? The central authority will have no other grounds on which to decide but the past performance of the entrepreneur. But how are they to decide whether the risks he has run in the past were justified? And will its attitude towards risky undertakings be the same as if he risked his own property?

Consider first the question how his success or failure will be tested. The first question will be whether he has succeeded in preserving the value of the resources entrusted to him. But even the best entrepreneur will occasionally make losses and sometimes even very heavy losses. Is he to be blamed if his capital has become obsolete because of an invention or a change in demand? How is it to be decided whether he was entitled to take a certain risk? Is the man who never makes losses because he never takes a risk necessarily the man who acts most in the interest of the community? There will certainly be a tendency to prefer the safe to the risky enterprise.

But risky and even the purely speculative undertakings will be no less important here as under capitalism. Specialization in the function of risk-bearing by professional speculators in commodities will be as desirable a form of division of labour as it is to-day. But how is the magnitude of the capital of the speculator to be

determined and how is his remuneration to be fixed ?
How long is a formerly successful entrepreneur to be
suffered to go on making losses ?   If the penalty for loss
is the surrender of the position of " entrepreneur " will
it not be almost inevitable that the possible chance of
making a loss will operate as so strong a deterrent that
it will outbalance the chance of the greatest profit ?
Under capitalism, too, loss of capital may mean loss of
status as capitalist.   But against this deterrent is always
the attraction of the possible gain.   Under socialism
this cannot exist.   It is even conceivable that general
reluctance to undertake any risky business might drive
the rate of interest down to nearly zero.   But would
this be an advantage to society ?   If it were only due to
the satiation of all the absolutely safe channels of investment it would be bought at a sacrifice of all experimentation with new and untried methods.   Even if
progress is inevitably connected with what is commonly
called waste, is it not worth having if on the whole gains
exceed losses ?

But, to turn back to the problem of the distribution
and control of resources : there remains the very serious
question of how to decide in the short run whether a
going concern is making the best use of its resources.
Even whether it is making profit or losses is a matter
which will depend on one's estimate of the future returns
to be expected from its equipment.   Its results can only
be determined if a definite value is to be given to its
existing plant.   What is to be the decision if another
entrepreneur promises to get a higher return out of the
plant (or even an individual machine) than that on which
the present user bases his valuation ?   Is the plant or
machine to be taken from him and to be given to the

other man in his mere promise ? This may be an extreme case, yet it illustrates only the constant shift of resources between firms which goes on under capitalism and which would be equally advantageous in a socialist society. In a capitalist society the transfers of capital from the less to the more efficient entrepreneur is brought about by the former making losses and the latter making profits. The question of who is to be entitled to risk resources and with how much he is to be trusted is here decided by the man who has succeeded in acquiring and maintaining them. Will the question in the socialist state be decided on the same principles ? Will the manager of a firm be free to reinvest profits wherever and whenever he thinks it is worth while ? At present he will compare the risk involved in further expansion of this present undertaking with the income which he will obtain if he invests elsewhere or if he consumes his capital. Will consideration of the alternative advantages which society might derive from that capital have the same weight in this computation of risk and gain as would have his own alternative gain or sacrifice ?

The decision about the amount of capital to be given to an individual entrepreneur and the decision thereby involved concerning the size of the individual firm under a single control are in effect decisions about the most appropriate combination of resources.[1] It will rest with the central authority to decide whether one plant located at one place should expand rather than another plant

[1] For a more detailed discussion of how the size of the individual firm is determined under competition and of the way in which this affects the appropriateness of different methods of production and the costs of the product, cf. E. A. G. Robinson, *The Structure of Competitive Industry* (Cambridge Economic Handbooks, Vol. VII), London, 1931.

situated elsewhere. All this involves planning on the part of the central authority on much the same scale as if it were actually running the enterprise. And while the individual entrepreneur would in all probability be given some definite contractual tenure for managing the plant entrusted to him, all new investment will necessarily be centrally directed. This division in the disposition over the resources would then simply have the effect that neither the entrepreneur nor the central authority would be really in a position to plan, and that it would be impossible to assess responsibility for mistakes. To assume that it is possible to create conditions of full competition without making those who are responsible for the decisions pay for their mistakes seems to be pure illusion. It will at best be a system of quasi-competition where the person really responsible will not be the entrepreneur but the official who approves his decisions and where in consequence all the difficulties will arise in connection with freedom of initiative and the assessment of responsibility which are usually associated with bureaucracy.[1]

10. THE GENERAL SIGNIFICANCE FOR SOCIALIST THEORY OF THE RECOURSE TO THE " COMPETITIVE SOLUTION "

Without pretending any finality for this discussion of pseudo-competition it may at least be claimed that it has been shown that its successful administration presents considerable obstacles and that it raises numerous difficulties which must be surmounted before we can believe that its results will even approach those of competition

[1] For further very illuminating discussion of these problems, see the works of Mr. R. G. Hawtrey and Mr. J. Gerhardt quoted in Appendix B.

237

which is based on private property of the means of production. It must be said that in their present state, even considering their very provisional and tentative character, these proposals seem rather more than less impracticable than the older socialist proposals of a centrally planned economic system. It is true, even more true than in the case of planning proper, that all the difficulties which have been raised are " only " due to the imperfections of the human mind. But while this makes it illegitimate to say that these proposals are impossible in any absolute sense, it remains not the less true that these very serious obstacles to the achievement of the desired end exist and that there seems to be no way in which they can be overcome.

Instead of discussing any further the detailed difficulties which these proposals raise, it is perhaps more interesting to consider what it really implies that so many of those of the younger socialists who have seriously studied the economic problems involved in socialisms have abandoned the belief in a centrally planned economic system and pinned their faith on the hope that competition may be maintained even if private property is abolished. Let us assume for the moment that it is possible in this way to come very near the results which a competitive system based on private property achieves. Is it fully realized how much of the hopes commonly associated with a socialist system are already abandoned when it is proposed to substitute for the centrally planned system, which was regarded as highly superior to any competitive system, a more or less successful imitation of competition ? And what are the advantages which will remain to compensate for the loss of efficiency which, if we take account of our earlier objections it seems will be the inevitable effects of the fact, that without private property competition will necessarily be somewhat restricted and that therefore some of the decisions will have to be left to the arbitrary decision of a central authority?

The illusions which have to be abandoned with the idea of a centrally planned system are indeed very considerable. The hope of a vastly superior productivity of a planned system over that of chaotic competition has had to give place to the hope that the socialist system may nearly equal the capitalist system in productivity. The hope that the distribution of income may be made entirely independent of the price of the services rendered and based exclusively on considerations of justice, preferably in the sense of an egalitarian distribution has to be replaced by the hope that it will be possible to use part of the income from the material factors of production to supplement income from labour. The expectation that the " wage system " would be abolished; that the managers of a socialized industry or firm would act on entirely different principles from the profit-seeking capitalist has proved to be equally wrong. And although there has been no occasion to discuss this point in detail, the same must be said of the hope that such a socialist system would avoid crises and unemployment. A centrally planned system, although it could not avoid making even more serious mistakes of the sort which lead to crises under capitalism, would at least have the advantage that it would be possible to share the loss equally between all its members. It would be superior in this respect in that it would be possible to reduce wages by decree when it was found that this was necessary in order to correct the mistakes. But there is no reason why a competitive socialist system should be in a better position to avoid crises and unemployment than competitive capitalism. Perhaps an intelligent monetary policy may reduce their severity for both, but there are no possibilities in this respect under competitive socialism which would not equally exist under capitalism.

Against all this there is of course the advantage that it would be possible to improve the relative position of the working class by giving them a share in the returns from land and capital. And this is, after all, the main aim of socialism. But that it will be possible to improve their position relative to that of those who were capitalists does not mean that their absolute incomes will be increased or that they will even remain as high as before. What will happen in this respect depends entirely on the extent to which general productivity is reduced. It must again be pointed out here that general considerations of the kind which can be advanced in a short essay can lead to no decisive conclusions. Only by intensive application of analysis on these lines to the phenomena of the real world is it possible to arrive at approximate estimates of the quantitive importance of the phenomena which have been discussed here. On this point opinions will naturally differ. But even if it could be agreed that what exactly the effects of any of the proposed systems on the national income would be, there would still be the further question of whether any given reduction, either of its present absolute magnitude or its future rate of progress, is not too high a price for the achievement of the ethical ideal of greater equality of incomes. On this question, of course, scientific argument must give way to individual conviction.

But at least the decision cannot be made before the alternatives are known, before it is at least approximately realized what the price is that has to be paid. That there is still so little clarity on this point, that it is still possible to deny that it is impossible to have the best of both worlds, is mainly due to the fact that most socialists have little idea of what the system they advocate is really to be like, whether it is to be a planned or a competitive system. It is at present one of the strongest tactics of contemporary socialists to leave this point in the dark, and, while claiming all the benefits which used to be associated with central planning, refer to competition when they are asked how they are going to solve a particular difficulty. But nobody has yet demonstrated how planning and competition can be rationally combined ; and so long as this is not done one is certainly entitled to insist that these two alternatives are kept clearly separate, and that anybody who advocates socialism must decide for one or the other and then demostrate how he proposes to overcome the difficulties inherent in the system he has chosen.

## 11. Conclusion

No pretence is made that the conclusions reached here in the examination of the alternative socialist constructions must necessarily be final. One thing, however, seems to emerge from the discussions of the last years with incontrovertible force : that to-day we are not intellectually equipped to improve the working of our economic system by " planning " or to solve the problem of socialist production in any other way without very considerably impairing productivity. What is lacking is not " experience " but intellectual mastery of a problem which so far we have only learnt to formulate but not to answer. No one would want to exclude every possibility that a solution may yet be found. But in our present state of knowledge serious doubt must remain whether such a solution can be found. We must at least face the possibility that for the past fifty years thought has been on the wrong lines, attracted by a notion which on examination at close range proved not to be realizable. If this were so, it would be no proof that it would have been desirable to stay where we were before this tendency set in, but only that a development in another direction would have been more advantageous. And there is indeed some reason to suppose that it might, for instance, have been more rational to seek for a smoother working of competition than to obstruct it so long with all kinds of attempts of planning that almost any alternative came to seem preferable to existing conditions.

But if our conclusions on the merits of the beliefs which are undoubtedly one of the main driving forces of our time are essentially negative, this is certainly no cause for satisfaction. In a world bent on planning nothing could be more tragic than that the conclusion should prove inevitable that persistence on this course must lead to economic decay. Even if there is already some intellectual reaction under way, there can be little doubt that for many years the movement will continue in the direction of planning. Nothing, therefore, could do more to relieve the unmitigated gloom with which the economist to-day must look at the future of the world than if it could be shown that there is a possible and practicable way to overcome its difficulties. Even for those who are not in sympathy with all the ultimate aims of socialism there is strong reason to wish that now the world is moving in that direction it should prove practicable and a catastrophe be averted. But it must be admitted that to-day it seems, to say the least, highly unlikely that such a solution can be found. It is of some significance that so far the smallest contributions to such a solution have come from those who have advocated planning. If a solution should ever be reached this would be due more to the critics, who have at least shown what the problem is, even if they have despaired of finding a solution.

# APPENDIX A

## THE MINISTRY OF PRODUCTION IN THE COLLECTIVIST STATE

### By E. BARONE

#### I. THE SCOPE OF THIS ARTICLE

1. IN the consideration of production in a collectivist State there are two questions entirely distinct from each other. The first is : Will it be beneficial for some of the capital [1] to become collective property and for production to be socialized ? The second is this : How, in a collectivist régime, ought production to be directed ? One can discuss the second question quite independently of the answer one gives to the first. My particular purpose here is to make a study of the second question, setting the problem in as precise a form as is possible.

Hence I do not write for or against Collectivism. I assume it to be established in a certain social group and I propose to establish certain general lines of the solution which the Ministry of Production ought to give to the vast problem with which it is faced.

Many believe that they have confuted Collectivism when they have shown that some propositions, of Marx or of others, contain errors and contradictions. But the mere confutation of these propositions has not, in fact, any value, because without falling into such errors and contradictions one can very well imagine an economic system which would realize the spirit of the Marxist system. Logical absurdities can be eliminated. But it is necessary to have a clear idea of what the nature of the

[1] [The term capital is here and throughout this article used in the comprehensive sense introduced by Professor Irving Fisher. It includes land as well as the produced means of production.—*Ed.*]

245

system could be after eliminating such absurdities. The elucidation of this system is the object of the following pages.

2. In this article I use mathematics for the simple reason that I do not know another method which, with similar precision and brevity, allows me to put certain questions in unequivocal terms and to give a precise exposition of certain propositions. . . .[1]

3. Since many, who speak of arguments which they do not understand, show that they believe that the Mathematical School and the Austrian School are identical and that the former must necessarily make use of some of the fundamental concepts of the latter, I propose to prove also, that to define the economic equilibrium—be it in a régime of free competition, in one of monopoly, or in the Collectivist State—there is no need to have recourse to the concepts of *utility*, of the *final degree of utility*, and the like ; and neither is it necessary to have recourse to Pareto's concept of the *Indifference Curve*, although it represents a notable step in freeing the Mathematical School from all that seems metaphysical. The old and simple ideas of demand, supply and cost of production, suffice, not only to construct into a system of equations the most important interrelations of economic quantities, but also to treat the various dynamic questions which relate to the greater or smaller welfare of individuals and of the community.

4. In this article—in which I have used freely the works of my predecessors, and especially that of Vilfredo Pareto, to which I have added my original contribution—I propose to determine in what manner the Ministry concerned with production ought to direct it in order to achieve the maximum advantage from its operations. Some of the arguments I use and some of the conclusions at which I arrive have already been made available to us, as the special contribution of the indefatigable and prolific work of that solitary thinker of Céligny. Others are my own. This I say not in order to draw attention to the original element

---

[1] [In the passages which were left out Barone referred to a further instalment of this article in which he intended to present the problem in the form of a discourse which the Minister of Production of the Socialist State delivers to his colleagues. This part was unfortunately never published.—*Ed.*]

in my work. Rather, it is my purpose to make sure that readers little familiar with the new theories should not attribute to me that which belongs to Walras and Pareto.

## II. THE INDIVIDUALIST RÉGIME

5. *The Data and the Unknown Quantities.*—This régime is essentially one in which free competition, monopolies and cartels are all present.

Let us state the conditions of equilibrium, dealing first with free competition, afterwards introducing monopolies and cartels.

The data are : the quantity of capital (including free capital) possessed by each individual ; the *relations*, in a given state of technique, between the quantity produced and the factors of production ; and the *tastes* of the various individuals. On these last we will make no pre-supposition, no preliminary inquiry, limiting ourselves simply to assuming the fact that at every given series of prices of products and productive services, every single individual portions out the income from his services between consumption and saving in a certain manner (into the motives of which we will not inquire) by which, at a given series of prices, the individual makes certain demands and certain offers. These quantities demanded and offered vary when the series of prices vary.

Thus we disengage ourselves from every metaphysical or subtle conception of utility and of the functions of indifference, and rely solely on the authenticity of a fact.[1]

6. Let us represent among the data the quantities of the different kinds of capital possessed by single individuals. Let the different kinds of capital be $S, T$ . . . to $n$ terms. The total quantities of these existing in the group will be $Q_s, Q_t$ . . . Among these $n$ kinds of capital there is also working capital, and also the kinds $H, K$ . . . (to $n$ terms) of new capital in process of construction.

[1] In my elementary treatise, ' Principi di economia politica ' (Bibliotica del *Giornale degli economisti*), I used the conception of utility, because it seemed to me the simplest and clearest method to explain to the beginner some of the most notable results of the new theories. This treatise will be referred to in future by the short name ' Principi '.

Let the technical coefficients be $a_s$, $a_t$, . . ., $b_s$, $b_t$ . . ., indicating, respectively, the quantity of services $S$, $T$ . . . necessary for the manufacture of every unit of $A$, $B$ . . . which are the various kinds of products, $m$ in number.

For the present we will not count the technical coefficients among the unknown ; let us suppose them given, temporarily. We shall see afterwards that they are determined by the condition of minimum cost of production.

The unknowns are set out in the following table :

| | Quantity. | Number of Unknowns. |
|---|---|---|
| *Products :* | | |
| Quantity demanded and produced . . | $R_a$, $R_b$, ... | $m$ |
| with cost of production . . . . . | $\pi_a$, $\pi_b$, ... | $m$ |
| and prices . . . . . . . . | $1$, $P_b$, ... | $m - 1$ |
| *Existing Capital :* | | |
| Quantity of their services directly consumed [1] . . . . . . . . . | $R_s$, $R_t$, ... | $n$ |
| prices of services . . , . . . . | $P_s$, $P_t$, ... | $n$ |
| *New Capital :* | | |
| Quantity manufactured . . . . . | $R_h$, $R_k$, ... | $n'$ |
| with cost of production . . . . . | $\Pi_h$, $\Pi_k$, ... | $n'$ |
| Total excess of income over consumption, expressed in numerical terms [2] . . | $E$ | $1$ |

[1] Thence the quantities $Q_s - R_s$, $Q_t - R_t$ ... are devoted to the manufacture of new capital and of final products.

[2] This excess serves for the manufacture of new capital and the constitution of new working capital.

There are altogether $3m + 2n + 2n'$ unknowns.

The question now is to see if there is an equal number of independent equations.

7. *Equations expressing the R's and E as Functions of Prices.*— Let us begin with individual budgets. It is convenient to suppose—it is a simple book-keeping artifice, so to speak—that each individual sells the services of all his capital and re-purchases afterwards the part he consumes directly. For example, $A$, for eight hours of work of a particular kind which he supplies, receives a certain remuneration at an hourly rate. It is a matter of indifference whether we enter $A$'s receipts as the proceeds

of eight hours' labour, or as the proceeds of twenty-four hours'
labour less expenditure of sixteen hours consumed by leisure.
The latter method helps to make easier the comprehension of
certain maxims of which we shall speak later. Naturally we
shall not use this artifice, when (§ 22) we deal with the case of
services being monopolized by an individual or a group.

The individual then, selling at prices $p_s, p_t \ldots$ the quantities
$q_s, q_t \ldots$ of the services of capital of which he disposes, devotes
the proceeds to certain products $r_a, r_b \ldots$ and certain services
$r_s, r_t \ldots$ which he consumes, saving $e$.

The individual, then, within the limits of the equation

$$p_a r_a + p_b r_b + \ldots p_s r_s + p_t' r_t + \ldots + e = p_s q_s + p_t q_t + \ldots,$$

which the economic society in which he lives imposes, after
having sold all his services, reserves a part of his receipts for
saving.

We shall not inquire into the criteria on which this distribution is made. It is a *fact*, and here we confine ourselves to
formulating it ; and to showing that if the series of prices were
different, he would demand final products and consumable
services in different amounts and would save a different amount.

Hence each of these quantities demanded (and likewise the
amount of the individual's savings) depend on the entire series
of prices, according to certain functions which it is not necessary
to define here. By saying that the individual $r$'s and $e$ are functions, intricate though they be, of all prices, we are only stating
a *fact* of universal experience. And that is enough.

Given, then, a series of prices, the $r$'s and $e$ are determinate ;
and consequently the $R$'s and $E$ are determinate as functions of
prices. Note that each one of these $m + n + 1$ quantities is a
function of *all* the $m + n - 1$ prices of products and services.

8. *The Equations of the Equilibrium.*—Beside $m + n + 1$, which
express the $R$'s and $E$ in functions of all the prices of final goods
and services, the following relationships can be established :

The first system of equations expresses the physical necessities of production : the total of the services of existing capital
must suffice for final goods and services and for the manufacture
of new capital, including new working capital :

I. $\begin{cases} Q_s = R_s + a_s R_a + b_s R_b + \ldots + h_s R_h + k_s R_k + \ldots \\ Q_t = R_t + a_t R_a + b_t R_b + \ldots + h_t R_h + k_t R_k + \ldots \end{cases}$

There are $n$ of these equations.

Then we have an equation, which says that the excess of incomes over consumption is used in the manufacture of new capital :

II. $\quad E = \Pi_h R_h + \Pi_k R_k + \ldots$

Another system of equations gives the cost of production of final goods and new capital as functions of prices of productive services :

III. $\begin{cases} \pi_a = a_s p_s + a_t p_t + \ldots & \Pi_h = h_s p_s + h_t p_t + \ldots \\ \pi_b = b_s p_s + b_t p_t + \ldots & \Pi_k = k_s p_s + k_t p_t + \ldots \\ \cdot\ \cdot\ \cdot\ \cdot\ \cdot\ \cdot\ \cdot\ \cdot\ \cdot\ \cdot\ \cdot\ \cdot\ \cdot & \cdot\ \cdot\ \cdot\ \cdot\ \cdot\ \cdot\ \cdot\ \cdot\ \cdot\ \cdot\ \cdot\ \cdot \end{cases}$

They are $m + n'$ in number.

Lastly, another system expresses one of the characteristics of free competition that the price of final products and of services of new capital equal their cost of production :

IV. $\begin{cases} 1 = \pi_a & p_h = \Pi_h \cdot p_e \\ p_b = \pi_b & p_k = \Pi_k \cdot p_e \\ \cdot\ \cdot\ \cdot\ \cdot & \cdot\ \cdot\ \cdot\ \cdot\ \cdot\ \cdot\ \cdot \end{cases}$

There are $m + n' - 1$ of these equations, because among the varieties of new capital is new working capital, the price of which is $p_e$.

For new capital the condition of the price of the services being equal to the cost of production means that the net rate of yield of new capital is equal everywhere to the interest $p_e$ on free capital (included among the $p$'s of the various services).

9. Counting the number of the equations of the four systems and adding the $m + n + 1$ relations which express the $R$'s and $E$ in functions of all prices, we find in all $3m + 2n + 2n' + 1$ equations. These exceed by 1 the number of the unknowns ; but, as it is easy to see, one of the equations is the result of the others. In fact, summing up on the one hand the equalities of the individual formulae, we arrive at

$$R_a + p_b R_b + \ldots + p_s R_s + p_t R_t + \ldots + E$$
$$= p_s Q_s + p_t Q_t + \ldots,$$

which is the same result as is obtained by adding together, on the other hand, those of system (I) after having multiplied by $p_s$, $p_t$ . . . and taking account of (II), (III) and (IV).

Thus we have the same number of equations as of unknowns. The entire economic system is thus determinate.

10. We have considered the technical coefficients as given quantities ; now let us determine them. Some are constants ; others are variables and related to each other and to the quantity produced by certain relations. These relations are those of increasing or decreasing returns, as is shown by experience. This *economic variability* of the technical coefficients is related to phenomena of the greatest importance. On these matters Vilfredo Pareto has made a most useful contribution to our science. To proceed gradually, let us begin by considering the limiting case of free competition, when, that is, the profits of enterprise are absent, and production is in the hands of one or more entrepreneurs, whose firms are similar to each other, and who are producing at the same cost. It is easy to see by what relations the technical coefficients and the sizes of the firms are determined.

To give the problem its most general solution, let us suppose that between the $n$ technical coefficients of the product $B$ there are $k$ relations $(k < n)$ of the form :

$$f_\theta(b_s b_t \ . \ . \ . \ Q_b) = 0 \ . \ . \ . \ \theta = 1 \ . \ . \ . \ k$$

$n - k + 1$ equations are necessary to determine the $n$ coefficients and the quantity $Q_b$. And these precisely we have, giving the minimum $\pi_b = b_s p_s + b_t p_t + \ . \ . \ .$, in which the prices are considered as constant and $b$ and $Q_b$ related by $f_\theta$. Thus is constituted the well-known theory of maximum and minimum relations.

11. Now let us consider, taking a step towards the real case, several competitive enterprises and their profits.

Profit, in which there is an element in addition to the wages of management, i.e. there is a differential gain, appears as soon as the competing entrepreneurs are *not* manufacturing under the same conditions. For it is evident—in the realistic case—that it is necessary to admit that, besides the technical relations between the technical coefficients, there are, for each entrepreneur, special *economic* relations, which are usually based either on the want of ability to discern and to put into action a plan which combines the technical coefficients to the greatest economic advantage, or on the impossibility of arranging that combination of maximum advantage because of the limitation on the available supply of some factor. Hence originates the *transitory* profit of various enterprises, even in static conditions.

It is easy to see how even in this case the problem may be determined. It is a question of $\alpha$ competing entrepreneurs. There are $\alpha$ new unknowns representing the respective individual profits $g_1, g_2 \ldots g_\alpha$, and $\alpha$ new unknowns representing the respective quantities produced.

Now in this case each entrepreneur, in organizing his production in a manner to obtain the maximum profit $Q_b(p_b - \pi_b)$, will consider as constants (because he is not able to change them himself) the prices of the product and of the services, and as variables the quantities to be produced and the technical coefficients. These are the conditions in which the quantity produced and the technical coefficients for each firm are determined. The profits per unit are :

$$p_b = b'_s p_s + b'_t p_t + \ldots + g_1 = b''_s p_s + b''_t p_t + \ldots + g_2 = \ldots \,^1$$

If a marginal producer $\alpha$ makes no profit, $g_\alpha = 0$.

But, reserving for later discussion the profits of the various enterprises, let us confine ourselves now to the limiting case to which free competition tends, in which there are one or more competing entrepreneurs who make no profit and who produce at the same cost.

12. *The ' Maximum ' of Free Competition.*—The system of equilibrium equations which we have just seen can be simplified in the following manner :

the system of $R$'s and $E$ in functions of prices ;

the system (I) which expresses the physical necessities of production and which, obviously, will be found in any other economic régime ;

the following system (II) :

---

[1] The reader will find a graphic illustration of equilibrium, taking account of the profits of the undertakings, in ' Principi ', §§ 8–13.

$$(\text{II})\begin{cases} 1 = a_s p_s + a_t p_t + \ldots & p_h = p_e(h_s p_s + h_t p_t + \ldots) \\ p_b = b_s p_s + b_t p_t + \ldots & p_k = p_e(k_s p_s + k_t p_t + \ldots) \\ \ldots\ldots\ldots\ldots\ldots & \ldots\ldots\ldots\ldots\ldots \end{cases}$$

which is characteristic of free competition ;

finally the system in which the technical coefficients are determined in such a manner that the costs of production may be at a minimum ; and this case also, as that of the price being equal to the cost, is characteristic of free competition.

13. A noteworthy property of this equilibrium is that the partial differential of

$$\Phi = R_a + p_b R_b + \ldots + p_s R_s + p_t R_t + \ldots + E$$

is zero when prices are considered as constants.

The quantity $\Phi$ can also be put in the form

$$\Phi = R_a + p_b R_b + \ldots + p_s R_s + p_t R_t + \ldots \frac{1}{p_e}(p_h R_h + p_k R_k + \ldots)$$

We will show first that the partial differential of $\Phi$, taking prices as constants, is zero ; afterwards we will interpret the economic significance of it.

In fact

(a) Leaving fixed all the other quantities $R$, suppose an increase in the quantity of one of the products, say $B$, of $\Delta R_b$, allowing for the services required. Then we have in $\Phi$ on one side the increment of $p_b \Delta R_b$, and on the other the decrease $(p_s b_s + p_t b_t + \ldots)\Delta R_b$ ; and therefore $\Delta \Phi$ is nil because $p_b = p_s b_s + p_t b_t + \ldots$

(b) Leaving fixed all the other quantities $R$, suppose an increase in new capital of some kind, of $\Delta R_h$ allowing for the necessary services. Then we have in $\Phi$ on the one side the increment $\frac{1}{p_e} p_h \Delta R_h$ and on the other the decrease $(p_s h_s + p_t h_t + \ldots)\Delta R_h$ ; and therefore $\Delta \Phi$ is nil, because $p_h = p_e(p_s h_s + p_t h_t + \ldots)$.

(c) Leaving fixed all the other quantities $R$, suppose that in the manufacture of $B$ there are used more of $S$ and less of $T$ ($b_s$ and $b_t$ are independent), adding or subtracting the services consumable by them. Then the variation of $\Phi$ will be $(p_s \Delta b_s + p_t \Delta b_t)R_b$. But this variation is zero, because the technical coefficients were determined with the condition of $\pi_b$ minimum.

Consequently, precisely by virtue of the conditions which are characteristic of free competition (that is, the cost of production equals the prices and the costs of production are at a minimum) given the quantity of services available, the partial differential of $\Phi$ *when prices are considered constant* is zero.

Of this proposition we may give further demonstration.

If that equilibrium is changed in any manner whatever (for example, by changing the technical coefficients so that the costs of production are no longer the minimum ; or by disturbing the equality of prices to the costs of production) so that the $R$'s and $P$'s are changed, since always, according to the individual equations, there must be

$$R_a + p_b R_b + \ldots + p_s R_s + p_t R_t + \ldots + E = p_s Q_s + p_t Q_t + \ldots,$$

the total variation of the first section will be composed of two parts. The former is that $\Delta\Phi$, just now considered by us, which is obtained by differentiating with the $p$'s *regarded as constant* and the $R$'s as variables. The second, on the other hand, is obtained by differentiating with the $R$'s regarded as constants and the $p$'s as variables. It is easy to see immediately that the first part, our $\Delta\Phi$, is zero if in the equilibrium the equations (IV) hold. It is enough to multiply (I) by $\Delta p_s$, $\Delta p_t$ . . . and to sum up.

Note that this partial differential $\Delta\Phi$, just now considered, can be put [as it is easy to verify, finding the total differential and taking account of equations (III)] in the form $\Sigma R(\Delta\pi - \Delta p)$, which expression is zero if the costs of production are minimum and prices equal costs and it becomes *negative*, as might be expected, if, on the other hand, one or more prices become higher than the respective minimum costs of production.

14. Let us remember now that $\Phi$ is the sum of all individual quantities analogous to

$$\phi = r_a + p_b r_b + \ldots + p_s r_s + p_t r_t + \ldots + e,$$

which we have seen in the individual equations.

Let us remember, moreover, that if the individual $A$, by an alteration in the economic equilibrium, obtains a positive $\Delta\phi$, *considering prices constant*, his situation *is improved. Vice versa*, his situation deteriorates if a negative $\Delta\phi$ results. Let us demonstrate this, specifying the significance of that *improvement and deterioration*. Then let us suppose that prices vary and therefore the different *r*'s of the individuals vary. In the individual equations which express the usual relations the total variation of the first section is composed of two parts : the first is our $\Delta\phi$, *considering prices constant*, the second, on the other hand, is obtained by differentiating with prices as variables and the *r*'s as constants. Then

$$\Delta\phi = q_s\Delta p_s + q_t\Delta p_t + \ldots - (r_b\Delta p_b + \ldots + r_s\Delta p_s + r_t\Delta p_t + \ldots).$$

When this $\Delta\phi$ is positive, that is to say, if the individual holds his consumption unchanged at the new prices, he will have an excess of income over expenses. Therefore, however the individual disposes of this excess in new consumption, and independently of whatever criterion is the basis of this distribution, his situation will be improved, because even if he spends *all* the increase on a *single item* of consumption, taking all the others as at first, he will now achieve a more advantageous combination than before, improving his situation in a sense which cannot give rise to equivocation.

As for a negative change, this necessarily constrains the individual to adopt a combination $\beta$, less advantageous than the former combination $\alpha$, since if it did not, it would mean that in passing from $\beta$ to $\alpha$ with a positive $\Delta\phi$, the individual would not obtain a more advantageous combination ; we have already seen that, in this latter case, a more advantageous combination *is* obtained. From these premises we come to a most important conclusion.

This conclusion is, that if in any way whatever the conditions alter, the costs of production falling and the prices remaining equal to costs, $\Delta\Phi$ will be negative, that is to say, the individual $\Delta\phi$'s will either be all negative (i.e. every individual will suffer loss) or there will be some positive and others negative, the negative preponderating. That is to say, some individuals will be benefited, others will suffer loss ; the loss to the latter will be decidedly greater than the advantage to the former, in the sense that even taking all their gain from those who have gained in the change (which takes them back to their former condition) and giving it to those who have lost by it, the latter, even with such an addition, remain in a worse situation than originally : or indeed, what comes to the same thing, some of the latter with such an addition might be brought back to their former situation, but all of them certainly could not.

To explain more clearly this conception, which is of great importance, let us think of three individuals only. When that equilibrium is attained at which $\Delta\phi_1 + \Delta\phi_2 + \Delta\phi_3$ is zero, it is implicit that every divergence from the equilibrium conditions expressing the minimum costs of production and the equality of prices to costs renders that sum $(\Delta\phi_1 + \Delta\phi_2 + \Delta\phi_3)$ negative. If all three terms are negative the positions of all the three individuals will become worse. If some are positive and some negative—e.g. $\Delta\phi_1>0$, $\Delta\phi_2>0$, $\Delta\phi_3<0$—while in absolute value $\Delta\phi_3>\Delta\phi_1 + \Delta\phi_2$, if the gain of individuals 1 and 2 were transferred to 3 (who has lost) the latter would still be left with less than he had formerly.

15. One can say then, with regard to this maximum, that production organized with the two conditions characteristic of free competition does not itself maximise, as it is often erroneously said, the *sum of the products* which are afterwards distributed among the group by the competitive system. If we may be allowed for the moment to use that incorrect expression and unscientific concept " the sum of the products " (which is greater, the " sum " of a hundred litres of grain and ten of wine or that of ninety of grain and fifteen of wine ?) it is not at all true that this sum of the products is maximized, because if, e.g. the individuals would be satisfied with less leisure the " sum of the products " could be increased. If the use of the word " sum " is tolerated, the only " sum " which is maximized is that of products and services, including leisure.

Nor is it correct to say that free competition leads to this maximum because within the limits of the equation

$$r_a + p_5 r_b + \ldots + p_s r_s + p_t r_t + \ldots + e = q_s p_s + q_t p_t + \ldots$$

each individual is free, with the services which he supplies, to make that choice between consumption of products, consumption of services and saving, which pleases him best ; because obviously, in other régimes, although the expression and form of that equation might be different it is perfectly conceivable that the individual may be left free within the same limits to make whatever choice he pleases between consumption of products and consumption of services and saving.

And lastly, the maximum of free competition certainly does not imply that, in such a régime, every individual, with the services at his disposal, obtains a higher scale of choice than that which is possible in any other régime.

It is quite incorrect to suppose that this maximum has any such implications.

16. The maximum, we repeat, simply means this : that by substituting other conditions for one or more of the characteristics of free competition (minimum costs of production, equality of prices and costs of production) the conditions of *all* could not be improved. On the contrary, if some are benefited by this substitution their gain is less than the loss of those who suffered. So that if all their gain is taken from those who gained by the substitution, and is given to those who suffered loss by it, the latter could never retrieve their former position and some would always remain losers.

17. Such is the significance of the maximum, from which we deduce these corollaries :

(1) That each substitution of other conditions, for one or more of the characteristic conditions of free competition, is a *destruction of wealth*, in the sense that wealth which could have been produced with the available resources is not obtained.

(2) That if it is considered desirable to benefit some at the expense of others, it is much better—rather than by altering the conditions of free competition to obtain such a result *indirectly* —to make direct transfers from the latter to the former, because by such a method the harm inflicted on the latter is less, in proportion to the gain made by the former. Naturally, this is true only so far as this method of direct transfer does not noticeably alter the conditions of production.

The old economists had a *vague idea* of all this ; but they had not a precise conception, nor were they able to give a rigorous demonstration. Consequently sometimes by clumsy arguments (which have a curious effect on those who are used to most rigorous logic) they arrive at conclusions which in the main are correct. These conclusions they had in fact perceived by intuition, though they believed they had demonstrated them. To have defined precisely this fundamental conception, to which we shall often refer later, and to have given it a thorough demonstration is the great merit of using mathematical analysis in political economy.

18. Before passing to monopolies and cartels, let us illustrate the genesis and the significance of a more or less graphical method, of which we shall sometimes make use later. It is a quick way, useful for obtaining immediately—provided it is adopted with due caution—a rough idea of certain results, which it would be much more laborious to deduce by using directly the system of equations of equilibrium.

For product $B$, for example, we have seen (7) that the price is a function not only of $R_b$, but of all the $R$'s; as, *vice versa*, the quantity $R_b$ is a function not only of $p_b$, but of all the $p$'s. Hence it is not possible to imagine any cause whatever which makes one $p$ vary without altering all the others and all the $R$'s, sooner or later, according to the friction, as we say, which the economic system presents to the propagation of these movements; even without altering the technical coefficients which, by their economic variability, are bound up in the entire system.

But it is possible to imagine an intermediate period between one equilibrium and another, in which $p_b$ alone varies, with the consequential changes of the $R$'s, without the movement of variation being transmitted by $p_b$ to all the other prices. Then for the small variations of $p_b$ we could hold

$$dR_b = \frac{\partial R_b}{\partial p_b}dp_b.$$

That partial derivative is generally negative, as experience shows. Whence arises the conception of a small movement along *the smooth curve of demand* on either side of the position of equilibrium.

In this intermediate period, since the equation

$$R_a + p_bR_b + \ldots p_sR_s + p_tR_t + \ldots + E = p_sQ_s + p_tQ_t + \ldots$$

must always hold good, the usual variation of $\Phi$, the single price $p_b$ being varied, will be

$$dR_a + p_bdR_b + \ldots + p_sdR_s + p_tdR_t + \ldots + dE = - R_bdp_b.$$

This means that after the variation of the single $p_b$ and before the variation is transmitted to the other prices, the mass of individuals has experienced a change, as if the sum of all the productive services $Q_s p_s + Q_t p_t + \ldots$ had undergone a variation $-R_b dp_b$; which, apart from the second order of small quantities, is the shaded area shown in Fig. 1. Thence is derived the concept of the *variation* of the *consumers' surplus*. This variation gives in an approximate way, for small oscillations around the position of equilibrium $M$, an idea of the variation of the state of the individuals : how much they are affected by the variations of a single price $p_b$. This is subject to the hypothesis that this variation of one price has not so far been transmitted to other prices.

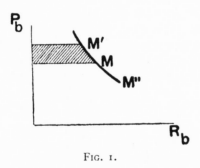

FIG. 1.

This procedure is adopted with the same caution with which, in infinitesimal calculus, one makes use of certain graphical *illustrations*, as distinct from graphical *proofs*; just as in the formula for the radius of curvature of a smooth curve it is said that it is equal to the infinitesimal length of the arc divided by the angle which the two tangents at the extremities of the same arc make, without taking into consideration the known infinitesimal curvilinear triangle.

19. *Monopolies and Cartels.*—Equilibrium in an individualist régime exists in a medley of free competition, monopolies and cartels.

We note that in the equilibrium previously studied, which represented the full régime of free competition, each individual in the market, either as a consumer or as a producer, or as an entrepreneur, acts pursuant to the maximization of his own gain but *subject to* the market prices of products and services. He is subject to them in the sense that, as he cannot influence them in any appreciable manner by increasing or restricting the demands or offers which he makes, he will consider such prices as given constants (11). On the other hand, monopolies and cartels are characterized precisely by the fact that by increasing or decreasing supplies they can noticeably influence the prices. They therefore take account of the variability of these prices and of the influence they can exercise directly in order to increase their own profits.

20. The Monopolies which are most interesting are those of a single entrepreneur manufacturing a product and a single seller of a productive service.

Let us repeat that the origin of the difference between equilibrium in this case and equilibrium in the preceding case is that in the case of free competition the manufacturer of a product or the seller of a service cannot, by decreasing or increasing the quantity of the product or service, influence in a noticeable manner the total supply in the market, and therefore he cannot directly influence the price, which he must consider as constant. In the case of monopoly, on the other hand, by changing $R$ the respective $p$ can be influenced; and therefore in solving his own problem of maximizing his gains a supplier will consider this price as a variable function of the quantity he supplies and will therefore adjust the quantity to his own advantage. Now we will proceed.

21. Let us suppose the manufacture of product $B$ to be monopolized. The entrepreneur seeks to maximize the profit $(p_b - \pi_b)R_b$ from his monopoly. If, as is the most general case, he can act only on the selling price of the product and not at all on the cost of production (because he is obliged to accept the prices of services as they are and cannot influence them directly, because he finds himself demanding services in competition with the manufacturers of *other* products), then, to obtain his maximum profit, he must consider $p_b$ and $R_b$ as variables (the latter as an independent variable)

and $\pi_b$ as a constant. Then the condition of this maximum is

$$p_b - \pi_b + R_b\frac{\partial p_b}{\partial R_b} = 0 \quad \text{or} \quad p_b + R_b\frac{\partial p_b}{\partial R_b} = \pi_b \ . \qquad . \ (\alpha)$$

which in system (IV) is substituted for $p_b = \pi_b$.

22. Let us suppose one of the services, say $S$, is monopolized. Then the quantity at the disposal of the market is no longer *given*: it is a new unknown, which it is in the power of the monopolist to augment or diminish. At the same time there is added to the system of equations one which formulates that the sole possessor of such a productive service will try to obtain the maximum $Q_s p_s$; this equation is

$$p_s + Q_s\frac{\partial p_s}{\partial Q_s} = 0 \ldots \qquad . \qquad . \qquad . \ (\beta)$$

If instead of a single monopolist there is a cartel, that is a syndicate of $\theta$ individuals, the possessors of a service which, to their own advantage they can monopolize, the preceding equation is used for the determination of $Q_s$, the new unknown, and in the expression of the individual relationship the $q_s$ of each individual is determined in the second term, by the way in which $Q_s$ is distributed between them (i.e. how each individual contributes to the total $Q_s$ of the cartel).

Consequently also in these cases the equilibrium is perfectly determinate. It is not true that the cartelization renders the problem of price and quantity indeterminable. Given any particular agreement among members of the cartel on the distribution of the individual contributions to the total $Q_s$ supplied to the market, and on the distribution of receipts, the entire equilibrium is determinate. But whatever may be this division of $Q_s$ into individual contributions and this division of $Q_s p_s$ between the members, it is obviously always advantageous to all that $Q_s$ shall be such that $Q_s p_s$ is maximized.

23. Our analysis of the complications introduced by cartels and monopolies can be illustrated graphically.

Let us look at the case of the cartel (Fig. 2). The quantity $R_s$ is a function, as we know, of all prices. But if all the prices except $p_s$ are considered constant (and the syndicate will consider them as such in aiming at its maximum profit) the relations between $R_s$ and $p_s$ can be represented by a smooth curve (18).

The point $M$ of the equilibrium of the cartel (we will call

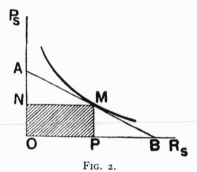

FIG. 2.

it Cournot's point) is that in which the shaded rectangle is maximized ; it has the property that the projection $PB$ is equal to the abscissa $OP$, also $AN = NO$.

And, since $OP$ is the $Q_s$, $p_s + Q_s \dfrac{\partial p_s}{\partial Q_s} = 0$, therefore $NO = p_s$

and $AN = - Q_s \dfrac{\partial p_s}{\partial Q_s}$.

Let us now look at the case of monopoly (Fig. 3). The

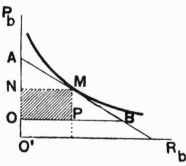

FIG. 3.

problem is to maximize the shaded rectangle ($OO'$ is the cost of production). It is maximized when $AN = NO$ ; or when

$$- R_b \dfrac{\partial p_b}{\partial R_b} = p_b - \pi_b.$$

262

24. As we said so much about it in section 17, there is no need for another demonstration of the proposition that monopolies and syndicates create a difference from the equilibrium of free competition which may be described as a destruction of wealth, in the sense that if some (the monopolists) obtain a profit by it, others (the consumers) lose more. The latter would lose less if, without altering the conditions of productions of free competition, they surrendered freely to the former that increase of wealth which the constitution of monopolies and syndicates would have procured for those people.

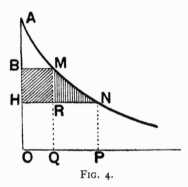

FIG. 4.

Using (as in Section 18) the crude graphical representation, we note that precisely the same conclusion is revealed (Fig. 4). Indeed, in passing from the point $N$ (free competition, price equal to cost) to point $M$ (monopoly, with the condition of $BMRH$ maximized) the loss of some is $BMNH$ and the gain of the monopolist is $BMRH$ : the loss of the former, then, is greater than the gain of the monopolist by $MRN$. There would have been less disadvantage to all if $BMRH$ had been taken away directly and been given freely to the monopolist, leaving production as before : the destruction of $MRN$ would have been avoided.[1]

24A. *Money*.—Economic equilibrium is the starting-point for all further inquiry. Consideration of as many other problems as we please naturally rise from that point, as branches from the trunk of a tree.

[1] See ' Principi ', §§ 16–18.

Let us take an example : money.

In order to see things with a greater clarity, let us suppose—a temporary hypothesis which we will modify immediately—that the merchandize $A$, instead of *money*, be the *numeraire* (that is, that in terms of which the prices are expressed) and that one of the productive resources, $M$, already included in the equilibrium, is *money*, *i.e.* it has that special function which, in production and exchange, it fulfils independently of its numerical quality in the sense now defined. Individuals and entrepreneurs will not require a quantity, $R_m$, of money, but a certain quantity, $R_m \Pi_m$ ($\Pi_m$ is the price of money expressed in the *numeraire*) which is a function of all the prices. For this money-good, as for everything else, the quantity, $R_m$, the $\Pi_m$ and $p_m$ (the price for the use of it), will be determined in the equilibrium. Likewise there will be a definite quantity, $R_a$, of $A$, which is both a commodity and the *numeraire*. All is determinate.

Now let us reject that temporary hypothesis and identify $M$ with $A$, in the system, making $A$ become not only a commodity and the *numeraire* but also money. It is easy to see that even now the problem is entirely determinate. Indeed, in the system of equations of the equilibrium we have only to introduce these variations :

(1) In the place of $m_s$, $m_t$ . . . write $a_s$, $a_t$ . . .

(2) In the place of $R_m$ write $R_{am}$ understanding this to be the quantity of $A$ money, to distinguish it from the quantity of $R_a$ goods.

(3) To introduce the new equation $\Pi_m = \pi_a$. But it is easy to see there is another way. Indeed, of the three

$$\Pi_m = a_s p_s + a_t p_t + \ldots$$
$$\pi_a = a_s p_s + a_t p_t + \ldots$$
$$\Pi_m = \pi_a$$

one is the consequence of the other two.

The problem of the monetary equilibrium, then, is determinate. The quantity of $A$ goods is given here as $R_a$, and the quantity of $A$ money, $R_{am}$. The equilibrium is stable, and in dynamic changes the equalization of the prices of $A$ goods and $A$ money (both the prices equal to 1) is maintained by shifting the commodity to or from the monetary use. That is, of course, in a closed market.

25. The reader will notice that all this theory of the economic equilibrium, in which we have compressed into a system of equations many varied circumstances, of which we take account at one moment [1]—all this theory, we say, we have expounded without it being necessary to refer to any concept of *utility*, the *final degree of utility* or to effort-costs and such-like. " Synthetic economics " can do without all that, without a single one of its theories suffering for it. It does not need to avail itself of any other concepts but those old, well-known and clear ones of demand, supply and cost of production expressed in a *numeraire*, and not in terms of vague " efforts and sacrifices ".

This is the best proof that there is no necessary bond between the new theories of " synthetic economics " and the theories of the final degree of utility.

It is useless to make out that economics would not have been able to attain the degree of *synthesis* of the new theories unless mathematical *analysis* had been previously applied to it.

And now we pass to the Collectivist Régime.


## III.—THE COLLECTIVIST RÉGIME

26. *The Statement of the Problem.*—Some resources remain the property of the individuals (e.g. that which they devote to personal uses) : let them be $M, N \ldots$ to $l$ terms. Let the resources which become the collective property of the State (e.g. fixed capital and land capital) be $S, T \ldots$ to $n - l$ terms.

The Ministry of Production has to solve the problem of combining these individual and collective services in order to procure the *maximum welfare* for its people. We shall see in what precise sense this vague formula can be understood. The Ministry has studied the very complex problem and has solved it, on the basis of a certain formula of distribution which has been established by the community, on certain ethical and social

---

[1] Since this is what the recently developed doctrines amount to, it seems more appropriate to describe them as " synthetic economics " than as " mathematical economics ".

criteria, with which we do not propose to concern ourselves directly. Such a formula of distribution we suppose (we shall deal with the wherefore later) may be embodied in a certain law, according to which is distributed between the members of the community, what in the old régime was the *yield* of resources now appropriated by the State and what was the profit from various enterprises now administered directly by the State (i.e. socialized). We shall see later whether *all* this *income* can be effectively distributed among the community.

27. If the exposition of the solution of the problem were to follow step by step the route followed in the inquiry, it would be long and confusing.

Therefore, with a view to brevity and clarity of exposition, we shall first enunciate the conditions in which the Ministry is faced with the task of solving the problem. We shall see how in such conditions, and with the criterion of the maximum collective welfare, it succeeds in determining the equilibrium perfectly, with as many equations as unknowns.

*Later* we shall return to the conditions which it has imposed on itself and we shall show how, if the conditions were different, scientific collectivism would break down either because the problem was indeterminate (the number of conditions insufficient to determine the equilibrium), or because the problem is not only practically but also logically insoluble (the number of equations exceeding the number of quantities to be determined), or, indeed, even when the number of conditions equals the unknowns and the equilibrium is therefore determinate, because the maximum of collective welfare obtainable in this equilibrium would be less than that necessary to provide the distribution formulated.

Hence it is preferable for it to plan production in its own way, and if it still wishes to correct the distribution it should work directly on the formula of distribution, varying certain coefficients $\gamma$ which we shall define later, rather than directing production on lines inconsistent with the fundamentals of its own arrangement.

Hence the reader must expect that the conditions which we have posited here will be discussed later (§§ 39–54), after the solution of the problem, when a comparison will be made between those conditions and others which could have been posited.

28. Here are the conditions in which the Ministry of Production faces the problem :

(1) There is no money. There are *products* of a certain work of a given kind. There are no *prices* : but the Ministry maintains, for no other purpose than the social accounts, some method of determining ratios of *equivalence* between the various services and between the various products and between products and services.

(2) On the basis of these equivalents [1] the individuals themselves bring their *products* to the *socialized shops* to obtain consumable goods or to obtain from the social administration permission to use some resources of which the State is the proprietor.

The Ministry also maintains ratios of equivalence between the services of socialized resources and other goods, because it is agreed (we shall state the reasons later) that it would be a grave social loss to cancel arbitrarily the equivalences of these socialized resources. Let $1, \lambda_b \ldots \lambda_m, \lambda_n \ldots \lambda_s, \lambda_t \ldots$ be the equivalences determined upon.

29. (3) The members of the community can enjoy the benefit of the quantity $Q_s\lambda_s + Q_t\lambda_t + \ldots$ which we will call $X$ (remember that $Q_s, Q_t \ldots$ are the quantities of collectively-owned resources) either by an *indirect* distribution, the equivalents of the products being reduced, or by a *direct* distribution, that is giving to the members a *supplement* (to income) which is a quota of $X$.

The Ministry of Production has agreed that, generally, from the point of view of the greatest collective welfare, the *direct* distribution is preferable to the *indirect*.

The same cannot always be said for certain economic quantities which appear in the collectivist equilibrium and which are analogous to the *profits* of the old régime. We shall discuss them later.

---

[1] We will discuss later if and when it is convenient, in the interests of the community, to establish different equivalences for the same goods according to the various categories of the individuals.

30. (4) Being obliged to proceed with the system of *direct* distribution of $X$, the Ministry has decided, in agreement with the people, to try a certain system of distribution of $X$ as a supplement to incomes. To each individual belongs $\gamma X$. The $\gamma$ could be different for every individual or different for different groups or arranged in such other ways as are possible. We shall discuss these different arrangements afterwards. For now and throughout the greater part of our discussion, let us suppose that $\gamma$ is determined and differs from one individual to another. It is clear that $\Sigma\gamma = 1$.

31. (5) As for saving, the Ministry, although the people do not wish to hear the words " saving " and " interest ", still ought to arrange so that all its productive services are not directly consumed or employed in the production of goods for consumption. Capital, or if we do not wish to speak of capital, the *means of production*, is used up and unless something is substituted for it, it will be necessary to reserve a part of the productive services for the manufacture of it.

But that is not all. The Ministry knows that if it devotes an *adequate* portion of productive services to this manufacture of the *means of production* it will in the future assure a still greater benefit to its people. The Ministry therefore requires some saving to be done. If it is left to individuals to save as much as they like (they then being obliged to lend the savings freely to the State), the amount of saving may not be sufficient to provide for the manufacture of that quantity of new capital which will be considered of maximum social advantage. It could impose a greater saving on individuals ; but what if these are not content and prefer a greater present consumption to a greater one in the future ? It could deduct from $X$, before proceeding to the direct distribution of it, that amount which it thinks appropriate for the manufacture of new capital ; but it is agreed (we shall see later, in the sequel, the reason for this) that by such a method it would attain a collective maximum *less* than that which is possible by adopting the following method : let it choose at random a rate of *premium* for *deferred consumption* ; let it then see how much saving on the basis of this premium its people put freely at its disposition. Then let it find out if with this sum of saving it is possible to manufacture such a quantity of new capital that it will be able, in the future, to put at the disposition of the people a quantity of products and consumable services so great that it can really give them the promised premium for deferred consumption. And by trial and error, raising and reducing the promised premium, it will eventually make its promise in terms which can be realized. By such a method it could provide for their greater future welfare without disturbing their freewill and without interfering with that distribution which each one makes of the *income* he receives for his work, between his present and future needs.

It could, if it wished—and nothing prevents it—prohibit the savers from lending their savings to others and oblige them to lend them to the State so that the production of some goods would be the monopoly of the Government. In the collectivist régime, the Ministry of Production orders the use of individual saving to be sold *only* to the Government.

32. (6) In distributing his earnings, which he receives in exchange for his services—according to the established equivalents of the Ministry—and that amount which he receives as a supplement to distribution ($X$), between consumption of various kinds and saving the individual is left free to choose, according to his own pleasure.

The Ministry of Production, after mature reflection, imposes these same conditions on itself in striving to provide the maximum collective welfare. Consequently it ought to order production so as to obtain the maximum benefit for its people with the services of which the State disposes and those of which the individuals dispose. These have the freedom, in ordering their own individual economies, to make the choice they believe most convenient, consistent with the equation

$$r_a + \lambda_b r_b + \ldots \lambda_s r_s + \lambda_t r_t + \ldots + e = \lambda_m q_m + \lambda_n q_n + \ldots + \gamma X.$$

33. *The Collective Maximum.*—The Ministry of Production commences with the adoption of the technical coefficients which happen to exist at the time (but which satisfy their technical equations). It does not for the present preoccupy itself with the economic variability of these coefficients. It fixes, moreover, at random, a series of $R$'s which, however, accord with the

physical necessities of production (that is System (I) of § 8). It is absolutely essential that, having chosen the technical co-efficients, whatever afterwards may be the system of production which it wishes to follow, the quantity of productive services available must always be precisely that which is necessary to provide for services which are consumed directly and for the manufacture of products and of new capital.

Let it give now, a *random* series of equivalents and the modifications which may be necessary in order that these technical conditions of production (System (I)) may be satisfied. It is understood that there is not a *single* system of equivalents which satisfies these conditions. If it, indeed, announced at random $m + n - 1$ equivalents of products and productive services, each of its people will make, as we say, a schedule. The individual schedules will give, for the series of equivalents selected by chance, the individual $r$'s and $e$, whence are derived the totals $R$'s and $E$. But as System (I) gives a number of relations between these $R$'s and the $E$, less than the number of equivalents, which are $m + n - 1$, the system of equivalents satisfying System (I) will admit an infinite number of solutions. Then the Ministry decides on one among those which satisfy System (I) as a starting-point. It will then make adjustments in such a way as to attain the end of the maximum collective welfare.

34. What concrete and unequivocal significance must be attached to this very vague expression "maximum collective welfare"?

If the Ministry corrects one of the equivalents consistently with (I), the individual will make a new choice, which will be more or less advantageous than the preceding choice according as

$$\Delta r_a + \lambda_b \Delta r_b + \ldots + \lambda_s \Delta r_s + \lambda_t \Delta r_t + \ldots + \Delta e$$

which we call $\Delta \theta$, is positive or negative (14) according to which, we will say, for the sake of brevity, the individual will be *higher* or *lower*.

The meaning of the *collective maximum* would be patent if, by successive attempts, the Ministry could arrive at such a series of equivalents that every further modification of it would place *all* individuals lower. *But such a series of equivalents does not exist; it is useless to try to find it.* It would be necessary to find such a series of equivalents, that by modifying one of them by a very small quantity, the $\Delta\theta$ for each individual would be reduced to zero. And that is *impossible* ; since, as we shall now see, the sole condition for reducing to zero not the individual $\Delta\theta$'s but their sum $\Sigma\Delta\theta$,[1] implies as many conditions as are sufficient to determine completely all the equivalents.

We must bear in mind the possibility that, by making use of the great freedom with which the individual $\gamma$'s can be varied (subject to the sole condition that $\Sigma\gamma = 1$), we can obtain a series of $\gamma$'s and of such equivalents that not only $\Sigma\Delta\theta$ is zero but all individual $\Delta\theta$'s are zero also. We will show in an appropriate place (53) that this is impossible.

35. What does the reduction of $\Sigma\Delta\theta$ signify ? To eliminate

$$\Delta R_a + \lambda_b\Delta R_b + \ldots + \lambda_s\Delta R_s + \lambda_t\Delta R_t + \ldots + \Delta E$$

means that every other series of equivalents, different from that which accords with this condition, would make that sum negative. That is to say, either it causes a decline in the welfare of all or, if some decline while others are raised, the gain of the latter is less than the loss of the former. (So that, even taking all their gain from those who gained in the change, reducing them to their former position, to give it completely to those who lost, the latter would always remain in a worse situation than their preceding one, without the situation of the others being improved.) Since it is absurd to attempt to resolve the *impossible* problem of finding such a series of equivalents that every further alteration would produce a reduction of welfare for everyone, we will consider that the sole criterion of maximum welfare which the Ministry of Production can use is $\Sigma\Delta\theta = 0$.

36. *How the Equilibrium is Determined.*—$\Sigma\Delta\theta$ can be put in the form

$$\Delta R_a + \lambda_b\Delta R_b + \ldots + \lambda_s\Delta R_s + \lambda_t\Delta R_t + \ldots + \Delta_h\Delta R_h + \Delta_k\Delta R_k \ldots$$

calling $\Delta_h$, $\Delta_k \ldots$ the quantities of saving necessary for the manufacture of a unit of $H, K \ldots$

Let us remember that in the first approximate solution the

[1] Which does not mean eliminating every *individual* $\Delta\theta$, for the individuals may not be *identically* provided with the resources and have *identical* tastes.

271

Ministry of Production had assumed a series of technical co-efficients *at random* (though satisfying their technical equations) and one of such possible series of equivalents and of $R$'s as will satisfy System (I)

Now it is necessary to correct this series of quantities so long as successive corrections always give a positive $\Sigma\Delta\theta$, and stop at that point at which further corrections give a zero increment, a sign that the maximum is attained and that further modifications would give rise to a decline in welfare.

37. The technical coefficients are not changed at first : this task is reserved for later.

Keeping an eye on the System (I) of the physical necessities of production which must always be satisfied :

(*a*) $R_b$ is increased by $\Delta R_b$, the necessary services being taken from those directly consumed. Then $\Sigma\Delta\theta$ is constituted by the increment $\lambda_b\Delta R_b$ in the product *less* the diminution

$$(\lambda_s b_s + \lambda_t b_t + \ldots)\,\Delta R_b,$$

in the consumable services. Therefore in these changes the Ministry ought to stop when the total increment is zero, which can never happen except when

$$\lambda_b = \lambda_s b_s + \lambda_t b_t + \ldots \quad . \quad . \quad . \quad (\alpha)$$

For the purpose of verification, and because thereby the significance of this argument will appear still more clear, let us begin by considering a situation in which the equivalent of $B$ (which is afterwards the *price*, under another name, expressed in terms of that special kind of work which is called the *goods*) is greater than the cost of production. In such a case, the Ministry of Production, in the interests of the community, agrees to increase $R_b$ and to decrease the consumable services, because by manufacturing more of $R_b$, the addition being $\Delta R_b$, there is for $\Sigma\Delta\theta$ on the one hand the increase $\lambda_b\Delta R_b$, by the increase in $B$, and on the other hand the diminution $(\lambda_s b_s + \lambda_t b_t + \ldots)\Delta R_b$, by the diminution in consumable services. The net result of this is evidently advantageous because, by hypothesis, $\lambda_b$ exceeds $\lambda_s b_s + \lambda_t b_t + \ldots$ The maximum will be achieved only when there is no more advantage to be gained by such adjustments, which is when $\lambda_b = \lambda_s b_s + \lambda_t b_t + \ldots$

(b) Increase one of the new productive resources $H$ by $\Delta R_h$, taking the services necessary from those directly consumed. Then for $\Sigma\Delta\theta$ there will be on the one hand the increase $\Delta_h\Delta R_h$ and on the other the decrease

$$(\lambda_s h_s + \lambda_t h_t + \ldots)\Delta R_h \,;$$

and hence, with the same reasoning as before, we arrive at the condition

$$\Delta_h = \lambda_s h_s + \lambda_t h_t + \ldots \qquad \cdot \qquad \cdot \quad (\beta)$$

(c) Now let us proceed to the savings. The Ministry disposes of a quantity of saving

$$E = \Delta_h R_h + \Delta_k R_k + \ldots + R_e,$$

with which it must increase as much as is possible the total quantity of services available for subsequent production. It will approach this maximum, by transferring new capital from one use to another, until, $\lambda_h \lambda_k \ldots \lambda_e$ being the equivalents of the services of the new kinds of capital[1] $\lambda_h R_h + \lambda_k R_k + \ldots \lambda_e R_e$ reaches the maximum.

This condition of the maximum is only satisfied, evidently, when

$$\frac{\lambda_h}{\Delta_h} = \frac{\lambda_k}{\Delta_k} = \ldots = \lambda_e \quad \cdot \qquad \cdot \qquad \cdot \quad (\gamma)$$

(d) Now we proceed to the technical coefficients. The Ministry, in the first approximate solution, had chosen them in such a way that they should simply satisfy their technical equations. But we know that some of them are variables, in the sense that some can be diminished while in others there is a compensating increase. Let $S$ and $T$ be the services for which in the manufacture of $B$ these variations can be made. Then, per unit of $B$, more of $S$ and less of $T$ will be employed as far as is advantageous from the point of view of the collective maximum. The $\Sigma\Delta\theta$ is constituted, with regard to the consumable services, by an addition $\lambda_t R_b \Delta b_t$ and a diminution $\lambda_s R_b \Delta b_s$. Therefore the variation is zero if

$$\lambda_s \Delta b_s + \lambda_t \Delta b_t = 0$$

which is one of the conditions of the $\lambda_b$ minimum when the *economic* variability of the technical coefficients is considered.

[1] $\lambda_e$ is the *premium* for deferring for one unit of time consumption of one unit of saving.

38. Taking account of what we have just said on the technical coefficients and glancing at the relations $(\alpha)$, $(\beta)$, $(\gamma)$ of § 37, it is immediately evident :

(1) That the system is perfectly determined : there are as many equations as unknowns.

(2) That the Ministry of Production in this perfecting of its first approximate and indeterminate solution (the sole criterion of perfection being the maximum collective welfare) comes to the conclusion that production should be so organized that (with the systems of technical coefficients, of the $\lambda$'s and $R$'s) *the cost of production may be minimized* and that the *equivalents for the products* and *for the additions to capital may be such as will correspond to their respective costs of production.*

(3) That the system of the equations of the collectivist equilibrium is no other than that of the free competition.

Which only means that with equal resources (the quantities $Q$) the economic quantities of the collectivist equilibrium ($\lambda$, $R$, etc.) will be the same as those in the individualist equilibrium ; and that is due to the presence of that *supplementary term $\gamma X$* in the individual equations of the collectivist régime, which does not occur in the individual equations of the individualist régime.

39. *The Distribution of X.*—Now is the time to discuss the conditions (§§ 28 to 32) which the Ministry has considered as the basis of its problem.

There are five problems concerned here : the distribution of services possessed by the State ; saving and the creation of new capital ; the distribution of the profits from the undertakings ; multiple prices ; and the supplements to income $(X)$.

Let us discuss them in order.

If the productive resources $S$, $T$ . . . ($n{-}l$ in number) are the property of the State, there are two different ways of enabling the community to reap the benefit of this collective property : either that which we have assumed as one of the conditions in the solution of the problem of the collectivist equilibrium (that is, the *direct* division of $X$, giving to each individual a supplement to his income $\gamma X$) ; or that of reducing to zero, in the cost of production, the equivalent of the services of resources which are the property of the State, and taking as the equivalent of each product (the $\lambda$, which is subsequently the *price*) the cost of the direct personal services which are required for its production. When the product is made with others, this cost is found by dividing the total cost in personal services by the entire quantity produced.

40. This system of indirect distribution, coupled with the reduction of the equivalents of the services of collective property to zero, is, at bottom, Marx's theory of value.

Those people who have criticized Marx have justly directed attention to the fact that such a system would be far from achieving the result, " to each person the entire product of his labour ", which is asserted to be connected therewith, because it is evident that a certain quantity of work of a given kind would be rewarded by a greater or smaller quantity of a certain product, according to the quantity and quality of the State-property with which it is employed. Hence the distribution of the product, made by such a system, is very far from realizing the formula of " the whole produce ". But showing that this formula is not realized does not mean that indirect distribution is shown to be unsuitable. With more effect is it remarked that even when some resources are collective property the State can do no less than fix a price for their services, since there would otherwise be an enormous waste of these, with a consequent destruction of wealth. These services would be used in a large measure, not for further production, but as consumable services, and of those employed productively there might easily be an excess in one kind of production, which excess would be more useful socially in another industry in which there was a deficiency of resources.

This is the correct and fundamental argument against indirect distribution and in favour of direct distribution : the impossibility of obtaining a maximum as high as that which could be achieved with the latter method.

41. Of such a truth we can give, in a few words, a more general and " synthetic " demonstration which can be applied equally to all those systems which propose to reduce to zero the equivalents of all or some of the services of those resources which become collective property.

To wish that the $n-l$ quantities $\lambda_s$, $\lambda_t$ . . . may be equal to zero, is to introduce into the general system of equilibrium, which we have seen *entirely* determined, $n-l$ new equations. Hence either there is an impossible problem (the number of equations greater than the number of unknowns), or, to make it at least logically possible, it is necessary to exclude from the system $n-l$ of the equations which are already there. And as this exclusion cannot be done by taking the equations of the $R$'s from System (I), because they express the physical necessities of production which any economic order whatever must necessarily respect; then to make the problem possible, it would be necessary to exclude as many equations as those which express the minimum costs or the equality of prices and costs. This means that it is necessary to exclude as many equations from those which express the obtaining of that certain maximum; exclusions by virtue of which it certainly could only obtain a lower maximum. The Ministry of Production, instead of rising to the limit, would be forced to stop half-way.

Hence one can affirm that the better way for the Ministry of Production to provide for the welfare of its subjects, is not that of indirect distribution (i.e: the reduction to zero of the $\lambda$'s of the services of collective property), but that of *direct* distribution of supplements to income.

42. The collectivists persist in defending themselves, by expounding, with subtle and laborious interpretations, certain propositions which are either contrary to facts or do not bear a penetrating analysis. They do not appear to think that, if they are to remain collectivists, they must now cast off these gross errors which they derived from a nebulous vision of the phenomenon and from a muddled idea of the mutual dependence of economic quantities.

Of course their attitude in this respect is reminiscent of the reluctance with which the dogmas of a religion are discussed, especially when the latter has great propaganda value.

In addition there is a consideration of great moment in a collectivist régime : that is, that indirect distribution is rigid and does not permit certain ethical and social criteria to be observed with all that liberty which is realized (by giving opportunity values to the $\gamma$'s) by direct distribution.

43. *Saving and the Creation of New Capital.*—For the dis-

cussion of the condition which the Ministry has imposed on itself concerning saving and the creation of new capital it will be enough for us to make :

(1) A brief observation on what we should call the productivity of capital.

(2) A comparison between the method followed by the Ministry of Production and another which it would be possible to follow, by deducting from $X$, before distributing it, that part which is necessary for the manufacture of new capital. Here it will be easy to show that by this second method it would realize a lower collective maximum than that which it can secure with the system preferred.

44. As for the first point, it is necessary to understand well that whether some capital is the property of individuals or whether it is collective property, does not upset the technical fact, that by once subtracting a part of the disposable productive services from the production of consumption goods, and then to produce new capital (new *means of production*, if that term is preferred), there is secured for always an increase of production greater than the *amortization* of capital.

Let us express this conception, which is the crux of the matter, with greater precision.

With the quantities $R_s + R_s'$ and $R_t + R_t'$ of the services $S$ and $T$ it may be possible for us to manufacture the quantity $R_b + R_b'$ of the product $B$. We are speaking of a given unit of time, e.g. one year. In this unit of time we may sacrifice the consumption $R_b'$ and with the services $R_s'$ and $R_t'$ we may manufacture instead some capital $R_k$. And let us call $\varepsilon$ the fraction of $R_k$ which it is necessary to manufacture every year in order to maintain the quantity intact (amortization).

In the next unit of time, and so in continuation, with the same services $R_s + R_s'$ and $R_t + R_t'$ along with $R_k$, after having taken away from those services the part which is necessary for the reintegration of $R_k$, we could have, instead of the product $R_b + R_b'$ which we obtained formerly, a quantity of product which we shall call $\bar{R}_b$, which is obviously given by these equations :

$$R_s + R_s' = b_s\bar{R}_b + \varepsilon k_s R_k$$
$$R_t + R_t' = b_t\bar{R}_b + \varepsilon k_t R_k$$
$$R_k = b_k\bar{R}_b.$$

## APPENDIX A

It often happens technically—and the most obvious experience shows it—that with the choice of an appropriate method $\bar{R}_b > R_b + R_b'$ ; thus this is the criterion on which the decision, whether to manufacture capital or not, is based. That condition is necessary though not always sufficient. Then with the sacrifice of $R_b'$ once made, there is an everlasting additional product $\bar{R}_b - (R_b + R_b')$. Hence there is the possibility of a premium on deferred consumption of $\dfrac{\bar{R}_b - (R_b + R_b')}{R_b'}$ for every unit of $B$ subtracted from present consumption.[1] It is precisely this purely *objective* technical fact, which does not depend in the slightest on whether the capital is individual property or collective property, which gives the Ministry the means to promise a premium on deferred consumption to those who are willing to provide it with savings for the construction of the new means of production. In substance, these people promise not to present a part of their earnings at the general shops to obtain goods, but to deposit it (though it continues to be their property) with the Ministry. The Ministry is thereby enabled to manufacture, with the total available services, a smaller quantity of final products and to set aside a part of the same services for the manufacture of new means of production. These new means of production will then be available to it in successive periods of production. It is precisely this *objective* fact which is the origin of what may be called the *economic productivity* of savings employed in production even in the collectivist régime.

45. Now we pass to another point : is it advantageous that the Ministry of Production, instead of having recourse to individual saving and promising (in order to secure a sufficient quantity of it) a premium on deferred consumption to those individuals who supply it, should, before distributing $X$, deduct that part of it which is considered necessary for the creation of new capital ?

The criterion is, and must be, always the same : the greatest welfare for society.

Let us leave aside the consideration that by the second method

[1] For a very elementary illustration, see ' Principi ', § 37.

the Ministry would take no account of the wishes of its subjects, who might prefer a greater $\gamma X$ to-day to a smaller future increment; and let us also leave aside the consideration that the Ministry would by such a method be without any means of determining the most advantageous quantity of new capital to create. We will confine ourselves here to viewing the case exclusively from the point of view of the collective maximum.

Then, in order to manufacture by this second method the same quantities of new capital $R_h$, $R_k$ . . . the Ministry distributes to the community an amount reduced by $E$. But each individual, even without the promise of a premium for deferred consumption, and simply for the provision of future needs, might for his own advantage decide not to consume all his *earnings*, but to save a certain amount. Hence there is a certain sum of individual saving, which we will call $E_i$ to distinguish it from the quantity $E$ which the Ministry, by reducing $X$, uses for the manufacture of new capital.

$E_i$ is the sum of all the $e_i$'s which result from the individual equations, which now become like this:

$$r_a + \lambda_b r_b + \ldots + \lambda_s r_s + \lambda_t r_t + \ldots e_i = q_m \lambda_m + q_n \lambda_n + \ldots + \gamma(X - E).$$

Or for the community:

$$R_a + \lambda_b R_b + \ldots + \lambda_s R_s + \lambda_t R_t + \ldots + E_i + E$$
$$= Q_m \lambda_m + Q_n \lambda_n + \ldots + Q_s \lambda_s + Q_t \lambda_t + \ldots$$

That is to say, that with this second method (i.e. the method of the Ministry deducting from $X$ the quantity $E$ necessary for the manufacture of new capital, before distributing $X$ among the people) the whole body of individuals is forced to limit the sum of goods and services consumed *more* than they did with the other system, with the prospect of a future increase of products and services *no greater* than that which the other system offers. Therefore evidently, in the interests of the maximum welfare of the community, the former method is preferable to the latter.

This conclusion will be more readily understood, if it is realized that this second method (which is not to be preferred) does not use, for increasing goods and services in the future, that sum of money which various individuals still save even without the promise of a premium for deferred consumption.

46. *The Distribution of the Profits of the Undertakings.*—The problem is in these terms : the product *B*, for example, is manufactured in two different ways, each with its own technical coefficients. Hence there is a *profit* for the method of production which costs less. The undertakings being socialized, this profit belongs to the community. It can be distributed among the members of the community in two ways : either *directly*, taking $\lambda_b$ equal to the higher cost and adding the profit *G* to the *X* which is distributed to the community ; or *indirectly*, lowering the price to the *average* cost of production. Which is more advantageous ?

47. Such questions we can solve by a simple graphical device. Let the product *B* be manufactured in two ways at different costs,

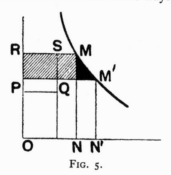

FIG. 5.

as Fig. 5 indicates. The quantity produced is *ON*, the higher cost *MN*, the profit of the lower cost undertaking *RSQP*. Let *M'N'* be the average cost, so that the obliquely shaded area will be equal to the profit *RSQP* of the lower cost enterprise. It is clear that at the average cost the consumption will be *ON'*. And it is also clear that if in passing from the production of *ON* to *ON'*—we will say in passing from *M* to *M'*—the average cost remains the same, the lowering of the price is preferable to the direct distribution of the profit, because with the latter method the community gains the shaded area, while with the method of reducing the price all the shaded area *plus* the black area is gained. Such a conclusion is true *a fortiori*, if in passing from *M* to *M'* the average cost diminishes.

But if, instead, the average cost increases, because the new consumption $NN'$ has to be produced at a higher cost than the two preceding ones or at a greater new cost, then according to the position, either the direct or indirect distribution of the profit is preferable.

In Fig. 6 $M'$ is the level of the previous average cost when the production is $ON$. The profit is shown by the horizontally and vertically shaded areas combined. $M''$ is the level of the new average cost when the production becomes $ON''$. Let us call the two shaded areas $a$ and $b$ respectively ($a$ the horizontally shaded and $b$ the vertically shaded) and the black area is $c$. It is clear that with the system of direct distribution of the profit the community gains $a + b$. With the system of indirect dis-

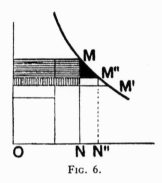

Fig. 6.

tribution, that is, with the lowering of the price to the average cost, it gains $a + c$. Hence the first or second method will be the more advantageous according as $b$ is greater than $c$ or *vice versa*.

48. We have said this because such an aspect of the question cannot be avoided in our analysis.

However, as experience shows, the total sum of the profits is in reality unlikely to be large (there are losses as well as profits) ; and it will still be necessary to use a part of these profits as remuneration for the work of those people who, as assistants of the Ministry, are engaged in endeavouring to keep the cost of production as low as possible ; and lastly, as we have already noticed, every method of indirect distribution implies a loss of freedom—curtailing the liberty of giving to the $\gamma$'s the most advantageous values from ethical and social aspects. For these reasons the Ministry would decide that there was no case for departing from the general principle of *direct* distribution, even in the sphere of profits. This decision would be reinforced by the fact that any such departure would give rise to further practical complications, and the Ministry would, apart from this, as we shall see later, already find itself in the midst of a multitude of complications arising out of the *practical* resolution of the equations of the equilibrium.

49. *Multiple Prices.*—The consumption of the product $B$, for example, may be $ON$, with the price $MN$ which is equal to the cost of production (Fig. 7). To extend the consumption of the product and to render it more widely accessible, we can

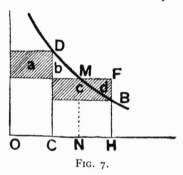

FIG. 7.

increase the price of a part of the supply, in order to lower the price of the other part, making the adjustment by a redistribution of the total cost : for example, the amount $OC$ could bear the price $CD$, while for $CH$ the price would be $HB$. If when the output is increased the cost of production does not vary (then the two shaded rectangles are equal) it is obvious that this proceeding implies a destruction of wealth ; for it is better to take directly from some to give to others ; or it is better to work on the $\gamma$'s.

In fact, passing from the position of equilibrium with a single price to that with a double price, in this case of costs remaining constant when output increases, a destruction of wealth, $MBF$, is caused. This may be easily verified by considering what, in passing from one state to the other, will be the variation of the consumers' surplus : as a result of the change it decreases by $a + b$ for one part and increases by $b + c$ for the other, a net increase of $c - a$ ; but $a = c + d$ because the average cost per unit is $HF$ ; therefore, on the whole, the consumers' surplus is diminished by $d$.

50. In order that there shall be no loss, it is necessary (though not sufficient) that the cost should fall as output increases. Then a system of multiple prices can be advantageous, when, as it is easy to verify (Fig. 8), by increasing consumption from $M$ with a single price to $N$ with multiple prices, with the lessening of the unit cost, the obliquely shaded surface may be bigger than the vertically shaded area. This is demonstrated in a few words, in spite of the apparent complication. Indeed, if there

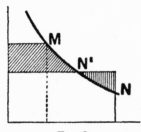

Fig. 8.

is a change from position $M$ with a single price to position $N'$, still with a single price, the gain is the obliquely shaded area. If from position $N'$ with a single price there is further change to position $N$ with multiple prices, the loss (according to what we saw just now) is represented by the vertically shaded area ; thus in passing from $M$ with a single price to $N$ with multiple prices, there is a gain represented by the first area (oblique shading) and a loss by the second (vertical shading).

Hence, when the first area is larger than the second it is possible that multiple prices may be consistent with increased welfare for the community. And as such a proceeding is more possible practically when production is socialized, this is in reality a sound argument in defence of socialized production, in certain cases, when such conditions are proved to exist.

51. Now, without rejecting the notion that in some particular

case the proceeding may be applicable, the Ministry of Production, since it has under its control the determination of the $\gamma$'s of the supplements to income, with which it can *directly* modify distribution, does not (having regard to the practical necessity of not adding other complications to those which it must solve in the immense problem with which it is faced) think it opportune to depart from the criterion of the single price in general. At the same time it may consider some particular cases in which the multiple price system can noticeably increase the collective welfare. For example, it might treat as special cases some products for wide consumption, by extending the production of which it would make possible a considerable lessening of the cost of production.

In such cases the sale of one part under cost and of another above cost, can produce advantage for some such as could be obtained by an increase in their $\gamma$'s only by reducing the $\gamma$'s of the others by much more than the latter would lose by having to pay a price above cost.

There are cases also, in which the multiple price system, with the increase of production which it makes possible, can lead to such a lessening of cost that the new price above cost would remain below the old single price equal to the cost of production. And in such cases, of evident and great advantage to the community, nothing debars the Ministry of Production from adopting the multiple price system in place of the single price. It is an error to believe that the single price is the better system *in every case.*

52. *The Supplement to Incomes.*—The origin of all the supplements distributed to the various individuals is constituted by the price of the services of which the State has become the possessor. This sum is divided according to certain rules fixing the individual $\gamma$'s. It would be erroneous to conclude from this that in the collectivist régime the individuals are benefited by all that which in the old régime formed the *income* of the possessors of this capital. In fact, with the mass of all the disposable services—which, save for the different appropriation, let us suppose for the purpose of comparison, are not changed— in the old régime, the consumption of products, the consump-

tion of services and saving for the formation of new capital were provided for. If it is desired that in the new régime existing capital should not be destroyed and that creation of new capital should be continued at a rate no less than that which was obtained in the old régime, the community must save as formerly. Hence its consumption (of products and consumable services) would be unchanged ; and thus in the new régime the community could not appropriate for consumption the *income* of the old possessors of resources, but at most only that part of this income which they consumed.

53. The distribution of that certain quantity

$$X = Q_s \lambda_s + Q_t \lambda_t + \ldots,$$

the price of the services of the resources possessed by the State, can be made in many different ways. For example : *in equal parts*, making $\gamma$ identical for all individuals ; by *classes*, giving to the individual a fraction $\gamma_1 X$, $\gamma_2 X$, etc., according to the class to which he is assigned.

It may be asked (34) if it is not possible for the Ministry of Production, in exercising its power to vary the individual $\gamma$'s, subject only to the condition of $\Sigma \gamma = 1$, to arrive at a series of $\gamma$'s, with the equivalents and the technical coefficients such that not only $\Sigma \Delta \theta$ is zero but also the single $\Delta \theta$'s are zero. Then an absolutely indisputable maximum would be realized, because then such an economic system would be worked out, that every alteration from it in the $\gamma$'s, in the equivalents and in the technical coefficients would produce a decline in welfare for everyone : the ideal of economic systems. *But such a system of $\gamma$'s does not exist.*

In fact, the individual $\gamma$'s must be a function of the $\lambda$'s and satisfy the condition that the variation of a $\lambda$ involves a variation of the $\gamma$ which makes the former equal zero.

The function $\gamma$ must therefore satisfy the conditions

$$-r_b + X \frac{\partial \gamma}{\partial \lambda_b} = 0 \ldots, \quad q_m - r_m + X \frac{\partial \gamma}{\partial \lambda_m} = 0 \ldots, \quad \gamma Q_s - r_s + X \frac{\partial \gamma}{\partial \lambda_s} = 0$$

(let us recollect that the individual equation is

$$r_a + \lambda_b r_b + \ldots + \lambda_m r_m + \lambda_n r_n + \ldots + \lambda_s r_s + \lambda_t r_t + \ldots + e$$
$$= \lambda_m q_m + \lambda_n q_n + \ldots + \gamma X) ;$$

285

that is, it must satisfy the conditions

$$\frac{\partial \gamma}{\partial \lambda_b} = \frac{1}{X} r_b \cdots, \quad \frac{\partial \gamma}{\partial \lambda_m} = \frac{1}{X}(r_m - q_m) \cdots, \quad \frac{\partial \gamma}{\partial \lambda_s} = \frac{1}{X}(r_s - \gamma Q_s).$$

It is easy to see that the function $\gamma$ which satisfies such conditions does not exist; since describing as $\gamma_b \cdots \gamma_m \cdots \gamma_s$, its partial derivatives, the known conditions of integrability are not satisfied.

$$\frac{\partial \gamma_b}{\partial \lambda_m} = \frac{\partial \gamma_m}{\partial \lambda_b}; \quad \frac{\partial \gamma_b}{\partial \lambda_s} = \frac{\partial \gamma_s}{\partial \lambda_b}; \quad \frac{\partial \gamma_m}{\partial \lambda_s} = \frac{\partial \gamma_s}{\partial \lambda_m}.$$

Hence there does not exist a function of the $\lambda$'s, which, used for the regulating of the $\gamma$'s, can lead to the marvellous result that the individual $\Delta\theta$'s may equal zero, so that any subsequent alteration in the equivalents would cause a *decline in welfare for everyone*.

54. The effects of distribution on production would vary with the different methods by which $X$ is distributed.

We have already noted (38) how the complete resemblance between the equations of free competition and the equations of the collectivist equilibrium, established with the idea of obtaining the maximum collective benefit, only means that there being in the group the same quantities of capital in one case as in the other, the appropriation alone being different, the economic quantities of the equilibrium will be equal to those of the other, there still being in both cases equations expressing the conditions of minimum cost and of prices equal to costs; that is precisely on account of that supplement added to the income of each individual. The distribution, which is made of that $X$ in one way or another according to the various values which are given to the $\gamma$'s, influences diversely these economic quantities. The study of these diverse influences gives rise to interesting speculations, one of the most remarkable (though not unexpected) results being that there would be a sharp rise in the premium for deferred consumption—which is the parallel to *interest* on saving in the old régime—which according to most superficial collectivist doctrines would be abolished. Precisely the opposite is the case !

55. *The Equations of the Equilibrium insoluble a priori.*—For

the solution of the problem it is not enough that the Ministry of Production has arrived at tracing out for itself the system of equations of the equilibrium best adapted for obtaining the collective maximum in the well-known sense (to which we need not return). It is necessary to solve the equations afterwards. And that is the problem.

Many of the writers who have critized collectivism have hesitated to use as evidence the practical difficulties in establishing on paper the various equivalents ; but it seems they have not perceived what really are the difficulties—or more frankly, the impossibility—of solving such equations *a priori*.

56. If, for a moment, we assume that the economic variability of the technical coefficients may be neglected and we take account of their technical variability only, it is not impossible to solve on paper the equations of the equilibrium. It would be a tremendous—a gigantic—work (work therefore taken from the productive services) : but it is not an *impossibility*.

It is conceivable, in fact, that with a vast organization for this work it would be possible to collect the individual schedules for every given series of the various equivalents, including the premium for deferred consumption. Hence it is not inconceivable that with these schedules collected—always supposing the technical coefficients known and invariable—it would be possible by a paper calculation to find a series of equivalents, which would satisfy the equations expressing the physical necessities of production and the equalization of costs of production and the equivalents, which become the *prices*. There is no analytical difficulty about it : it is a problem of very simple linear equations. The difficulty arises rather from the very great number of individuals and goods of which we must take account ; but it is not inconceivable that, with still more arduous work, such difficulty could be overcome.

57. But it is frankly *inconceivable* that the *economic* determination of the technical coefficients can be made *a priori*, in such a way as to satisfy the condition of the minimum cost of production which is an essential condition for obtaining that maximum to which we have referred. This *economic* variability of the technical coefficients is certainly neglected by the collec-

tivists ; but that it is one of the most important sides of the question Pareto has already very clearly shown in one of his many ingenious contributions to the science.

The determination of the coefficients economically most advantageous can only be done in an *experimental* way : and not on a *small scale*, as could be done in a laboratory ; but with experiments on a *very large scale*, because often the advantage of the variation has its origin precisely in a new and greater dimension of the undertaking. Experiments may be successful in the sense that they may lead to a lower cost combination of factors ; or they may be unsuccessful, in which case that particular organization may not be copied and repeated and others will be preferred, which *experimentally* have given a better result.

The Ministry of Production could not do without these experiments for the determination of the *economically* most advantageous technical coefficients if it would realize the condition of the minimum cost of production which is *essential* for the attainment of the maximum collective welfare.

It is on this account that the equations of the equilibrium with the maximum collective welfare are not soluble *a priori*, on paper.

58. Some collectivist writers, bewailing the continual destruction of firms (those with higher costs) by free competition, think that the creation of enterprises to be destroyed later can be avoided, and hope that with *organized* production it is possible to avoid the dissipation and destruction of wealth which such *experiments* involve, and which they believe to be the peculiar property of ' anarchist ' production. Thereby these writers simply show that they have no clear idea of what production really is, and that they are not even disposed to probe a little deeper into the problem which will concern the Ministry which will be established for the purpose in the Collectivist State.

We repeat, that if the Ministry will not remain bound by the traditional technical coefficients, which would produce a destruction of wealth in another sense—in the sense that the greater wealth which could have been realized will not be realized —it has no other means of determining *a priori* the technical coefficients most advantageous economically, and must *of necessity* resort to experiments on a large scale in order to decide *afterwards* which are the most appropriate organizations, which it is advantageous to maintain in existence and to enlarge to obtain the collective maximum more easily, and which, on the other hand, it is best to discard as failures.

59. *Conclusions.*—From what we have seen and demonstrated hitherto, it is obvious how fantastic those doctrines are which imagine that production in the collectivist régime would be ordered in a manner substantially different from that of " anarchist " production.

If the Ministry of Production proposes to obtain the collective maximum—which it obviously must, whatever law of distribution may be adopted—all the economic categories of the old régime must reappear, though maybe with other names : prices, salaries, interest, rent, profit, saving, etc. Not only that ; but always provided that it wishes to obtain that maximum with the services of which the individuals and the community dispose, the same two fundamental conditions which characterize free competition reappear, and the maximum is more nearly attained the more perfectly they are realized. We refer, of course, to the conditions of minimum cost of production and the equalization of price to cost of production.

60. This conclusion could have been reached, at first sight, by a " synthetic " argument ; but it could not have acquired the value of a demonstrated truth, without the phenomenon being subjected to a minute quantitative analysis, as has been done in the preceding pages. The argument would be this : to hand over some capital to the State and afterwards to distribute the yield thereof among the individuals, according to a certain law, whatever it is, is like starting from a situation in the individualist régime, in which the individuals, besides having their own capital, may be possessors of certain quotas of capital of which the State has become the controller, quotas corresponding to that same law of distribution which we supposed adopted.

In such a situation what are the technical coefficients and what is the system of equivalents which allow the attainment of the maximum ? Those which give the equalization of price to cost of production and the minimum cost of production !

61. That supplement to income distributed among the individuals—whatever may be the system of distribution—does not augment, as we have seen, the consumption of products and consumable services of the group, by the total *income* which in the old régime the possessors of capital received and which is appropriated by the State in the new régime, even when this appropriation takes place without some promise of compensation to the expropriated owners. When there is no intention of restricting saving and the creation of new capital to narrower limits than in the old régime (to this we shall return in a moment) the total consumption of products and of consumable services can be scarcely different from what it was before.

Hence, given that there is no wish to check the creation of new capital in the new régime, the distribution of consumable goods and services among the people must inevitably be restricted within the limits of what in the old régime the possessors of the capital, which is now socialized, consumed, not the whole of what they received as income. Besides this, account must be taken of the necessary remuneration of the army of officials whose services would be devoted not to production but to the laborious and colossal centralization work of the Ministry (assuming the practical possibility of such a system).

62. If it were so desired, it would be possible to augment consumption, at the expense, however, of the formation of new resources, but of *all* the new resources, even at the expense of the birth-rate. To promise increased welfare and to propose to " organize " production and to preach about free love in the new régime is simply ridiculous nonsense. If the State does not wish the collective maximum to decrease rapidly in time, the accumulation of capital must be regulated according to the birth-rate ; or, conversely, the latter must be restricted within the limits set by the former.

# APPENDIX B

## SELECTED BIBLIOGRAPHY

L. v. Mises : Die Wirtschaftsrechnung im sozialistischen Gemeinwesen, *Archiv für Sozialwissenschaft*, Vol. 47, 1920.

A. W. Cohn : *Kann das Geld abgeschafft werden?* Jena, 1920.

Max Weber : *Wirtschaft und Gesellschaft* (Grundriss der Sozialökonomik, Part III), Part I, Ch. II, 9–14. Tübingen, 1921.

L. v. Mises : *Die Gemeinwirtschaft.* Jena, 1922, 2nd ed., 1932.

E. Heimann : *Mehrwert und Gemeinwirtschaft.* Berlin, 1922.

K. Polanyi : Sozialistische Rechnungslegung, *Archiv für Sozialwissenschaft*, Vol. 49, 1922.

O. Leichter : *Die Wirtschaftsrechnung in der sozialistischen Gesellschaft.* Wien, 1923.

L. v. Mises : Neue Beiträge zum Problem der sozialistischen Wirtschaftsrechnung, *Archiv für Sozialwissenschaft*, Vol. 51, 1924.

J. Marschak : Wirtschaftsrechnung und Gemeinwirtschaft, *Archiv für Sozialwissenschaft*, Vol. 51, 1924.

T. Weil : Gildensozialistische Rechnungslegung, *Archiv für Sozialwissenschaft*, Vol. 52, 1924.

K. Polanyi : Die funktionelle Theorie der Gesellschaft und das Problem der sozialistischen Rechnungslegung, *Archiv für Sozialwissenschaft*, Vol. 52, 1924.

O. Neurath : *Wirtschaftsplan und Naturalrechnung.* Berlin, 1925.

R. G. Hawtrey : Chapter on " Collectivism " in *The Economic Problem.* London, 1926.

J. Bowen : *Conditions of Social Welfare.* London, 1926.

G. Halm : *Ist der Sozialismus wirtschaftlich möglich?* Berlin, 1926.

E. Horn : *Die ökonomischen Grenzen der Gemeinwirtschaft.* Halberstadt, 1928.

L. v. Mises : Neue Schriften zum Problem der sozialistischen Wirtschaftsrechnung, *Archiv für Sozialwissenschaft*, Vol. 60, 1928.

B. Brutzkus : *Die Lehren des Marxismus im Lichte der russischen Revolution.* (First published in Russian in 1921-2.) Berlin, 1928.
   An English translation of this book forms the first part of *Economic Planning in Soviet Russia.* Routledge, London, 1935.

E. Heimann : Ueber Konkurrenz, Monopol und sozialistische Wirtschaft, *Die Arbeit*, 1929.

F. M. Taylor : The Guidance of Production in a Socialist State, *American Economic Review*, Vol. XIX, 1929.

W. Crosby Roper : *The Problem of Pricing in a Socialist State.* Cambridge (Mass.), 1929.

F. Pollock : *Die planwirtschaftlichen Versuche in der Sowjetunion 1917-1927*, Leipzig, 1929.

G. Halm : Ueber Konkurrenz, Monopol und sozialistische Wirtschaft, *Jahrbücher für Nationalökonomie und Statistik*, Vol. 133 (III. F. 78), 1930.

*Grundprinzipien kommunistischer Verteilung und Produktion.* Gruppe internationaler Kommunisten (Holland) hrsg. v.d. Allgemeinen Arbeiterunion Deutschlands. Berlin, 1930.

H. D. Dickinson : The Economic Basis of Socialism, *Political Quarterly*, Sept.-Dec., 1930.

J. Gerhardt : *Unternehmertum und Wirtschaftsführung.* Tübingen, 1930.

L. Pohle and G. Halm : *Kapitalismus und Sozialismus.* Berlin, 1931.

C. Landauer : *Planwirtschaft und Verkehrswirtschaft.* München, 1931.

G. Morreau : De Economische Struktur eener Socialistische Volkshuishouding, *De Economist.* s'Gravenhage, 1931.

K. Tisch : *Wirtschaftsrechnung und Verteilung im zentralistisch organisierten sozialistischen Gemeinwesen* (Doctorial thesis, University of Bonn). Wuppertal-Elberfeld, 1932.

W. Schiff : *Die Planwirtschaft und ihre ökonomischen Hauptprobleme.* Berlin, 1932.

R. Kerschagl : Die Möglichkeit einer Wirtschaftsrechnung in der sozialistischen Planwirtschaft, *Ständisches Leben,* Vol. 2, 1932.

A. A. van Rhijn : De Economische Calculatie in het Socialism, *De Economist.* s'Gravenhage, 1932.

E. Heimann : *Sozialistische Wirtschafts und Arbeitsordnung.* Potsdam, 1932.

T. E. Gregory : An Economist looks at Planning, *Manchester School,* Vol. IV, 1933.

H. D. Dickinson : Price Formation in a Socialist Community, *Economic Journal,* June, 1933.

H. D. Dickinson : Freedom and Planning. A Reply to Dr. Gregory, *Manchester School,* Vol. IV, 1933.

M. Dobb : Economic Theory and the Problem of a Socialist Economy, *Economic Journal,* December, 1933.

B. Wootton : *Plan or No Plan.* London, 1934.

R. Frisch : Circulation Planning : Proposal for a National Organization for a Commodity and Service Exchange, *Econometrica,* Vol. II, July, 1934.

H. Zassenhaus : Ueber die ökonomische Theorie der Planwirtschaft, *Zeitschrift für Nationalökonomie,* Vol. V, September, 1934.

A. P. Lerner : Economic Theory and Socialist Economy, *Review of Economic Studies,* Vol. II, October, 1934.

K. Mandelbaum and G. Mayer : Planwirtschaft, *Zeitschrift für Sozialforschung,* Vol. III, 1934.

E. Heimann : Planning and the Market System, *Social Research,* Vol. I, 1934.